Dummies 101: FrontPage® 98

A Quick Tour of FrontPage

CHEAT SHEET

S0-BXH-615

☑ Progress Check

The FrontPage Explorer

The FrontPage Explorer is where you create and manage Web sites. Here are some of the things you can do using the Explorer: create new and import existing Web sites, add blank pages to Web sites, organize the site's files and folders, view the site's system of links, map the site's navigational flow, apply a graphical theme to the Web site, make sure that the site's links work properly, and maintain a running task list. You also use the Explorer to publish your Web site.

Views bar   Menu bar   Title bar   Toolbar

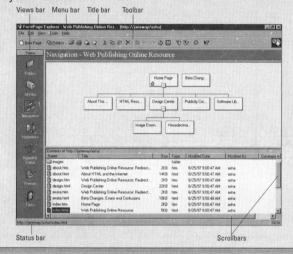

Status bar   Scrollbars

The FrontPage Editor

The FrontPage Editor is where you make changes to individual Web pages. Using the Editor, you can add and format text, create hyperlinks and navigation bars, work with graphics and image maps, create tables, build interactive forms, work with frames, and use dynamic FrontPage features.

Table toolbar Title bar Menu bar Standard toolbar Format toolbar Forms toolbar

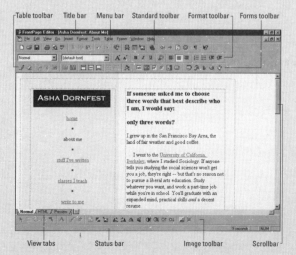

View tabs   Status bar   Image toolbar   Scrollbar

Dummies 101:™ FrontPage® 98

CHEAT SHEET

Basic FrontPage Tasks

▶ **Starting FrontPage:** On the taskbar, click the Start button, choose Programs, and then choose Microsoft FrontPage.

▶ **Creating a new Web site:** Choose options in the Getting Started dialog box (this dialog box appears when you first launch FrontPage), or in the Explorer, choose File⇨New⇨FrontPage Web.

▶ **Opening a Web page using the Explorer:** In the Explorer's All Files View, Folders View, Hyperlinks View, or Navigation View, double-click a page icon.

▶ **Opening a Web page using the Editor:** On the Standard toolbar, click the Open button, or choose File⇨Open.

▶ **Creating a new Web page using the Explorer:** On the toolbar, click the Create New Page button, or choose File⇨New⇨Page.

▶ **Creating a new Web page using the Editor:** On the Standard toolbar, click the New button, or choose File⇨New.

▶ **Saving a page:** On the Editor's Standard toolbar, click the Save button, or choose File⇨Save.

Accessing the Files on the CD

Appendix C contains everything you need to know about the CD that comes with this book, including detailed installation instructions. The CD does not contain Microsoft FrontPage 98 software — you need to purchase FrontPage separately.

Where to Go for More Help

Choose Help⇨Microsoft FrontPage Help. On the Contents tab of the Help dialog box, double-click Contacting Microsoft Technical Support. There you find a full array of Microsoft Technical support options.

DUMMIES 101™: FRONTPAGE® 98

by Asha Dornfest

IDG BOOKS WORLDWIDE

IDG Books Worldwide, Inc.
An International Data Group Company

Foster City, CA ✦ Chicago, IL ✦ Indianapolis, IN ✦ Southlake, TX

Dummies 101™: FrontPage® 98

Published by
IDG Books Worldwide, Inc.
An International Data Group Company
919 E. Hillsdale Blvd.
Suite 400
Foster City, CA 94404
www.idgbooks.com (IDG Books Worldwide Web site)
www.dummies.com (Dummies Press Web site)

Library of Congress Catalog Card No.: 97-80413

ISBN: 0-7645-0166-6

Printed in the United States of America

10 9 8 7 6 5 4 3 2 1

1B/QU/RR/ZX/IN

Distributed in the United States by IDG Books Worldwide, Inc.

Distributed by Macmillan Canada for Canada; by Transworld Publishers Limited in the United Kingdom; by IDG Norge Books for Norway; by IDG Sweden Books for Sweden; by Woodslane Pty. Ltd. for Australia; by Woodslane Enterprises Ltd. for New Zealand; by Longman Singapore Publishers Ltd. for Singapore, Malaysia, Thailand, and Indonesia; by Simron Pty. Ltd. for South Africa; by Toppan Company Ltd. for Japan; by Distribuidora Cuspide for Argentina; by Livraria Cultura for Brazil; by Ediciencia S.A. for Ecuador; by Addison-Wesley Publishing Company for Korea; by Ediciones ZETA S.C.R. Ltda. for Peru; by WS Computer Publishing Corporation, Inc., for the Philippines; by Unalis Corporation for Taiwan; by Contemporanea de Ediciones for Venezuela; by Computer Book & Magazine Store for Puerto Rico; by Express Computer Distributors for the Caribbean and West Indies. Authorized Sales Agent: Anthony Rudkin Associates for the Middle East and North Africa.

For general information on IDG Books Worldwide's books in the U.S., please call our Consumer Customer Service department at 800-762-2974. For reseller information, including discounts and premium sales, please call our Reseller Customer Service department at 800-434-3422.

For information on where to purchase IDG Books Worldwide's books outside the U.S., please contact our International Sales department at 415-655-3200 or fax 415-655-3295.

For information on foreign language translations, please contact our Foreign & Subsidiary Rights department at 415-655-3021 or fax 415-655-3281.

For sales inquiries and special prices for bulk quantities, please contact our Sales department at 415-655-3200 or write to the address above.

For information on using IDG Books Worldwide's books in the classroom or for ordering examination copies, please contact our Educational Sales department at 800-434-2086 or fax 817-251-8174.

For press review copies, author interviews, or other publicity information, please contact our Public Relations department at 415-655-3000 or fax 415-655-3299.

For authorization to photocopy items for corporate, personal, or educational use, please contact Copyright Clearance Center, 222 Rosewood Drive, Danvers, MA 01923, or fax 508-750-4470.

is a trademark under exclusive license to IDG Books Worldwide, Inc., from International Data Group, Inc.

About the Author

On her first day of college, Asha Dornfest took a bold step: She replaced her broken typewriter with a PC.

Asha did not consider herself a geek; her computer was simply a tool to help her write papers and reports. But by her senior year, she had defended her clunky PC against so many insults from Mac-loving roommates, she came to regard her computer with a sense of kinship. (Okay, so that's a little geeky.)

After graduation, Asha trudged into the real world with a liberal arts degree and strong computer skills. (Which do you think got her a job?) She quickly realized that she enjoyed showing people how computers could simplify their lives (when the things weren't making life more difficult, that is).

In 1994, Asha discovered the Internet. Soon after, she and her husband Rael started a Web design business in their dining room and began hawking their electronic wares. Mind you, this venture began during the Web-publishing Stone Age; some people had never even heard of the World Wide Web. A savvy friend quipped that ...*For Dummies* books about Web publishing might one day hit the shelves. Asha laughed.

Today, Asha writes books and articles about Web publishing and other Internet-related topics. She welcomes visitors to her virtual home at www.ashaland.com.

ABOUT IDG BOOKS WORLDWIDE

Welcome to the world of IDG Books Worldwide.

IDG Books Worldwide, Inc., is a subsidiary of International Data Group, the world's largest publisher of computer-related information and the leading global provider of information services on information technology. IDG was founded more than 25 years ago and now employs more than 8,500 people worldwide. IDG publishes more than 275 computer publications in over 75 countries (see listing below). More than 60 million people read one or more IDG publications each month.

Launched in 1990, IDG Books Worldwide is today the #1 publisher of best-selling computer books in the United States. We are proud to have received eight awards from the Computer Press Association in recognition of editorial excellence and three from *Computer Currents'* First Annual Readers' Choice Awards. Our best-selling *...For Dummies®* series has more than 30 million copies in print with translations in 30 languages. IDG Books Worldwide, through a joint venture with IDG's Hi-Tech Beijing, became the first U.S. publisher to publish a computer book in the People's Republic of China. In record time, IDG Books Worldwide has become the first choice for millions of readers around the world who want to learn how to better manage their businesses.

Our mission is simple: Every one of our books is designed to bring extra value and skill-building instructions to the reader. Our books are written by experts who understand and care about our readers. The knowledge base of our editorial staff comes from years of experience in publishing, education, and journalism — experience we use to produce books for the '90s. In short, we care about books, so we attract the best people. We devote special attention to details such as audience, interior design, use of icons, and illustrations. And because we use an efficient process of authoring, editing, and desktop publishing our books electronically, we can spend more time ensuring superior content and spend less time on the technicalities of making books.

You can count on our commitment to deliver high-quality books at competitive prices on topics you want to read about. At IDG Books Worldwide, we continue in the IDG tradition of delivering quality for more than 25 years. You'll find no better book on a subject than one from IDG Books Worldwide.

John Kilcullen
CEO
IDG Books Worldwide, Inc.

Steven Berkowitz
President and Publisher
IDG Books Worldwide, Inc.

*Eighth Annual
Computer Press
Awards 1992*

*Ninth Annual
Computer Press
Awards 1993*

*Tenth Annual
Computer Press
Awards 1994*

*Eleventh Annual
Computer Press
Awards 1995*

Dedication

For my family and friends, with love.

Author's Acknowledgments

Having one's name on a book cover is misleading because it gives the impression the author deserves 100% of the credit for the book. I'm not complaining, mind you — I'd just like to set the record straight.

I worked with an excellent editorial team at IDG Books Worldwide. I'd like to thank Kelly Oliver for her excellent direction despite a schedule crammed with other projects, Christa Carroll for her thoughtful copyediting, Gareth Hancock for tapping me for the project, and the CD trio of Kevin Spencer, Joyce Pepple, and Heather Dismore. Thank you also to Regina Snyder, Kate Snell, Drew Moore, Jane Martin, Christine Berman, Nancy Price, Betty Kish, Maridee Ennis, Angie Hunckler, Brent Savage, and Joel Draper.

I was lucky to snag Michael Lerch as my technical editor. I appreciate Mike's attention to detail, his sense of humor, and his amazing dedication.

My sincere thanks to Microsoft FrontPage 98 Product Manager Kevin Shaughnessy for his friendly insight and assistance from Day One. Kevin made a special effort to keep me updated on FrontPage happenings no matter how busy he was — for that I am very grateful. I'd also like to thank Microsoft FrontPage 98 Technical Support mensch Courtney Crawford for his commitment to a challenging beta program.

As always, David Rogelberg, Sherry Rogelberg, and Brian Gill of Studio B Productions shored me up with wise counsel and warm support. Thank you for everything you do.

I'd like to recognize the talent and generosity of Maia Matalon, whose artwork graces the CD. Thank you, Maia, for letting me use your picture in my book.

Without the reliable FrontPage Internet service provided by DNAI (www.dnai.com), I couldn't do what I do.

And finally, to my friends, my family, and especially my husband, Rael, thank you for standing with me through it all.

Publisher's Acknowledgments

We're proud of this book; please register your comments through our IDG Books Worldwide Online Registration Form located at: http://my2cents.dummies.com.

Some of the people who helped bring this book to market include the following:

Acquisitions, Development, & Editorial

Project Editor: Kelly Oliver

Acquisitions Editor: Gareth Hancock

Media Development Manager: Joyce Pepple

Associate Permissions Editor: Heather H. Dismore

Copy Editor: Christa Carroll

Editorial Manager: Leah P. Cameron

Editorial Assistant: Donna Love

Production

Project Coordinator: Regina Snyder

Layout and Graphics: Maridee Ennis, Jane E. Martin, Drew R. Moore, Angela F. Hunckler, Anna Rohrer, Brent Savage

Proofreaders: Betty Kish, Christine Berman, Joel K. Draper, Nancy Price

Indexer: Sharon Hilgenberg

Special Help

Andrea Boucher, Copy Editor; Constance Carlisle, Copy Editor; Tammy Castleman, Senior Copy Editor; Richard Graves, Product Development Administrator; Joe Jansen, Senior Copy Editor; Stephanie Koutek, Proof Editor; Barry Pruett, Strategic Partnerships Manager; Kevin Spencer, Associate Technical Editor

General & Administrative

IDG Books Worldwide, Inc.: John Kilcullen, CEO; Steven Berkowitz, President and Publisher

IDG Books Technology Publishing: Brenda McLaughlin, Senior Vice President and Group Publisher

Dummies Technology Press and Dummies Editorial: Diane Graves Steele, Vice President and Associate Publisher; Mary Bednarek, Acquisitions and Product Development Director; Kristin A. Cocks, Editorial Director

Dummies Trade Press: Kathleen A. Welton, Vice President and Publisher; Kevin Thornton, Acquisitions Manager

IDG Books Production for Dummies Press: Beth Jenkins, Production Director; Cindy L. Phipps, Manager of Project Coordination, Production Proofreading, and Indexing; Kathie S. Schutte, Supervisor of Page Layout; Shelley Lea, Supervisor of Graphics and Design; Debbie J. Gates, Production Systems Specialist; Robert Springer, Supervisor of Proofreading; Debbie Stailey, Special Projects Coordinator; Tony Augsburger, Supervisor of Reprints and Bluelines; Leslie Popplewell, Media Archive Coordinator

Dummies Packaging and Book Design: Patti Crane, Packaging Specialist; Lance Kayser, Packaging Assistant; Kavish + Kavish, Cover Design

♦

The publisher would like to give special thanks to Patrick J. McGovern, without whom this book would not have been possible.

♦

Files at a Glance

ABC 123

Here's a listing of all the CD files and where in the book you can find more information about that. See Appendix C for instructions about installing the files from the CD onto your computer. Please go to the appropriate lesson for further instructions about the particular file.

Part I

Lesson 1-4	Using FrontPage to Work with an Existing Web Site	design.htm, graphic.htm, index.htm, resource.htm, stripe.gif
Lesson 1-5	Adding Existing Files to a FrontPage Web Site	frontpg.htm
Lesson 2-3	Opening a Web Page from within the Editor	unit02.htm
Lesson 2-5	Converting Other File Formats into Web Pages	convert.doc

Part II

Lesson 3-1	Working with the *Dummies 101: FrontPage 98* Example Files	unit03.htm
Lesson 4-1	Prioritizing Information with Headings	unit04.htm
Lesson 5-1	Creating a Hyperlink	unit05.htm, resume.htm
Lesson 6-1	Inserting an Image	unit06.htm, fish.gif, backgrnd.gif, resume.htm, favorite.htm, and painter.gif
Lesson 6-4	Inserting a Background Image	backgrnd.gif

Contents at a Glance

Table of Contents

Introduction

If you picked up this book, you already know that Microsoft FrontPage 98 is one of the most powerful Web authoring tools around. With FrontPage, you don't have to be an Internet or design expert to create a beautiful, sophisticated Web site. The problem is, to create such a Web site, you *do* need to figure out how FrontPage works — a challenge in and of itself.

The best way to discover what software can do is to put the program to work on a real project. That's where *Dummies 101: FrontPage 98* comes in. This fun and easy tutorial demonstrates the capabilities of FrontPage using hands-on exercises and step-by-step examples. *Dummies 101: FrontPage 98* gets you involved with the program by leading you through the construction of a Web site.

I understand how busy you are, so instead of taking you through every single FrontPage feature, I focus on the most important skills you need to both get comfortable with FrontPage and to build a dazzling Web site. With a minimum of time and effort, you will soon be an experienced, savvy FrontPage user, ready to take on bigger and better projects.

What's Inside

This book chisels the daunting task of creating a Web site with FrontPage into a series of units. Each unit is divided into lessons that focus on specific tasks. The CD included with this book contains practice files you use as you follow each lesson, saving you lots of typing and providing you with ready-made examples of the information found in many Web sites.

Here is a preview of what you'll find inside:

Part I: Getting Your Feet Wet

Part I introduces you to the basic workings of the two major FrontPage components: the FrontPage Explorer and the FrontPage Editor. You find out how these programs work together to make Web publishing easier. You create a new Web site, and you find out how to use FrontPage to work with an existing Web site. You also get familiar with Web page basics, such as how to create and save pages and how to convert other file formats into Web pages.

Part II: The Art of Web Page Creation

The units in Part II put you to work on the stuff that sits *inside* a Web site, such as text, pictures, hyperlinks, and tables. These elements are the basic building blocks of a Web page, and you'll fall back on the skills you pick up in this part again and again.

Part III: A Web Site with All the Trimmings

In Part III, you start getting fancy. The units in this part show you how to add dynamic features to a Web site that aren't mandatory, but are definitely impressive. You create an interactive feedback form, you use frames to decorate your site, and you get your first look at FrontPage extras such as hit counters and keyword site searches.

Part IV: Publishing and Maintaining Your Web Site

Part IV takes you through the final and most exciting step, preparing your Web site for its worldwide premiere and publishing the site on the World Wide Web.

Part V: Appendixes

Appendix A contains an overview of the programs that tag along with FrontPage: Microsoft Internet Explorer 3.0 with Internet Mail and News, Microsoft Image Composer 1.5 with GIF Animator, Microsoft Personal Web Server, and the Web Publishing Wizard. Appendix B contains answers to all the book's quiz and test questions. Appendix C tells you how to use the CD that comes with this book.

What I Assume about You

You don't need any experience with Web publishing or FrontPage to follow the lessons in this book. I do, however, assume a few things about your computer setup and what you already know:

- ▶ You have access to a computer running FrontPage 98.
- ▶ You have an Internet connection through an Internet service provider or your company.
- ▶ You've seen — and hopefully explored — the World Wide Web.

◆ You know the basics of Windows 95/NT, such as how to use the Start menu, how to click toolbar buttons, how to select menu items, and how to use the Windows taskbar.

About the CD

The CD-ROM tucked inside the book's back cover contains all the exercise files you'll need as you work through the lessons in the book. In each lesson that uses one (or more) of these files, I tell you exactly what to do with the file. And as a bonus, I included sign-up software for MindSpring, an Internet service provider that fully supports FrontPage Web publishing.

The CD contains a handy installation program that copies the files to your hard drive in a very simple process. After you're finished with this book, you can follow an even simpler process to remove the files from your hard drive, if you want.

Check out Appendix C for all the details about the CD. Remember that the files are meant to accompany the book's lessons, so try to resist the urge to work with the files before I tell you to.

How to Use This Book

Dummies 101: FrontPage 98 reads very much like a workbook, with clearly-defined tasks and practical goals. Here's an overview of the book's layout.

Units and lessons

◆ **Order of events:** The first five units in this book demonstrate basic FrontPage and Web publishing skills, and are most useful if followed in order. After that, I strongly recommend continuing through each unit in order, just because each lesson builds on your previous work. If you feel like skipping around a little, however, I include completed practice files for each unit on the CD and I explain how to use them in each unit.

◆ **Objectives, prerequisites, and practice files:** Every unit begins with a list of objectives that tells you the skills you learn in that unit. I also list any prerequisites (things you already need to know how to do) before you begin each unit. If the unit makes use of practice files, I list filenames at the beginning of the unit.

◆ **Text conventions:** Each unit is divided into lessons. Lessons are full of practical, step-by-step examples in which you work with FrontPage. I use a few text conventions when I describe examples, as follows:

A notation such as "Choose File➪Open FrontPage Web" is a condensed version of "From the File menu, choose the Open FrontPage Web command."

When I say "Press Ctrl+N," it means "While holding down the Ctrl key on your keyboard, press the letter N."

If you are trying to cut down on your mouse usage, the underlined letters in the instructions indicate keyboard shortcuts. To activate a keyboard shortcut, do this: While holding down the Alt key on your keyboard, simultaneously press the first underlined letter to open the menu. Then press the next underlined letter (without holding down Alt) to activate the command. For example, to use keyboard shortcuts instead of choosing File➪Open FrontPage Web, you would press Alt+F and then you would press O.

▶ **Margin notes:** As you follow the lessons, be sure to glance in the page margins. There, I jot down notes to help you remember important points such as the names of toolbar buttons or the main point of that paragraph, among other things.

▶ **Recess:** Each unit packs in a ton of information, so I toss in a Recess when I think you may want a break. Use Recess as a time to rest and recharge your brain or to stretch your legs.

▶ **Progress check:** At the end of each lesson, I include a Progress Check — a list of things you should know how to do after you've finished the lesson.

▶ **Unit quizzes and exercises:** At the end of each unit, you find a short quiz and an exercise. If the idea of quizzes brings on a terrifying flashback of your fifth grade math teacher, don't worry. No one is hovering over you with a red pencil — the quizzes simply serve as a way to review the stuff you learned in the unit (you can check your answers in Appendix B). The exercises give you a chance to apply your new skills without step-by-step instructions.

Icons

The following icons in each unit point out special types of information:

heads up

If you see this icon, don't duck — instead, pay special attention to a potentially troublesome point.

on the test

This icon points out information that appears on a quiz or test. I don't give away *every* answer, but I do try to make it as easy as possible for you to remember important details.

extra credit

FrontPage contains hundreds of capabilities, some of which you need to know, and others that are fun or interesting but not mandatory. I point out many of these extras using this icon.

on the CD

This icon appears when you are about to use a practice file from the CD.

reminder: watch for margin notes

Part reviews and tests

At the end of each part, I summarize the main points of each unit and I give you a comprehensive test of the material covered in that part. Again, as with the unit quizzes, my goal isn't to intimidate you, it's to provide a way for you to know that you really *got* the stuff you learned. To be sure that you're on the right track, check your answers in Appendix B.

The highlight of the Part Review is the Lab Assignment. There, you get a chance to apply your new FrontPage skills to your *own* real-world Web project. The Lab Assignments help you get started on your own Web site, whether it's a personal home page, a professional Web site, or an internal department project.

Beta Changes and Errata

I wrote this book using a prerelease or *beta* version of FrontPage 98. Although we tested all the examples in this book using the final beta version, a slight chance exists that the version of FrontPage 98 you bought at the store contains minor differences from the version I used to write the book.

If the instructions listed in the book don't exactly match what you see on your screen, check to see that the computer and Internet connection are working properly. If everything checks out, you may have stumbled upon a beta change. I list all beta changes and errata on the Beta Changes and Errata page, located at www.ashaland.com/webpub/errata.html. Please check this page, and if you don't see what you need listed there, please write to me at webpub@ashaland.com. I want to be sure that this book is as perfect as it can be; plus I can integrate the bug fixes into future printings of *Dummies 101: FrontPage 98*.

One Last Thing . . .

I'd love to hear from you. If you ever want to get in touch, feel free to drop by my Web site at www.ashaland.com or send e-mail to webpub@ashaland.com.

Notes:

Getting Your Feet Wet

Part I

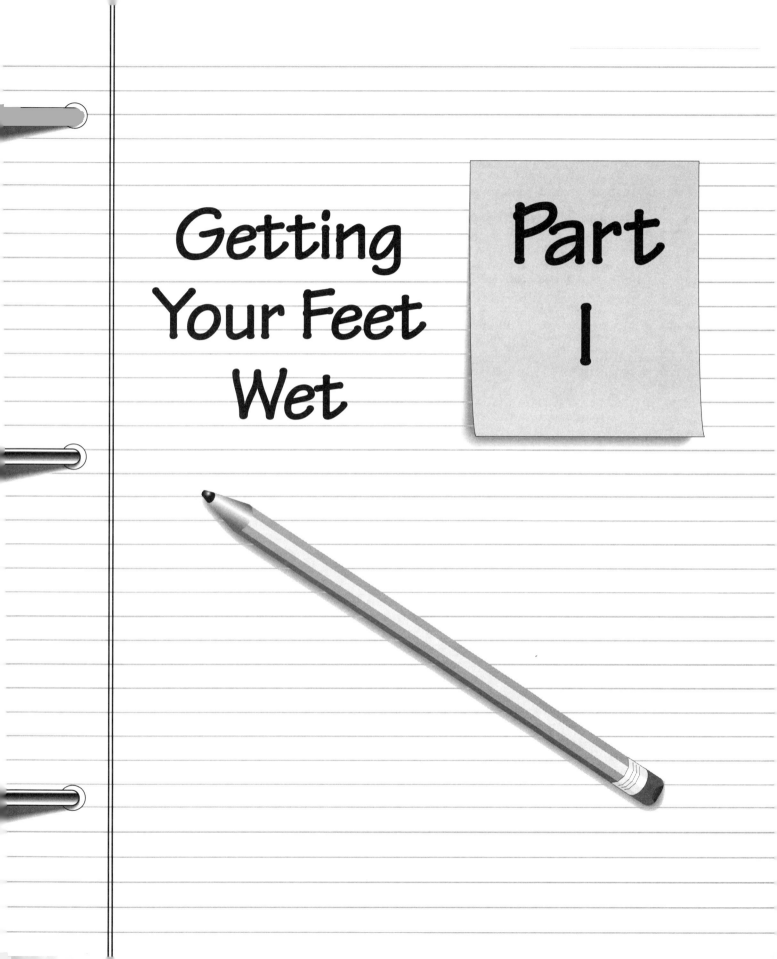

In this part . . .

I find that dipping my pinkie toe into a swimming pool is always easier than diving in head-first. Therefore, Part I provides a gentle introduction to Web publishing and the workings of FrontPage 98. Here, you gain basic FrontPage fluency you'll use throughout the rest of this book.

In this part, you find out what's involved in publishing a Web site, and, more importantly, how FrontPage simplifies the process. You become familiar with how FrontPage looks and acts. You tinker with its buttons and toolbars, and you experience how easy getting your Web site started can be.

Crafting Web Sites in the FrontPage Explorer

Prerequisites

▶ Installing FrontPage 98

▶ Installing the *Dummies 101* CD files (See Installation Instructions on the last page of the book.)

on the CD

▶ The importweb folder and its contents: design.htm, graphic.htm. index.htm, resource.htm, and the images folder (which contains the graphic file stripe.gif)

▶ frontpg.htm

Objectives for This Unit

✓ Understanding the Web publishing process

✓ Launching FrontPage

✓ Creating a new Web site

✓ Using FrontPage to work with an existing Web site

✓ Getting familiar with the Explorer's views

✓ Exiting FrontPage

The Internet, especially its colorful, seductively clickable cousin the World Wide Web, has taken the world by storm. Web addresses seem to be popping up everywhere: business cards, cereal boxes, and TV commercials all beckon us to log on and explore. If you're like many folks, you're excited by the benefits the Web offers — higher visibility among your customers, a cutting-edge reputation, a link to the global community — and you're ready to get involved. You want a Web site, *today*.

In this unit, you find out what's involved in publishing a Web site. Then you jump right in and start building Web sites with the help of the FrontPage Explorer, the component of FrontPage that's in charge of creating and managing Web sites.

Lesson 1-1

Understanding What *Web Publishing* Means

Web site = group of interconnected Web pages and files

don't need to know HTML to use FrontPage

to make a site visible on the Web, transfer site's files to a web server

☑ **Progress Check**

If you can do the following, you've mastered this lesson:

❏ Understand the basic Web publishing process.

on the test

Sure, FrontPage simplifies the Web site building process, but before you get started, you're better off understanding what the process entails. After you're armed with the big picture — even if the picture is a bit fuzzy — the individual Web-building steps make a lot more sense.

A *Web site* is your own personal corner of the World Wide Web. Anyone with an Internet connection and a web browser (a program such as Microsoft Internet Explorer or Netscape Navigator) can visit your site.

A Web site is simply a collection of interconnected files. The files you see when you visit someone's Web site are called *Web pages*. Web pages contain the text, graphics, and other nifty effects that make up your site's content. Web pages also contain *hyperlinks* — graphics or bits of text that visitors click to go to another location or page. Hyperlinks connect the pages in a Web site to one another, and they also connect the site to remote destinations on the Web. FrontPage contains all the tools you need to create Web pages full of text, graphics, hyperlinks, and more.

With FrontPage, you can create Web pages without having to know *HTML*. HTML (short for *Hypertext Markup Language*) is the set of structure and formatting codes that underlie all Web pages. Not long ago, if you wanted to create a Web site, you needed to know all the HTML codes. Learning HTML isn't difficult, but it can be rather time-consuming. FrontPage does all the HTML work for you, so you can concentrate on the fun stuff — the content and design of your Web site.

extra credit

Should I know HTML?

Although you don't *need* to know HTML to do wonders with FrontPage, a little HTML know-how deepens your understanding of Web publishing and enables you to keep your Web site on the cutting-edge of design. If you're even the teensiest bit interested in finding out about HTML, plenty of excellent tutorials are available on the Web. I list a few of my favorites at `www.ashaland.com/webpub/about.html`.

After your Web site is complete, you're ready to *publish,* or make the site visible on the Web. To do so, you must copy all the Web site files from your computer to a different computer called a *web server.* A web server runs special server software and is connected to the Internet 24 hours per day. If you're publishing a personal Web site, most likely you transfer your files to a computer maintained by your Internet service provider (ISP). If you're working on a corporate or *intranet* site, you'll most likely use your company's web server (an intranet is a company's internal network accessible only to employees). Whatever your situation, publishing your Web site is a simple task with FrontPage. Unit 13 demonstrates how to publish your Web site.

Launching FrontPage

on the test

Now that you have a sense of what's involved when you create and publish a Web site, you're ready to fire up FrontPage. FrontPage isn't a single program; it's a Web publishing suite that contains three distinct programs that work together.

> ◆ **FrontPage Explorer.** The Explorer is where you create, view, and manage the files that make up your Web site. Think of the Explorer as your FrontPage starting point; each time you launch FrontPage to create a new Web site or edit an existing site, you begin by working with tools in the Explorer.
>
> ◆ **FrontPage Editor.** After you've created or opened a Web site in the Explorer, you use the Editor to add text, graphics, and other stuff to the site's individual pages. (Unit 2 introduces you to the workings of the Editor.)
>
> ◆ **Personal Web Server.** The Personal Web Server works in the background as you build your Web site with FrontPage. This program enables you to test your Web site on your own computer without first having to publish the site on another computer.

heads up

The FrontPage program CD contains two different web server programs: the *FrontPage* Personal Web Server and the *Microsoft* Personal Web Server. Which server program you're using right now depends on choices you made when you installed FrontPage on your computer. When you installed FrontPage, the FrontPage Setup program may have encouraged you to install the Microsoft Personal Web Server before installing the rest of FrontPage. If you said Yes, the Setup program installed the Microsoft Personal Web Server and then proceeded to install FrontPage. If you said No, the Setup program installed FrontPage along with the less-powerful-but-perfectly-adequate FrontPage Personal Web Server.

If you're not sure which version of the Personal Web Server you're using right now, take a look at the taskbar. If you see this button on the taskbar, you're using the FrontPage Personal Web Server.

If you don't see a button but instead see this icon in the lower-right corner of the screen, you're using the Microsoft Personal Web Server.

The examples in this book assume that you are using the FrontPage Personal Web Server. If you are using the Microsoft Personal Web Server, a few minor details will be different. I point out these details as they come up.

If some of this information doesn't ring a bell right now, don't worry. I talk more about each piece of the FrontPage puzzle as you follow the lessons in this and upcoming units. The workings of FrontPage will also become clearer after you launch the program and peer inside the Explorer menus and poke around the toolbar.

FrontPage is made up of three distinct programs: the FrontPage Explorer, the FrontPage Editor, and the Personal Web Server

Notes:

🔌 Web Server idle

FrontPage Personal Web Server

🖥️

Microsoft Personal Web Server

🏁 Start

Start button

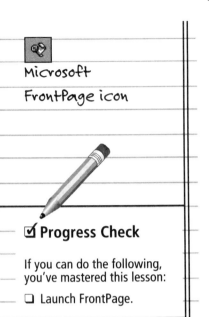

Microsoft
FrontPage icon

☑ **Progress Check**

If you can do the following,
you've mastered this lesson:

❑ Launch FrontPage.

Time to get started! To launch FrontPage, follow these steps:

1 **On the Windows 95 taskbar, click the Start button.**

The Start menu pops up.

2 **From the Start menu, choose Programs and then select the Microsoft FrontPage icon.**

I describe the default position of the Microsoft FrontPage icon. If you organize your Start menu differently, the icon may be sitting in a different position on the Start menu.

heads up

After you select the Microsoft FrontPage icon, the FrontPage Explorer launches, and the Getting Started dialog box appears (see Figure 1-1). (Don't worry if your screen doesn't look exactly like Figure 1-1. The contents of the Getting Started dialog box depend on your computer's individual settings.)

At this point, you can choose to open an existing site (FrontPage comes installed with a default Web site) or you can create a new Web site.

In the next lesson, you jump straight into Web-building by creating a new site. (Leave the Getting Started dialog box open because you'll use it in a moment.)

Lesson 1-3

Creating a New Web Site

the Explorer sets
up the site's
structure; the
Editor works with
the site's content

The traditional way to go about creating Web sites is to first create individual Web pages, and then link the pages together to form a cohesive Web site. FrontPage turns the process upside-down: First you create the Web site and then you add text and graphics to the site's pages.

Many first-time FrontPage users get tripped up by this seemingly chicken-and-egg scenario. After all, if a Web site is made up of Web pages, how can you create the site first and the pages later? The answer lies in the partnership between the Explorer and the Editor. You first use the Explorer to set up the site's basic structure (its file system and navigational flow). After the basic structure is established, you use the Editor to add and change the site's content (in Part II, you use the Editor to work with individual Web pages).

on the test

FrontPage gives you three options for creating a new Web site:

▶ You can use a *template* as a starting point.

▶ You can build your site from scratch.

▶ You can *import* an existing site into FrontPage.

In this lesson, you create one site using a FrontPage template, and you build another site from scratch. In Lesson 1-4, you import an existing site into FrontPage.

Creating a Web site using a template

If you're not sure where to begin, avail yourself of a FrontPage Web site template. Each template contains a set of generic pages to which you add your own distinctive content. The Explorer contains templates for five Web sites, as outlined here:

- **Customer Support Web.** This template is useful for companies that use the Web to share product help with customers. Customers access the Web site for product announcements, contact information, product discussions with other users, and more.

- **Personal Web.** Use this template as the basis for a personal home page. The Personal Web template contains space for a photograph collection, information about yourself, and a list of favorite sites.

- **Project Web.** This site tracks the status of a project and includes space for project team members, status reports, schedules, an archive, a search form, and a discussion forum.

- **Corporate Presence Wizard.** The Corporate Presence Web site contains everything necessary for a company site, including graphics and an interactive feedback form.

- **Discussion Web Wizard.** The Discussion Web site enables visitors to post comments and read others' replies about a given topic.

The Empty Web option isn't really a template because it doesn't create any pages; it simply sets aside space for pages you create yourself.

heads up

The Corporate Presence and Discussion Web sites are fairly complex. To assist you in the construction of these sites, FrontPage provides you with *Wizards*. A Wizard is a series of dialog boxes that leads you through a multistep process by prompting you for information. For details about how these Wizards work, refer to the FrontPage Help system by choosing <u>H</u>elp⇨<u>M</u>icrosoft FrontPage Help, or by pressing F1.

If you'll now follow me, I can show you how to create a Web site using the Project Web template.

1 **In the Getting Started dialog box, click the <u>C</u>reate a New FrontPage Web radio button and click OK.**

(If the Getting Started dialog box isn't visible, choose <u>F</u>ile⇨<u>N</u>ew⇨FrontPage <u>W</u>eb.)

The Getting Started dialog box closes, and the New FrontPage Web dialog box appears (see Figure 1-2).

2 **In the dialog box's From <u>W</u>izard or Template area, click Project Web.**

3 **In the Choose a <u>T</u>itle for Your FrontPage Web text box, type** Project. **Then click OK.**

After you click OK, a pause occurs. If the version of the Personal Web Server you're using requires an access password, the Name and Password Required dialog box appears.

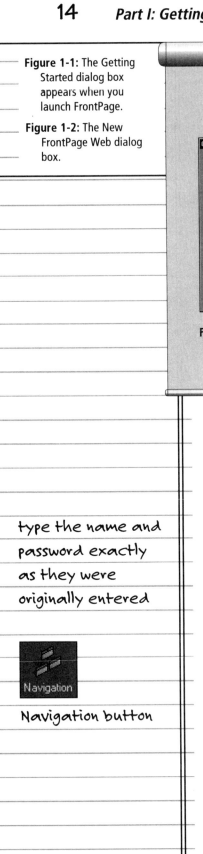

Figure 1-1: The Getting Started dialog box appears when you launch FrontPage.

Figure 1-2: The New FrontPage Web dialog box.

type the name and password exactly as they were originally entered

Navigation button

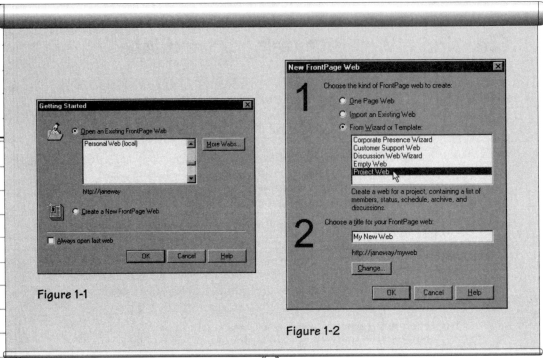

Figure 1-1

Figure 1-2

4 **In the Name and Password text boxes, type the administrator name and password you chose when you installed FrontPage and then click OK.**

After you click OK, the Name and Password Required dialog box closes, and FrontPage rumbles and grumbles as it sets up your Web site. (This takes a few moments.) Pretty soon, the Project Web site appears in the Explorer, as shown in Figure 1-3.

Right now, you are looking at the Project Web site as it appears in the Explorer's Navigation View (if your screen doesn't look like Figure 1-3, in the Views bar on the left side of the Explorer window, click Navigation). The Navigation View's upper portion (called the Navigation pane) contains a chart of the site's navigational structure; in this case, a main home page that directs visitors to six interior pages, each of which represents a different section of the site. The lower portion (called the Files pane) displays the site's system of files and folders.

If you were to use this template as the basis for your Web site, you would customize the site's content by opening each page in the FrontPage Editor and adding your own text and graphics. In upcoming units, you work with individual pages — right now, I show you another way to create a new Web site — by building it from the ground up.

Creating a Web site from scratch

If you already have an idea about how you want your site to look, you can forgo the canned FrontPage Web site templates and instead build your site page by page. You can use the Explorer to create a Web site containing a single blank page. You then add new pages to the site based on your own personal preferences.

In the following steps, you create a new Web site you use and add to in this and upcoming units. This Web site, called *My Web Site,* is like your FrontPage scratch pad; you scribble on it to prepare yourself for future masterpieces.

1 If the Getting Started dialog box is visible, click the Create a New FrontPage Web radio button and then click OK. Otherwise, choose File⇨New⇨FrontPage Web.

The New FrontPage Web dialog box appears.

2 In the dialog box, click the One Page Web radio button.

If you *really* wanted to build a site from scratch — that is, without even a home page to start off the site — you could choose the Empty Web template instead, but I find the One Page Web option much easier to use.

3 In the Choose a Title for Your FrontPage Web text box, type My Web Site.

Take special notice of the line that appears underneath the Choose a Title for Your FrontPage Web text box (it looks something like `http://servername/mywebsite`). This line is the address or *URL* of the Web site you are about to create. URL stands for *Uniform Resource Locator*, which is the technical name for a Web address. This particular URL points to the Personal Web Server on your computer (most URLs you've seen while Web surfing point to web servers elsewhere on the Internet).

4 In the New FrontPage Web dialog box, click OK.

The dialog box closes. FrontPage creates the one-page Web site, and in a moment, the site becomes visible in the Explorer.

If it isn't already visible, switch to the Navigation View (in the Views bar on the left side of the Explorer window, click the Navigation button).

This time, instead of the fleshed-out navigation structure produced by the Project Web template, the Navigation pane displays a single page: the Home Page. The Files pane displays the Web site's file structure, which, in this case, contains two folders and the home page named index.htm (if you're using the Microsoft Personal Web Server, the home page is named Default.htm).

heads up

Different makes and models of web servers recognize different names as the site's default home page. Most web servers recognize index.htm or index.html, but others recognize default.htm, welcome.htm, and home.htm. For now, don't worry about the home page filename. It only becomes an issue when you publish your Web site. I return to this issue in Unit 12.

FrontPage generates a URL for the new web site

Navigation button

Figure 1-3: This is how a site based on the Project Web template looks in the FrontPage Explorer's Navigation View.

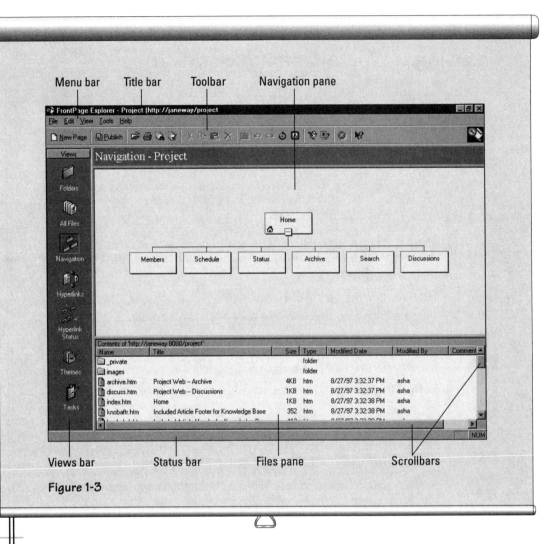

Menu bar   Title bar   Toolbar   Navigation pane

Views bar   Status bar   Files pane   Scrollbars

Figure 1-3

At this point, you can use the Editor to open and add stuff to the home page, or you can fill out the site with additional pages (I show you how to create new pages in Lesson 2-4). Instead, for now, put My Web Site aside. In upcoming units you flesh out the site.

Recess

It's time for a break and some back-patting because you have just created two new Web sites! Did you expect the first steps to be so easy? Congratulations — you're on your way to even bigger and better things in the upcoming lessons.

☑ **Progress Check**

If you can do the following, you've mastered this lesson:

❏ Create a new Web site using a template.

❏ Create a new one-page Web site.

Using FrontPage to Work with an Existing Web Site

Lesson 1-4

Quite a few new FrontPage users have already dabbled in Web design using other Web publishing programs. A few intrepid souls may have hand-crafted Web sites using HTML. If you're one of these people and you'd like to use FrontPage to update and maintain your Web site, you first need to *import* the Web site into FrontPage. You'll be glad to know that the Explorer's Import Web Wizard does most of the work for you.

on the CD

So you can experience the coolness of the Import Web Wizard firsthand, I included a complete sample Web site on the CD. The sample Web site's files are stored in a folder called importweb, which, in turn, is stored in the FP101 folder on your hard drive. (If, when you installed the CD files, you chose a location other than C:\FP101, the importweb folder is stored in the location you chose.)

To summon the Import Web Wizard, follow these steps:

1 **If the Getting Started dialog box is visible, click the Create a New FrontPage Web radio button and then click OK. Otherwise, choose File⇨New⇨FrontPage Web.**

The New FrontPage Web dialog box appears.

2 **In the dialog box, click the Import an Existing Web radio button.**

3 **In the Choose a Title for Your FrontPage Web text box, type Import Example. Then click OK.**

You can enter any name in the text box; I chose the name Import Example simply as a reminder that this Web site illustrates the import process.

The Create New FrontPage Web dialog box appears while FrontPage sets aside a space on the Personal Web Server for the new Web site. In a moment, dialog box closes, and the Import Web Wizard - Choose Source dialog box appears. In this dialog box, you specify the location of the Web site files you want to import.

4 **In the dialog box, click Browse.**

The Browse For Folder dialog box appears. This dialog box enables you to browse the contents of your computer and then select the folder that contains the files you want to import.

5 **Click the plus sign sitting next to the FP101 folder.**

The folders inside the FP101 folder become visible.

6 **Click the importweb folder.**

The folder opens (see Figure 1-4).

7 **Click OK.**

The Browse For Folder dialog box closes, and the Import Web Wizard — Choose Source dialog box becomes visible again, and the *path* to the importweb folder is visible in the Location text box (see Figure 1-5).

Notes:

Note: If your Internet connection is active, you can also import a site directly from the World Wide Web. To do so, in the dialog box, click the From a World Wide Web Site radio button and then enter the site's URL in the Location text box (a URL looks something like `www.microsoft.com`).

8 In the dialog box, click the Include Subfolders check box and then click Next.

The Import Web Wizard - Edit File List dialog box appears, with all the files contained in the importweb folder listed in the Files area. Notice that stripe.gif appears with a folder notation (images/) in front of its name. The folder notation tells you that the graphic file stripe.gif is stored in the images folder, which is, in turn, stored inside the importweb folder.

heads up

In this example, you want to import every file listed in the dialog box into the site. Sometimes, however, you import a complex site into FrontPage, and you don't want to import every single file contained in the folder. In that case, you can select the files you want to exclude by clicking their names in the text box and then clicking Exclude. If you change your mind and want to start over with a fresh file list, click Refresh.

9 Click Next again.

The Import Web Wizard - Finish dialog box appears, congratulating you on a job well done. This dialog box also gives you an opportunity to change any of your selections by clicking Back to return to previous dialog boxes. But because you're sure that you're ready to move on (right?) . . . .

10 Click Finish.

The Import Web Wizard does its thing, and in a moment, the Import Example Web site appears in the Explorer's Navigation View (see Figure 1-6).

The Web site is now primed and ready for FrontPage treatment. (In Unit 2, you get your first look at the FrontPage Editor by opening the pages inside this Web site.)

heads up

If the home page filename of an imported site doesn't match the filename the Personal Web Server uses to identify the home page, in order for FrontPage to display the Web site properly, FrontPage changes the filename when it imports the site. For example, say your Web site's home page filename is home.htm. If you are using the FrontPage Personal Web Server, when you import the Web site, FrontPage automatically changes the home page filename to index.htm. (If you are using the Microsoft Personal Web Server, FrontPage changes the home page filename to Default.htm.)

This little quirk only becomes an issue when it comes time to publish your Web site. I talk about the significance of home page filenames in Unit 12.

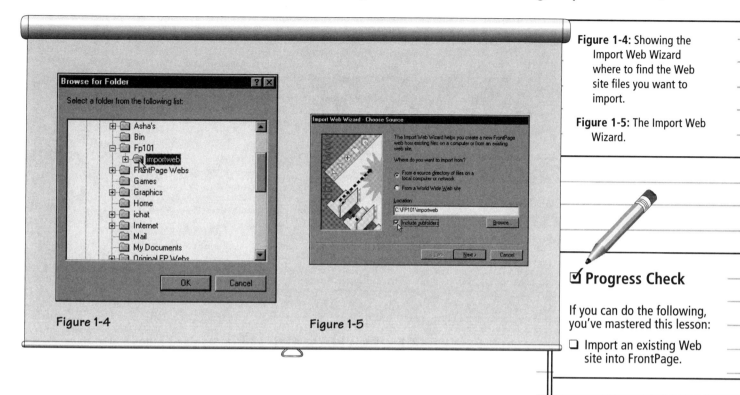

Figure 1-4: Showing the Import Web Wizard where to find the Web site files you want to import.

Figure 1-5: The Import Web Wizard.

Figure 1-4   Figure 1-5

☑ **Progress Check**

If you can do the following, you've mastered this lesson:

❑ Import an existing Web site into FrontPage.

Adding Existing Files to a FrontPage Web Site

Lesson 1-5

In Lesson 1-4, you imported an entire Web site into FrontPage. If, however, you want to import only single files or folders into a FrontPage Web site, you can do that, too.

For example, say that you take the Corporate Web Wizard for a spin and are now ready to begin customizing your corporate Web site. You realize you already have the entire company phone directory stored on your hard drive — as a Web page, no less. You can simply import that single Web page into Web site. You can even import pages and files directly from the World Wide Web.

on the CD

In the following steps, you import the file frontpg.htm (currently sitting in the FP101 folder) into the Import Example Web site.

1 **With the Import Example Web site open in the Explorer, choose File⇨Import.**

The Import File to FrontPage Web dialog box appears.

2 **In the dialog box, click Add File.**

The Add File to Import List dialog box appears. You use this dialog box to choose the files and folders you want to import.

Figure 1-6: The Import Web site, as it looks after being imported into FrontPage.

Figure 1-7: Importing a single file into a FrontPage Web site.

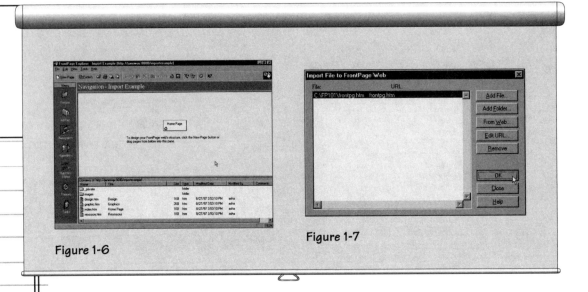

Figure 1-6

Figure 1-7

☑ Progress Check

If you can do the following, you've mastered this lesson:

❑ Import a file into a FrontPage Web site.

3 **In the dialog box, navigate your hard drive to the FP101 folder.**

The contents of the FP101 folder appear inside the dialog box's file list.

4 **In the file list, click frontpg.htm.**

5 **In the dialog box, click Open.**

The Add File to Import List dialog box closes, and the file's path appears in the import list in the Import File to FrontPage Web dialog box (see Figure 1-7).

6 **Click OK.**

The dialog box closes, and FrontPage imports frontpg.htm into the Import Example Web site.

In Unit 2, you find out how to create new pages to add to your Web site.

Lesson 1-6

Getting Familiar with the Explorer Views

on the test

After you create a FrontPage Web site, you can use the Explorer to display the site in different ways. In this lesson, I introduce you to each of the Explorer's seven views.

You can switch between views by clicking the icons sitting in the Views bar, which is the vertical strip on the left side of the Explorer window (see Figure 1-8).

Folders View

The Folders View works like a file cabinet; it shows you the files and folders that make up your Web site. The Folders View looks and acts much like the Windows 95 Explorer; use it when you want to make changes to the site's file system, such as renaming files or storing files in subfolders.

In the following steps, you find your way around the Folders View. In Unit 12, you return to the Folders View to rearrange the file system of My Web Site which, by then, will be full of pages and files.

1 **In the Views bar, click Folders.**

The Explorer switches to Folders View. The left pane contains a hierarchical outline of the Import Example Web site's folders. The right pane displays the contents of the folder that's open in the left pane.

2 **If it's not already open, in the left pane, click the top folder in the folder list.**

The contents of the folder appear in the right pane, as shown in Figure 1-9.

3 **Near the top of the right pane, click the Modified Date header label.**

The order of the file list in the right pane changes and is now sorted by the date the files were last modified.

4 **In the left pane, click the images folder.**

(If the images folder isn't visible in the left pane, click the plus icon next to the top folder to display the subfolders.)

The contents of the images folder become visible in the right pane — in this case, the image file stripe.gif.

5 **Keep exploring the Folders View until you feel like you know your way around.**

When you create Web sites in FrontPage, the Explorer automatically creates another folder in addition to the images folder: the _private folder. Files stored in the _private folder are hidden from web browsers and from the Search Form Active Element (you learn about Active Elements in Unit 11).

All Files View

If you simply want to see a no-nonsense list of the files in your site, check out the All Files View (see Figure 1-10). The All Files View gives you more detailed information about the files in your Web site. This View displays your files in a single list, eliminating the need to hunt and peck inside folders to find a particular file.

To display the All Files View, in the Views bar, click All Files. As with the Folders View, you can sort the file list by clicking the header labels at the top of the View.

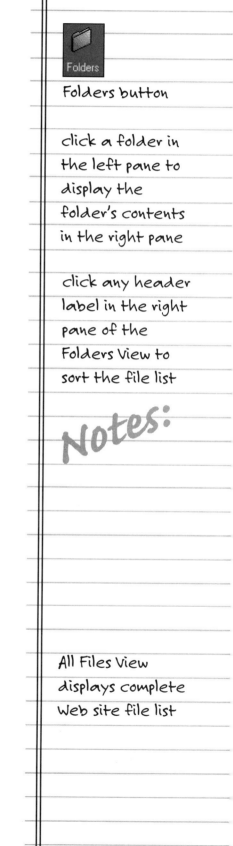

Folders button

click a folder in the left pane to display the folder's contents in the right pane

click any header label in the right pane of the Folders View to sort the file list

Notes:

All Files View displays complete Web site file list

Figure 1-8: The Explorer Views bar.

Figure 1-9: Working with the Folders View.

Figure 1-10: The All Files View.

Notes:

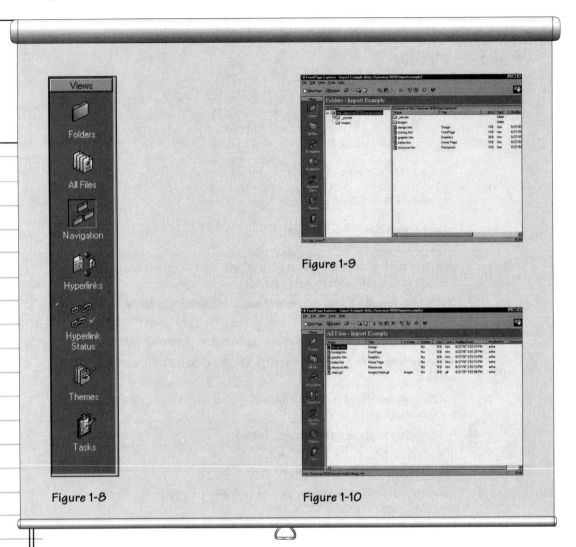

Figure 1-9

Figure 1-8   Figure 1-10

All Files button

Navigation button

Hyperlinks View
illustrates the Web
site's system of links

Navigation View

You already got a peek at the Navigation View in earlier lessons. This view enables you to design your site's navigational flow by building a graphical navigation structure inside the top Navigation pane. The lower Files pane displays a list of the site's files and folders.

You get to play with the Navigation View in Unit 5 when you create a navigational structure for My Web Site.

Hyperlinks View

The process of building a Web site can sometimes resemble urban sprawl: What starts out as a compact group of pages with a few links quickly grows into a collection of many pages with links leading every which way. The Hyperlinks View is like a road map — it helps you stay on top of your site's system of links as the site expands and becomes more complex.

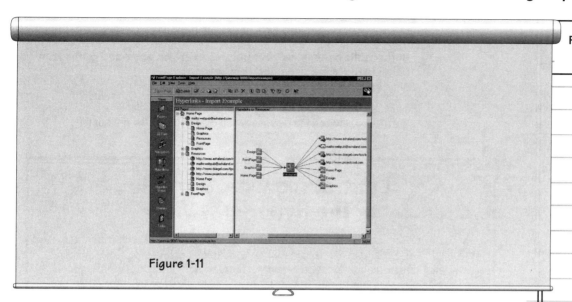

Figure 1-11

Figure 1-11: Working with
the Hyperlinks View.

You haven't yet experienced creating hyperlinks (you will in Unit 5), but that's
okay because the Import Example Web site already contains hyperlinks so that
you can see how the Hyperlinks View works.

1 **In the Views bar, click Hyperlinks.**

The Explorer switches to the Hyperlinks View. The left pane of the Hyperlinks
View contains an outline of the pages in the Import Example Web site, starting
with the site's home page. The right pane contains a magnified view of
whichever page is currently selected in the outline. In the right pane, the
hyperlinks leading to and from the page are listed with arrows.

2 **In the outline in the left pane, click the plus sign next to the page
titled Design.**

In the left pane, the outline expands to display the hyperlinks contained within
the Design page. The page contains hyperlinks leading to all the other pages in
the site (this setup enables visitors to explore the site easily because they can
jump to any page from any other page depending on where they want to go).

At the same time, in the right pane, the Design page moves to the center of the
magnified view. In the right pane, the pages with arrows leading to the Design
page represent the other pages in the Web site that contain links to that page
(these types of links are known as *incoming links*). The arrows leading away
from the Design page represent the links inside that page that lead to other
locations (otherwise known as *outgoing links*).

3 **In the left pane, click the plus sign next to the page icon titled
Resources.**

Again, the outline in the left pane expands to display the page's hyperlinks, and
the page moves to the center of the magnified view in the right pane (see
Figure 1-11). Like the previous page, this page contains hyperlinks to the other
pages inside the site. In addition, this page contains links to other sites on the
Web, as indicated in both panes with a globe icon. The page also contains a
link to an e-mail address (also known as a *mailto link*), which is marked with a
postal letter icon.

Hyperlinks button

⊞

click the plus sign

click an icon in the
left pane to
display a
magnified view of
the page's links in
the right pane

Hyperlinks to
Images button

Repeated
Hyperlinks button

Hyperlinks Inside
Pages button

☑ **Progress Check**

If you can do the following,
you've mastered this lesson:

❏ Switch between views in
the Explorer.

❏ Understand the
differences among the
seven views.

Hyperlink Status
button

---

4 **In the right pane, pass your pointer over the page-and-globe icon titled http://www.ashaland.com/webpub.**

If you can't see the icon, adjust the position of the view by moving the scrollbars on the bottom and right margins of the right pane, and by clicking the divider between the two panes and dragging it to the right or left.

extra credit

Controlling what's visible in the Hyperlinks View

As your site grows and becomes more involved, the Hyperlinks View can get crowded. Three toolbar buttons enable you to show and hide different types of links in the Hyperlinks View. By clicking these buttons, you can make visible only those links you want to see at any given time.

▶ **Hyperlinks to Images.** Clicking this button enables you to show or hide a listing of the images displayed inside each Web page (you can also choose View⇨Hyperlinks to Images).

▶ **Repeated Hyperlinks.** If a page contains more than one hyperlink

leading to the same location, the Explorer displays only one link. To make repeated links visible, you must click Repeated Hyperlinks or choose View⇨Repeated Hyperlinks.

▶ **Hyperlinks Inside Page.** If a page contains hyperlinks to locations within the page itself (better known as links to *bookmarks*), the Explorer doesn't display these links. To make links inside pages visible, you must click Hyperlinks Inside Page or choose View⇨Hyperlinks Inside Page.

When you pass the pointer over the icon, the arrow leading to the icon turns from blue to red, and a label that reads `External hyperlink: http://www.ashaland.com/webpub (Not verified)` appears. This label confirms that the hyperlink leads to a location outside this Web site, and reminds you that the link has not yet been tested to be sure it works (you test hyperlinks in Unit 12). You can pass your pointer over any icon in the right pane to get more information about that particular link. (Try it!)

5 **In the right pane, in the list of outgoing links, click the plus sign next to the page icon titled Graphics.**

The view expands to display the outgoing links contained in that page.

Being able to see your site's system of links at a glance helps you chart easy paths for your visitors to follow as they explore your site. As your site gets bigger, you'll find the Hyperlinks View an invaluable tool.

Hyperlink Status View

This view enables you to test and repair broken hyperlinks. You take this view for a spin in Unit 12.

Themes View

This view lists an array of graphical themes you can apply to your Web site. You find out about Themes when you add graphics to Web pages in Unit 6.

Themes button

Tasks View

This view enables you to maintain an ongoing to-do list of Web-building tasks. You don't use this view in this book, so to find out more about the Tasks View, refer to the FrontPage Help system by choosing <u>H</u>elp⇨Microsoft FrontPage <u>H</u>elp or by pressing F1.

Tasks button

Exiting FrontPage   Lesson 1-7

After you're done with Web-building for the day, you need to exit FrontPage. If a Web site is open in the Explorer when you exit the program, that's okay; FrontPage saves and closes the Web site as it shuts down.

To exit FrontPage, choose <u>F</u>ile⇨E<u>x</u>it, or click the Close button (X) in the upper-right corner of the FrontPage Explorer window. The FrontPage Explorer closes, and your Windows 95 desktop becomes visible.

heads up

When you exit FrontPage, the FrontPage Personal Web Server doesn't close automatically (if its button is visible in the taskbar, the FrontPage Personal Web Server is still running). To exit the Personal Web Server, right-click its taskbar button and then, from the shortcut menu that appears, choose Close.

If you're using the Microsoft Personal Web Server, by default, the server starts up each time you turn on your computer, and stays on all the time. This setup is just fine for most people, but if you want to turn the server off, on the taskbar click the Start button and then choose <u>S</u>ettings⇨<u>C</u>ontrol Panel. In the Control Panel window that appears, double-click Personal Web Server. The Personal Web Server Properties dialog box appears. At the top of the dialog box, click the Startup tab. In the Startup tab, click Stop. Click OK to close the Personal Web Server Properties dialog box. The Microsoft Personal Web Server is now off, and will start up again the next time you restart your computer.

If you turn off the Microsoft Personal Web Server, and later you want to use FrontPage (but don't want to restart your computer to launch the Microsoft Personal Web Server again), turn the server back on by following the same steps you followed to turn off the server, except click Start.

☒

Close button

don't forget to shut down the FrontPage Personal Web Server

☑ **Progress Check**

If you can do the following, you've mastered this lesson:

❑ Exit FrontPage.

Notes:

Unit 1 Quiz

Notes:

This short quiz will help you remember what you've discovered in this unit. If quizzes and tests intimidate you, try to relax. Unit quizzes simply give you a chance to review the unit's main points.

For each of the following questions, circle the letter of the correct answer or answers. Remember, I may throw in more than one right answer for each question. If you want to check your answers, turn to Appendix B.

1. **A Web site is . . .**

    A. A collection of individual Web pages that are linked together.

    B. A place you can visit on the World Wide Web.

    C. The local arachnid community.

    D. A computer connected to the Internet 24 hours per day.

    E. Peter Parker's house.

2. **FrontPage 98 is . . .**

    A. A single program that can create Web sites, fix cars, and clean windows.

    B. Several programs that work together to help you create Web sites.

    C. Useful only for advanced techies with HTML fluency.

    D. Useful for anyone who wants to build a Web site, whether they know HTML or not.

    E. The author's favorite Web publishing program.

3. **The FrontPage Explorer helps you create new Web sites by . . .**

    A. Providing site templates to help you get started.

    B. Providing Wizards that guide you through the process step-by-step.

    C. Automatically phoning your technically gifted niece and asking her to do it for you.

    D. Providing a New FrontPage Web button on the toolbar.

    E. Saying "You can do it!" every five minutes.

4. **To create a new Web site in the FrontPage Explorer . . .**

    A. Press Ctrl+N.

    B. Choose File➪New➪FrontPage Web.

    C. Choose an option from the Getting Started dialog box (the dialog box appears when you first launch FrontPage).

    D. Press F1.

    E. Click the New FrontPage Web button on the toolbar.

5. **If you want to use FrontPage to maintain or update an existing Web site, you must . . .**

   A. Sign a waiver promising never to use another Web publishing program again.

   B. Import the Web site into FrontPage using the Explorer's Import Web Wizard.

   C. Do nothing. You can't use FrontPage to work with an existing Web site.

   D. Learn how to tie cherry stems in a knot with your tongue.

6. **Which of the following items is NOT the name of an Explorer view?**

   A. Navigation.

   B. Odometer.

   C. All Files.

   D. Chores.

   E. Hyperlink Status.

7. **The purpose of the Hyperlinks View is to . . .**

   A. Create hyperlinks between pages in your Web site and to other sites on the Web.

   B. Display the hyperlinks between pages in your Web site and to other sites on the Web.

   C. Intimidate and confuse you.

   D. Help you keep track of the navigational paths visitors can follow when they explore your site.

   E. Display the files and folders in your Web site.

8. **The purpose of the Folders View is to . . .**

   A. Create hyperlinks between pages in your Web site and to other sites on the Web.

   B. Display the hyperlinks between pages in your Web site and to other sites on the Web.

   C. Intimidate and confuse you.

   D. Help you keep track of the navigational paths visitors can follow when they explore your site.

   E. Display the files and folders in your Web site.

Unit 1 Exercise

Notes:

1. Launch FrontPage.

2. Create a new Web site based on the Customer Support Web template.

3. Switch to the Hyperlinks View.

4. Expand and contract the outline in the left pane of the Hyperlinks View to display the links in different pages.

5. Switch to the Folders View to and poke around the site's file system.

6. Switch to the All Files View to see a complete list of files in the Web site (it contains quite a few!).

7. Exit FrontPage.

Working with Web Pages in the FrontPage Editor

Objectives for This Unit

✓ Understanding the relationship between the FrontPage Explorer and the FrontPage Editor

✓ Opening a Web site in the Explorer

✓ Launching the FrontPage Editor

✓ Creating a new Web page

✓ Opening an existing Web page

✓ Converting other file types into Web pages

✓ Saving a page

✓ Exiting the FrontPage Editor

Prerequisites

▶ Launching FrontPage (Lesson 1-2)

▶ Using FrontPage to work with an existing Web site (Lesson 1-4)

▶ Adding existing files to a FrontPage Web site (Lesson 1-5)

▶ Getting familiar with the Explorer's Views (Lesson 1-6)

on the CD

▶ frontpg.htm
▶ unit02.htm
▶ convert.doc

Unit 1 introduced you to the Explorer, the component of FrontPage responsible for creating and managing Web sites. In this unit, you get to know the other major FrontPage player: the FrontPage Editor. Here's where the real action occurs: Using the Editor, you add text, images, and hyperlinks (and more!) to the basic pages created by the Explorer. You can also use the Editor to create new pages to add to your Web site.

In this unit, I introduce you to the basic workings of the FrontPage Editor: using the Explorer and Editor together, opening Web pages, creating new pages, and saving pages. After you finish this unit, you're ready to start designing your own Web pages. (Part II is completely devoted to the art of Web page creation.)

Lesson 2-1

Opening an Existing Web Site in the Explorer

on the test

Every time you use FrontPage, your first step is to open the Web site you want to edit. After the Web site is open in the Explorer, you launch the Editor to make whatever changes you want to the Web site's individual pages. The Explorer and Editor work as a team; in fact, they work together so well, you may forget that you're working with two separate programs.

Tip: To help you remember which is which, keep in mind that the Explorer operates on entire Web *sites*, whereas the Editor works with individual Web *pages*.

If you haven't already followed the steps in Lessons 1-4 and 1-5 (in which you import the Import Example Web site and then add another page, named frontpg.htm, to the site), do so now. After you complete Lessons 1-4 and 1-5, choose File➪Close FrontPage Web, and then proceed with this lesson.

1 **If the program isn't already running, launch FrontPage.**

(If you can't remember how to launch FrontPage, refer to Lesson 1-2.)

The FrontPage Explorer opens, and the Getting Started dialog box appears.

If the Getting Started dialog box isn't visible, click Open FrontPage Web on the toolbar, or choose File➪Open FrontPage Web.

2 **In the dialog box's Open an Existing FrontPage Web area, click Import Example and then click OK.**

If `Import Example` isn't visible, follow the steps in the Extra Credit sidebar called "What to do if your Web site isn't listed in the Getting Started dialog box" at the end of this lesson.

The Getting Started dialog box closes. If you just launched FrontPage, and the version of the Personal Web Server you're using requires an access password, the Name and Password Required dialog box appears (the dialog box appears only the first time you create or open a Web site after launching FrontPage).

3 **In the Name and Password text boxes, enter the administrator name and password you chose when you installed FrontPage, and then click OK.**

The Name and Password dialog box closes, and in a moment, the Import Example Web site becomes visible in the Folders View.

to edit Web site's pages, first open site in FrontPage Explorer

Open FrontPage Web button

at bottom of the File menu, Explorer saves shortcuts to last four Web sites opened

heads up

What to do if your Web site isn't listed in the Getting Started dialog box

The Getting Started dialog box only lists recently opened Web sites. If the name of the Web site you want to open doesn't appear in the Getting Started dialog box, follow these steps:

1. **In the Getting Started dialog box, click More Webs.**

   The Open FrontPage Web dialog box appears.

2. **In the dialog box, if it's not already visible in the Select a Web Server or Disk Location list box, select the name of the Personal Web Server on your computer.**

   When you installed FrontPage, the installation program told you the name it assigned to the Personal Web Server. Choose that name in this step.

3. **In the dialog box, click List Webs.**

   After a moment or two of hard disk whirring, a list of FrontPage Web sites appears in the FrontPage Webs Found at Location area.

4. **In the FrontPage Webs Found at Location area of the dialog box, click the name of the Web site you want to open, and then click OK.**

   (The Name and Password Required dialog box may appear at this point. If the dialog box appears, enter your administrator name and password and then click OK to close the dialog box.)

   The Open FrontPage Web Site and the Getting Started dialog boxes close, and then the selected Web site opens in the Explorer.

You're now ready to open the Import Example Web site's pages.

☑ Progress Check

If you can do the following, you've mastered this lesson:

❑ Open a Web site in the Explorer.

Launching the FrontPage Editor   Lesson 2-2

Now that the Import Example Web site is open, you're ready to fire up the Editor to open the site's pages. The easiest way to launch the Editor is by simply opening one of the site's pages from within the Explorer (you do so in the steps that follow).

1 **If not already visible, make the Folders, All Files, Navigation, or Hyperlinks view visible.**

If you aren't sure how, refer to Lesson 1-6.

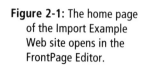

Figure 2-1: The home page of the Import Example Web site opens in the FrontPage Editor.

Notes:

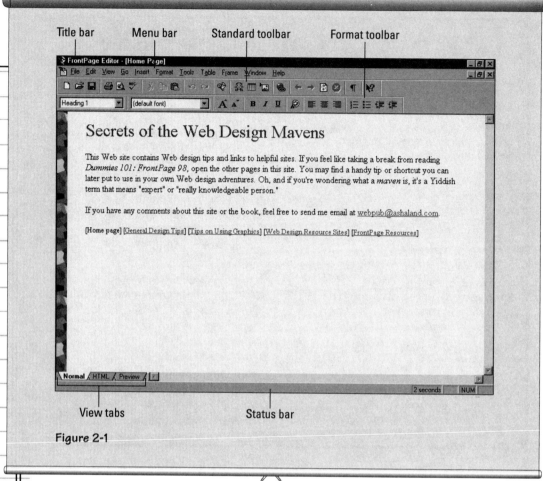

Title bar   Menu bar   Standard toolbar   Format toolbar

Secrets of the Web Design Mavens

This Web site contains Web design tips and links to helpful sites. If you feel like taking a break from reading *Dummies 101: FrontPage 98*, open the other pages in this site. You may find a handy tip or shortcut you can later put to use in your own Web design adventures. Oh, and if you're wondering what a *maven* is, it's a Yiddish term that means "expert" or "really knowledgeable person."

If you have any comments about this site or the book, feel free to send me email at webpub@ashaland.com.

[Home page] [General Design Tips] [Tips on Using Graphics] [Web Design Resource Sites] [FrontPage Resources]

View tabs   Status bar

Figure 2-1

Show FrontPage Editor button (on the Explorer toolbar)

☑ **Progress Check**

If you can do the following, you've mastered this lesson:

❑ Launch the Editor by opening a page from within the Explorer.

2 Double-click the home page icon.

If you use the FrontPage Personal Web Server, the home page is named index.htm. If you use the Microsoft Personal Web Server, the home page is named Default.htm.

After a few moments, the FrontPage Editor launches and opens the home page of the Import Example Web site (see Figure 2-1).

If you prefer to launch the Editor on its own without opening a Web page, click Show FrontPage Editor on the Explorer toolbar (or choose Tools⇨ Show FrontPage Editor).

Take a moment to gaze at the Editor's menu bar and toolbars. Notice anything familiar? If you've worked with other Microsoft Office programs — especially Microsoft Word — you may experience a little déjà vu. The Editor's tools parallel those available in other Microsoft Office applications, so if you're an Office user, you don't have to start at the absolute bottom of the learning curve. In fact, you're already a long way toward knowing how to create a Web page with FrontPage.

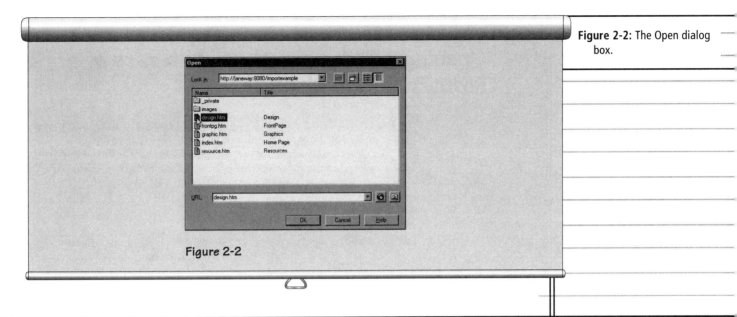

Figure 2-2: The Open dialog box.

Figure 2-2

Opening a Web Page from within the Editor

Lesson 2-3

After the Editor is up and running, you don't have to return to the Explorer to open another Web page. You can open pages directly from within the Editor. This capability is helpful when you want to edit more than one page at a time.

The most common way to use FrontPage is to open pages that are part of the Web site currently open in the Explorer (as is the Import Example Web site). The Editor also knows how to open pages that are stored elsewhere on your computer, and can even open pages directly from the Web.

Opening a page in the current Web site

When you work with FrontPage, most often you edit pages that make up a Web site you created or imported into the FrontPage Explorer. In the following steps, you open another page in the Import Example Web site.

1 **On the Editor's Standard toolbar, click Open. (If you don't see this button on your screen, first choose View⇨Standard Toolbar to make the toolbar visible.)**

Alternatively, choose File⇨Open, or press Ctrl+O.

The Open dialog box appears (see Figure 2-2), displaying a list of files and folders contained in the Import Example Web site.

2 **In the dialog box's file list, double-click design.htm.**

The Open File dialog box closes, and the General Web Design Tips page opens in the Editor.

And there you have it.

Open button

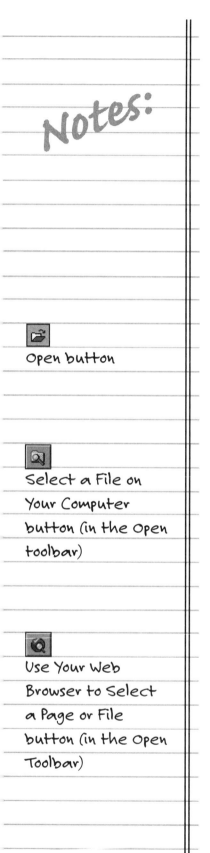

Notes:

Open button

Select a File on Your Computer button (in the Open toolbar)

Use Your Web Browser to Select a Page or File button (in the Open Toolbar)

Opening a Web page that isn't part of a FrontPage Web site

Every now and then, you may want to use the Editor to make changes to pages that *aren't* part of a FrontPage Web site. For example, say that you have a single Web page stored on your computer to which you want to make a few quick edits, but you don't want to go through the hassle of first importing the page into the Web site open in the Explorer. Or, the Web page in question is currently stored in a remote location on the Web. In either case, the FrontPage Editor can still come to your aid.

(Later, you can save the page as part of the Web site currently open in the Explorer, or you can save the page elsewhere on your hard drive. In Lesson 2-6, I show you how to save a page.)

on the CD

In the steps that follow, you open a page named unit02.htm, which is stored in the FP101 folder.

1 On the Editor's Standard toolbar, click Open.

The Open dialog box appears.

2 In the dialog box, click Select a File on Your Computer.

The Select File dialog box appears. This standard Windows dialog box enables you to browse the contents of your computer's drives to choose the file you want to open.

3 In the dialog box, navigate your hard drive to the FP101 folder.

The contents of the FP101 folder appear inside the dialog box's file list.

4 In the file list, double-click unit02.htm.

The Select File and Open dialog boxes close, and the page opens in the Editor.

extra credit

Opening a page directly from the Web

The Editor is so powerful, it can open any page on the Web. *Any* page. To do so, follow these steps:

1. **Activate your Internet connection.**

2. **On the Editor's Standard toolbar, click Open.**

   The Open dialog box appears.

3. **In the dialog box's URL text box, enter the page's URL.**

A Web URL looks something like the following address:

http://www.ashaland.com/write.htm.

If you can't remember the URL, you can launch your web browser by clicking Use Your Web Browser to Select a Page or File (this button sits in the Open dialog box). Using your browser, surf to the page you want to open, and then switch back to the FrontPage Editor viewing window. The page's URL appears in the URL text box.

3. In the Open dialog box, click OK.

The dialog box closes, and in a moment, the page opens in the Editor.

When you open a page directly from the Web, FrontPage opens a *copy* of the page for you to edit. FrontPage saves any changes you make to the copy (plus any graphics that are contained in the page) on your computer. For the changes to be visible on the Web, you must transfer the edited page back to the web server on which the original page is stored — in other words, you need to publish the page (I talk about how to publish your Web site in Unit 13).

Recess

If you feel like taking a break, close the book and open the other pages in the Import Example Web site. Look around for a while: I've packed the site full of helpful Web design tips I've picked up during my Net adventures.

☑ **Progress Check**

If you can do the following, you've mastered this lesson:

❑ In the Editor, open a page that's part of the site currently open in the Explorer.

❑ Open a page that's stored elsewhere on your computer.

Creating a New Web Page
Lesson 2-4

Opening pages is a useful enough skill, but *creating* Web pages — now that's what Web publishing is all about. You can use the Editor to create new pages to add to your site. If you need help with page design, you can choose one of the Editor's page templates, or you can just as easily create a new, blank page.

Page templates give you a design boost by providing a layout into which you plop your own text and graphics. You can choose a template based on a layout or geared toward a specific function (such as a Frequently Asked Questions page or a bibliography).

Want to see how the process works? Follow these steps to create a new page based on a template:

1 In the Editor, choose File⇨New (or press Ctrl+N).

The New dialog box appears, displaying a smorgasbord of templates.

(If you simply want to create a new, blank page, on the Format toolbar, click New. A new, empty page appears in the Editor, and you can skip the rest of the steps in this lesson.)

2 In the dialog box's template list, click Two-column Body.

(You may need to move the scroll bar inside the template list to make the template visible.)

use page templates for assistance with layout

New button creates a blank, new page

Figure 2-3: The New dialog box.

Figure 2-4: A new page based on one of the Editor's page templates.

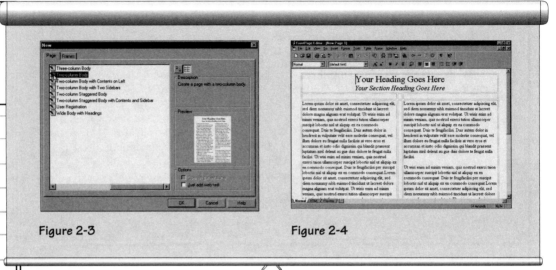

Figure 2-3   Figure 2-4

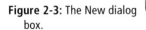

Create New Page button (on the Explorer toolbar)

☑ **Progress Check**

If you can do the following, you've mastered this lesson:

❏ Use the Editor to create a new Web page.

A description of the template appears in the Description area to the right of the template list, and a tiny version of the template appears in the Preview area (see Figure 2-3). The Preview is handy when you want to peek at the template before making your choice.

3 Click OK.

The New dialog box closes, and a new page based on the template appears in the Editor (see Figure 2-4).

(The dotted lines surrounding the blocks of text in this template signify the boundaries of a *borderless* table. Unit 8 tells you everything you need to know about tables, including how to build your own.)

From here, you simply replace the template's pseudo-content with your own, and you have a professionally designed page that would otherwise take a great deal of time to create.

Can't find a template you like? Create your own! I explain how in the Extra Credit sidebar "Creating your own Web page templates" later in this unit.

You may find adding pages to your site easier when you're able to look at the site as a whole. If so, create new, blank pages by using the Explorer. In the Folders, All Files, or Navigation Views, click Create New Page, or choose File➪New➪Page. A new page appears in the view with its filename highlighted. You don't need to click anywhere to change the file's generic filename — just type a new filename and then press Enter. When you're ready to fill the new page with text and other stuff, you can open the page in the Editor.

Converting Other File Formats into Web Pages

Lesson 2-5

If you're building a Web site to showcase your wares, chances are that much of the site's content already exists in other file formats. Product brochures, press releases, and financial reports — all of which began as word-processing documents or spreadsheets — can be reborn as Web pages without hours of retyping.

on the test

The Editor can convert the following popular document formats into Web pages, just by opening the files:

- Microsoft Word documents — for Windows, Versions 2.*x*, 6, and Word 97; and for Macintosh, Versions 4.0 to 5.1 and 6 (*.DOC, *.MCW)
- Microsoft Works 3.0 and 4.0 documents (*.WPS)
- WordPerfect 5.*x* and 6.*x* documents (*.DOC, *.WPD)
- Microsoft Excel and Lotus 1-2-3 worksheets (*.XLS, *.WK1, *.WK3, *.WK4)
- RTF documents (*.RTF)
- Text documents (*.TXT)

When you covert another file format into a Web page, the Editor maintains much of the document's formatting and layout by converting the formats to the closest HTML style. You'll probably need to do some stylistic tweaking once after the file has been converted because HTML can't accommodate all the sophisticated formatting effects other document formats can. For the most part, however, the Editor does a fantastic job of maintaining your document's style and structure.

on the CD

To demonstrate the Editor's file conversion wizardry, I include a Microsoft Word document in the FP101 folder named convert.doc. This word-processing document contains formatted text and tables. In the following steps, you open convert.doc in the Editor and watch it transform the document into a Web page.

1 **On the Editor's Standard toolbar, click Open.**

The Open dialog box appears.

2 **In the dialog box, click Select a File on Your Computer.**

The Select File dialog box appears.

3 **In the dialog box, navigate your hard drive to the FP101 folder.**

The contents of the FP101 folder appear inside the dialog box's file list.

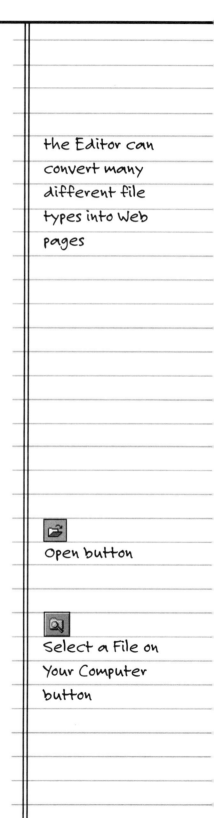

the Editor can convert many different file types into Web pages

Open button

Select a File on Your Computer button

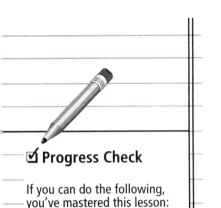

☑ Progress Check

If you can do the following, you've mastered this lesson:

❑ Convert a different file format into a Web page.

4 **In the dialog box's Files of Type list box, choose Word 6.0/95 for Windows&Macintosh (*.doc).**

The file list now only displays the Word documents stored in the FP101 folder.

5 **In the file list, double-click convert.doc.**

The Select File and Open dialog boxes close, the Editor translates the Word document into HTML, and in a moment, the new Web page appears in the Editor window. (The original Word document remains untouched in the FP101 folder.)

FrontPage makes the conversion operation look effortless, but plenty of fancy footwork went on in the few seconds it took to transform the document into a Web page. Before FrontPage existed, the conversion process may have taken an hour or two or hard work (and that's assuming HTML fluency!). So, rejoice in the time you just saved, and relax with a cup of herbal tea — or better yet, move on to the final lesson in this unit.

Lesson 2-6 Saving a Page

Creating sparkling Web pages is the snazzy part of Web design. Saving your work properly, although more humble, is just as central to the process. I'm loathe to mention the number of times I've had to retrace my steps because my computer got cranky or the power went out before I saved my masterpiece.

In this lesson, I show you how to save pages as part of your Web site. How you proceed depends on how the page was originally opened.

Saving pages that contain pictures involves a few extra steps. I describe the process in Lesson 6-5.

Saving a new page as part of your Web site

When you save a new page (that is, a page you created by using the Editor, a page that was converted from another file format, or a page opened from the World Wide Web), the page is automatically added to the Web site that's currently open in the Explorer.

These steps take you through saving the page you just converted from a Word document and, in the process, adding the new page to the Import Example Web site (the Web site that is currently open in the Explorer).

1 **With the converted page visible in the Editor, click Save.**

The Save As dialog box appears (see Figure 2-5). The Title text box contains the page's title (FrontPage automatically uses the page's first line of text). If you don't like the title, enter a new title in the Title text box. Based on the title, the Editor generates a filename that is visible in the URL text box.

Save button

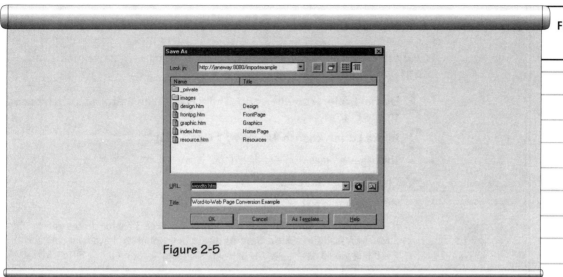

Figure 2-5

Figure 2-5: The Save As dialog box.

Notes:

2 **Click OK.**

The dialog box closes, and FrontPage saves the page and adds it to the Import Example Web site. To see the new addition, switch over to the Explorer.

3 **On the Standard toolbar, click Show FrontPage Explorer.**

The Explorer becomes visible. A new icon representing the page you just saved is visible in the Explorer. Switch between different Explorer views to see how the new page appears in each view.

Show FrontPage
Explorer button

heads up

The Editor attaches the three-letter filename extension .htm to all new Web pages. If you've spent much time on the Web, you may have noticed that many Web page filenames contain the four-letter filename extension .html rather than .htm. Most web servers recognize both filename extensions, so the choice is yours. If you prefer to use .html, change the filename when you save the file (or, rename an existing page — I show you how in Unit 12). For consistency, I recommend naming all your Web pages with the same filename extension.

Saving a page originally opened from elsewhere on your computer as part of your Web site

All new pages are automatically added to the Web site open in the Explorer. However, when you save an existing page that was originally opened from a location on your computer that's outside the FrontPage Web site, FrontPage saves the changes in the same location, thereby keeping that page separate from the Web site open in the Explorer. If you want to add the page to your Web site, you need to specifically tell the Editor to do so.

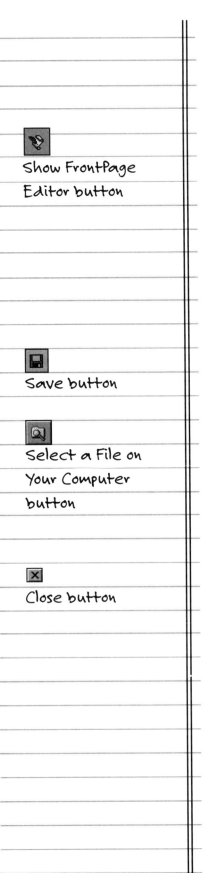

Show FrontPage
Editor button

Save button

Select a File on
Your Computer
button

Close button

heads up

In Lesson 2-3, you opened the page named unit02.htm, which is stored in the FP101 folder on your hard drive. In the following steps, you save unit02.htm as part of the Import Example Web site.

1 On the Explorer toolbar, click Show FrontPage Editor to switch back to the Editor.

2 In the Editor, choose Window➪3 Good Job!

The page becomes visible in the Editor.

3 Choose File➪Save As.

The Save As dialog box appears.

If, instead of choosing File➪Save As, you had clicked Save (or chosen File➪Save or pressed Ctrl+S), the Save As dialog box would not have appeared and the Editor would have saved the page in its original location in the FP101 folder.

If you want to give the page a new title and filename, go ahead. Otherwise . . .

4 Click OK.

FrontPage saves unit02.htm as part of the Import Example Web site.

After you save a page the first time, you can quickly save subsequent changes by clicking Save, choosing File➪Save, or pressing Ctrl+S. To save changes to all the pages open in the Editor at the same time, choose File➪Save All.

You don't *have* to save a page as part of the Web site open in the Explorer. You can tell the Editor to save the page anywhere in your hard drive. To do so, in the Save As dialog box, click Select a File On Your Computer (the same folder-and-magnifying-glass icon that appears in the Open dialog box) to display the Save As File dialog box. In the dialog box, navigate to the folder or drive where you want to save the file, and then click Save.

After you finish using the Editor, you're ready to exit the program. When you shut down the Editor, the Explorer still remains open so you can continue any unfinished business there.

To exit the Editor, select choose File➪Exit, or click the Close button in the upper-right corner of the FrontPage Editor window. (You still have one unsaved page open in the Editor: the page you created using the Two-column Body page template. Whether you save the page as part of the Import Example Web site is up to you.)

extra credit

Creating your own Web page templates

If you regularly update your Web site by using a standard page layout, save yourself time and energy by creating your own page template. The process is as simple as saving a regular Web page.

1. **With the page you want to save as a template open in the Editor, choose File⇨Save As.**

   The Save As dialog box appears.

2. **Click As Template.**

   (You don't have to fill in a page title or filename when you save a page as a template.)

   The Save As Template dialog box appears.

3. **In the Title text box, type a descriptive title.**

4. **In the Name text box, type a filename.**

Just type a short word — the Editor automatically applies the appropriate three-letter filename extension to the name you choose.

5. **In the Description text box, type a short description of the template's function.**

6. **Click OK.**

   FrontPage saves the page as a template.

   If the page you're saving contains pictures, FrontPage asks whether you want to save the pictures as separate files. Click Yes to save the graphics this way. (In Lesson 6-5, I describe how to save a page containing pictures in more detail.)

The next time you choose File⇨New or press Ctrl+N, the template appears with all the other FrontPage templates in the New dialog box.

☑ Progress Check

If you can do the following, you've mastered this lesson:

❑ Save a Web page.

❑ Exit the Editor.

Unit 2 Quiz

This quiz helps you review the important points in this unit. For each of the following questions, circle the letter of the correct answer or answers. Remember, I may offer more than one right answer for each question.

1. **The FrontPage Explorer and FrontPage Editor . . .**

   A. Are two separate programs that work independently without any relationship to each other.

   B. Are two separate programs that work together to help you create and manage Web sites and pages.

   C. Are two items available under the FrontPage File menu.

   D. Operate on different aspects of the Web publishing process: The Explorer is responsible for tasks involving the site as a whole, whereas the Editor is responsible for tasks pertaining to individual Web pages.

   E. Do basically the same things.

Notes:

2. **To launch the FrontPage Editor . . .**

   A. On the Explorer toolbar, click the Show FrontPage Editor button.

   B. Double-click the icon of a page that is part of a Web site open in the Explorer.

   C. Say "3 . . . 2 . . . 1 . . . we have liftoff!"

   D. In the Explorer, choose Tools⇨Show FrontPage Editor.

   E. Click the Start button and select the FrontPage icon.

3. **To use the FrontPage Editor to edit a Web page . . .**

   A. If the page is part of a FrontPage Web site, the site must be open in the FrontPage Explorer.

   B. The page must be stored on your computer.

   C. The page must already be saved in HTML format.

   D. The page must have been created by using the FrontPage Editor.

   E. The page must be part of a FrontPage Web site.

4. **To convert a Microsoft Word document into a Web page, you must . . .**

   A. Add HTML tags to the document, save the document as a text file, and then open the file in the Editor.

   B. In the Editor, select File⇨Convert⇨Microsoft Word document.

   C. In the Editor, select File⇨Open, and open the Microsoft Word document. The conversion process happens automatically.

5. **With the Editor, you can save a Web page . . .**

   A. As a Microsoft Word document.

   B. As part of a Web site open in the FrontPage Explorer.

   C. As a FrontPage page template.

   D. As a file stored elsewhere on your computer.

   E. For a rainy day.

Unit 2 Exercise

1. Launch FrontPage.

2. Create a new Web site, or open an existing Web site in the Explorer.

3. After the Web site is open, launch the FrontPage Editor by opening one of the site's pages from inside the Explorer.

4. In the Editor, create a new page based on a page template.

5. Save the new page as part of the Web site open in the Explorer.

6. Exit both the Editor and the Explorer.

Part I Review

Unit 1 Summary

▶ **What "Web publishing" means:** Web publishing is the process of creating a Web site — a collection of interlinked files called Web pages — and transferring the files to a computer called a web server. A web server is connected to the Internet 24 hours per day via a high-speed connection and is generally maintained by a company or an Internet service provider (ISP).

▶ **FrontPage, more than a single program:** FrontPage is a Web publishing suite comprised of several distinct programs: the Explorer, the Editor, and the Personal Web Server.

▶ **Launching the FrontPage Explorer:** Click the Start button on the Windows 95 taskbar to display the Start menu, and then select the Microsoft FrontPage icon.

▶ **Creating a new Web site:** In the Explorer, choose File⇨New⇨FrontPage Web. In the New FrontPage Web dialog box that appears, select the name of a Web site template (or choose to create a one-page Web), enter a title for the Web site, and then click OK.

▶ **Importing an existing Web site into FrontPage:** In the Explorer, choose File⇨New⇨FrontPage Web. In the New FrontPage Web dialog box that appears, select Import an Existing Web, enter a title for the Web site, and then click OK to launch the Import Web Wizard. Follow the Wizard's instructions to import the Web site into FrontPage.

▶ **The Explorer's views:** The Explorer contains seven views. The Folders View lists the Web site's files and folders. The All Files View displays a single list of all the files contained in the Web site. The Navigation View enables you to chart the site's navigational structure. The Hyperlinks View illustrates the Web site's system of links. The Hyperlink Status View lets you verify and repair broken hyperlinks. The Themes View lists an array of graphic themes you can apply to your Web site. The Tasks View keeps track of "to-do" items. To display a view, click its button in the Explorer's Views bar.

▶ **Exiting FrontPage:** In the Explorer, click the Close button, or choose File⇨Exit. To exit the Personal Web Server, right-click its taskbar button and select Close.

Unit 2 Summary

▶ **Opening a Web site in the Explorer:** Click the Open FrontPage Web button on the Explorer toolbar, or choose File⇨Open FrontPage Web. In the Open FrontPage Web dialog box that appears, click the List Webs button. From the list that appears in the FrontPage Webs text box, select the name of the Web site you want to open, and then click OK.

▶ **Launching the FrontPage Editor:** In the Explorer, click the Show FrontPage Editor button or choose Tools⇨Show FrontPage Editor. Alternatively, launch the Editor by opening one of the pages in the current Web site. To do so, in the All Files, Folders, Navigation, or Hyperlinks View, double-click the page's icon.

▶ **Opening a Web page from within the Editor:** In the Editor, click the Open button, choose File⇨Open, or press Ctrl+O. From the Open dialog box, double-click the file you want to open. The files and folders visible in the Open dialog box belong to the Web site currently open in the Explorer. You can also open Web pages stored elsewhere on your computer or local network, or directly from the Web.

Part I Review

- **Creating a new Web page:** In the Editor, choose File⇨New (or press Ctrl+N). From the New dialog box that appears, click the name of the template you want to use; then click OK. To create a new, blank page, click the New Page button, or select the Normal Page template in the New dialog box.

- **Converting other file formats into Web pages:** The FrontPage Editor can convert the following file formats into Web pages simply by opening the files: Microsoft Word documents (for Windows, Versions 2.*x*, 6, and Word 97; and for Macintosh, Versions 4.0 to 5.1 and 6) (*.DOC, *.MCW); Microsoft Works 3.0 and 4.0 documents (*.WPS); WordPerfect 5.*x* and 6.*x* documents (*.DOC, *.WPD); Microsoft Excel and Lotus 1-2-3 worksheets (*.XLS, *.WK1, *.WK3, *.WK4); RTF documents (*.RTF); and text documents (*.TXT).

- **Saving a Web page as part of the Web site open in the Explorer:** Click the Save button, or

choose File⇨Save, or choose File⇨Save As, or press Ctrl+S. In the Save As dialog box that appears, enter the page's title and filename and then click OK.

- **Saving a Web page elsewhere on your computer or local network:** Click the Save button, or choose File⇨Save, or choose File⇨Save As, or press Ctrl+S. In the Save As dialog box that appears, enter the page's title and filename and then click the Save as a File on Your Computer button. In the Save As File dialog box that appears, navigate to the folder in which you want to save the page and then click Save.

- **Saving a Web page as a template:** Click the Save button, or choose File⇨Save, or choose File⇨Save As, or press Ctrl+S. In the Save As dialog box that appears, click As Template. In the Save As Template dialog box that appears, enter a template title, filename, and description; then click OK.

Part I Test

This test covers much of the stuff mentioned in Part I, Units 1 and 2 (I often flag information that will appear on a test with an On The Test icon). The information in Part I lays the foundation for everything you'll learn in upcoming lessons, so now is your chance to make sure that you remember the material.

If you want to check your answers, refer to Appendix B.

True   False

T   F   1. FrontPage is a single program.

T   F   2. When you launch FrontPage, the program that opens first is the FrontPage Explorer.

T   F   3. Web publishing involves creating a Web site and then transferring the site's files to a dedicated web server.

T   F   4. To use FrontPage to update an existing Web site, the Web site must first be imported into the FrontPage Editor.

Part I Test

T   F   5. You use the FrontPage Explorer to edit individual Web pages.

T   F   6. The Explorer can display your Web site using one of seven views.

T   F   7. The Explorer contains templates and Wizards that simplify creating a Web site.

T   F   8. The Editor knows how to convert Microsoft Excel worksheets into Web pages just by opening the files.

T   F   9. If you create a Web page using another program, you cannot open that page in the Editor.

T   F   10. When you exit the Editor, the Explorer automatically shuts down as well.

Multiple Choice

For each of the following questions, circle the correct answer or answers. (I may sneak in more than one right answer for each question.)

11. Circle the item or items that describe how to use FrontPage to create or work with a Web site.

A. First create Web pages in the Editor, and then link the pages together using the Explorer.

B. First create Web pages in the Explorer, and then link the pages together using the Personal Web Server.

C. First create a Web site in the Explorer, and then open and edit the Web site's pages (and create new pages) using the Editor.

D. Launch the Explorer's Corporate Web Wizard to create a Web site by answering a series of questions and selecting options from dialog boxes.

E. Import an existing Web site into the Explorer, and then update the site by editing its pages with the Editor.

12. How do you create a new Web site in the Explorer?

A. Click the New FrontPage Web button.

B. Choose File➪New➪FrontPage Web.

C. Launch the Editor and, from the Editor's toolbar, choose File➪New Web.

D. Press Ctrl+N.

E. Turn on your computer's microphone and say, "New FrontPage Web."

13. In the Editor, you can open a Web page . . .

A. That is part of a FrontPage Web site.

B. That is located on another computer accessible via the Internet.

C. That isn't part of a FrontPage Web site.

D. That was created using another program.

E. That was hand-coded using HTML.

Part I Lab Assignment

Okay, here's the real stuff. Time to put what you've learned to work in the real world. This lab assignment is the first part of a lab project you will continue throughout the book, integrating tasks you've picked up in each book part. Lab assignments give you a chance to tinker with FrontPage at your own pace and in your own way. Instead of laying out specific steps for you to follow, I give you a project — building a Web site — that you can accomplish any way you like.

The content of the Web site you build as part of the lab project is up to you. If you've been wanting to create a personal home page but don't know where to begin, use these steps as a guideline. Or perhaps you'd like to use a Web site to spread the word about a volunteer organization you support. Maybe you'd like to take a shot at designing a corporate Web site. Whatever your goal, use the lab assignment as an opportunity to work on a real project that you want to complete.

If you get stuck on any of the steps, feel free to page back to the appropriate lesson for a refresher.

Step 1: Launch FrontPage and create a new one-page Web site

You can name the Web site anything you want.

Step 2: Launch the Editor by opening the Web site's home page

Step 3: In the Editor, create a new page based on the page template of your choice

Step 4: Save the page you just created

Give the page any title and filename you want.

Step 5: Switch back to the Explorer and notice the appearance of the new page in the Explorer's view

Step 6: Exit FrontPage

This step means exiting the Editor, the Explorer, and the Personal Web Server.

The Art of Web Page Creation

Part II

In this part . . .

Now that you're comfortable with basic FrontPage mechanics, you're ready to create attractive, colorful Web pages. That is, after all, why you bought FrontPage and this book, right?

In this part, you spend most of your time using tools in the FrontPage Editor. You create new Web pages, add and format text, create hyperlinks, insert pictures, build an image map, and construct a table.

Making Text Look Good

Objectives for This Unit

- ✓ Using the Dummies 101 example files in your Web site
- ✓ Adding text
- ✓ Formatting text with font and paragraph styles
- ✓ Aligning and indenting paragraphs
- ✓ Inserting symbols
- ✓ Previewing a page

Prerequisites

- ◗ Launching FrontPage (Lesson 1-2)
- ◗ Creating a Web site from scratch (Lesson 1-3)
- ◗ Opening an existing Web site in the Explorer (Lesson 2-1)
- ◗ Launching the FrontPage Editor (Lesson 2-2)
- ◗ Saving a page (Lesson 2-6)

◗ unit03.htm

on the CD

The Web makes it possible to communicate with hundreds of thousands — even millions — of people simply by pressing a few keys in the comfort of your office or den. This ability to reach out has captured the world's imagination. Every day, enthusiastic Web designers adorn their Web pages in an effort to grab a moment of attention. But beneath the flashing graphics and fancy effects, a Web site is simply a collection of words. Text is the Web's most fundamental — and most important — tool.

In this unit, you explore the FrontPage Editor's text tools. You add text to a page and then change its font, its color, its size, its alignment, and more. You also find out how to insert special characters (such as the © symbol), and you preview a Web page to get an accurate reflection of how the page will look to your visitors after the Web site is published.

Lesson 3-1

Working with the *Dummies 101: FrontPage 98* Example Files

From here on, you will be working with My Web Site, the scratch pad Web site you created in Lesson 1-3. This Web site will be your home base as you progress through the book. Each time you begin a unit, you start by setting up your FrontPage workspace: launching FrontPage, opening My Web Site, and, if necessary, opening or accessing one or more of the example files sitting in the FP101 folder. In this lesson, I lead you through these preparatory steps. In future lessons, I show you where to begin, but I refer you back to this lesson for detailed instructions. (After you go through these steps a few times, chances are that you won't need the details anymore.)

on the CD

In this and several other lessons, you use the Editor's nifty Insert⇨File command to work with example files. This command enables you to insert the contents of a separate file into the page currently open in the Editor, merging the two files into a single Web page. The file you insert can be a Web page, or it can be any file format the Editor knows how to convert, such as a Word document or a text file. In the following steps, you insert the contents of a Web page named unit03.htm into the home page of My Web Site.

1 **Launch FrontPage.**

2 **In the Explorer, open My Web Site.**

If you're not sure how to open a Web site, refer to Lesson 2-1. (If the name My Web Site doesn't appear inside the Getting Started dialog box, refer to the Extra Credit sidebar in Lesson 2-1 called "If your Web site isn't listed in the Getting Started dialog box.")

3 **Launch the FrontPage Editor by opening the Web site's home page.**

If you're not sure how to open a page from within the Explorer, refer to Lesson 2-2.

The Editor launches and displays the home page, which, at the moment, is blank. The insertion point flashes at the top of the page, urging you to tap on your keyboard.

4 **Type** My Web Site **and then press Enter to move the cursor onto a new line.**

5 **Choose Insert⇨File.**

The Select File dialog box appears (see Figure 3-1). This standard dialog box enables you to look through the files and folders on your computer to select the file you want to insert.

6 **In the dialog box, navigate through your computer's system of folders until the contents of the FP101 folder are visible in the file list.**

7 **In the file list, double-click unit03.htm.**

The dialog box closes, and FrontPage inserts the contents of unit03.htm into the home page.

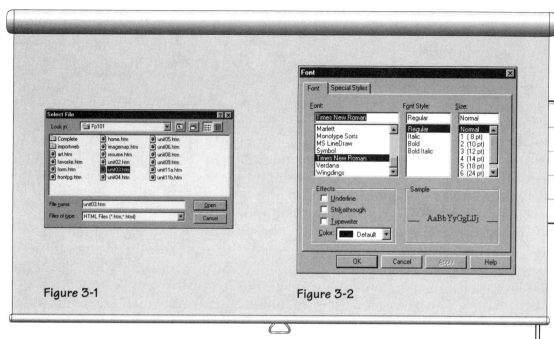

Figure 3-1   **Figure 3-2**

☑ **Progress Check**

If you can do the following you've mastered this lesson:

❑ Use the Insert⇨Files command to work with the *Dummies 101: FrontPage 98* example files stored in the FP101 folder.

The text you just inserted is nothing special; you could have easily typed it yourself. But why bother? I include it here simply to save you from doing a bunch of typing. It's a humble beginning, but it's all you need to fire up the Editor's text-tweaking tools.

Formatting Text with Font Styles   Lesson 3-2

Because working with the FrontPage Editor feels so similar to word processing, you will probably feel right at home with the Editor's text tools. This lesson is devoted to a set of tools called the *font styles*. Font styles can be applied to characters, words, sentences, and entire blocks of text.

The font style tools live inside the Font dialog box (see Figure 3-2). You can display the Font dialog box by choosing Format⇨Font. Buttons for the most commonly used font styles appear on the Editor's Format toolbar (shown in Figure 3-3). In the rest of this lesson, you'll experiment with a few of these styles.

You work with font styles by highlighting the text you want to format and then choosing the style you want to apply. To remove all font styles from selected text, choose Format⇨Remove Formatting, or press Ctrl+Spacebar.

Changing typeface

Typeface refers to the style and shape of your text's characters. The typeface you use in your Web pages can make text easier to read, and can contribute to your site's overall image. With the Editor, you can apply any typeface installed on your computer to the text in your Web pages.

Figure 3-3: The Format toolbar.

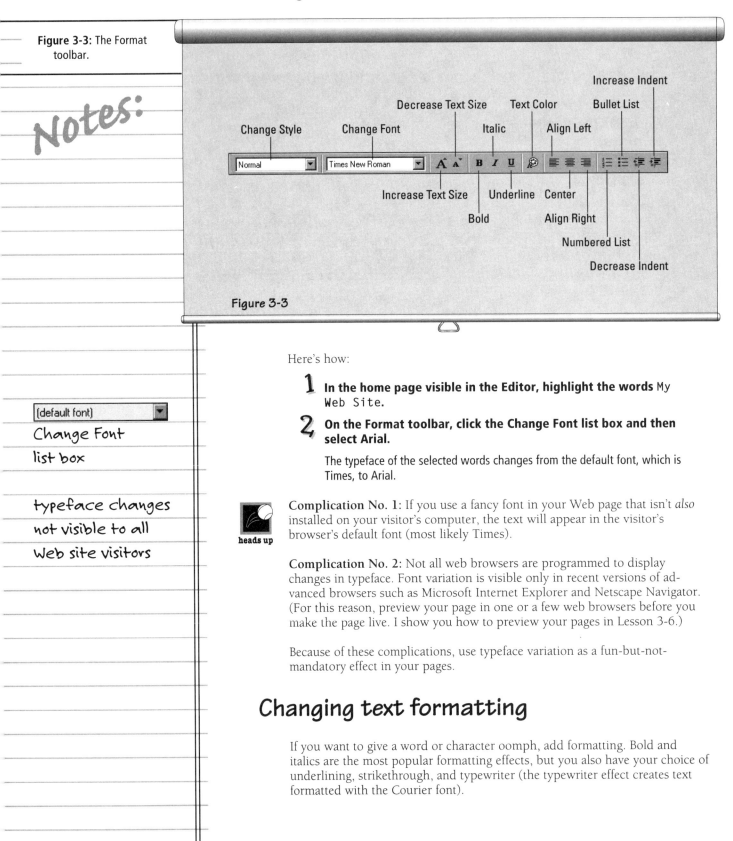

Change Style   Change Font   Decrease Text Size   Italic   Text Color   Align Left   Increase Indent   Bullet List

Increase Text Size   Underline   Center   Numbered List   Decrease Indent

Bold   Align Right

Normal   Times New Roman

Figure 3-3

Notes:

(default font)

Change Font list box

typeface changes not visible to all Web site visitors

Here's how:

1 **In the home page visible in the Editor, highlight the words** My Web Site.

2 **On the Format toolbar, click the Change Font list box and then select Arial.**

The typeface of the selected words changes from the default font, which is Times, to Arial.

heads up

Complication No. 1: If you use a fancy font in your Web page that isn't *also* installed on your visitor's computer, the text will appear in the visitor's browser's default font (most likely Times).

Complication No. 2: Not all web browsers are programmed to display changes in typeface. Font variation is visible only in recent versions of advanced browsers such as Microsoft Internet Explorer and Netscape Navigator. (For this reason, preview your page in one or a few web browsers before you make the page live. I show you how to preview your pages in Lesson 3-6.)

Because of these complications, use typeface variation as a fun-but-not-mandatory effect in your pages.

Changing text formatting

If you want to give a word or character oomph, add formatting. Bold and italics are the most popular formatting effects, but you also have your choice of underlining, strikethrough, and typewriter (the typewriter effect creates text formatted with the Courier font).

In the following steps, you try out two formatting effects: Bold and Italic.

1 **If not already selected, in the page, highlight the words** My Web Site.

2 **On the Format toolbar, click the Bold button.**

The selected words turn bold.

3 **With the text still selected, click the Italic button.**

The words turn bold and italic.

The Format toolbar contains a button for one other formatting effect: Underline. To use the Strikethrough and Typewriter effects, you need to use the Font dialog box, available by choosing Format➪Font.

Changing text size

Text size is just as easy to change. Here's how:

1 **Highlight the words** My Web Site.

2 **On the Format toolbar, click the Increase Text Size button.**

The selected words increase in size.

3 **With the text still selected, click the Decrease Text Size button.**

The words reduce in size.

on the test

If you take a look at the Size list box in the Font dialog box (available by choosing Format➪Font), you'll notice that each point size measurement is preceded by a number from 1 to 7. These numbers correspond to HTML size values, with 1 being the smallest text size, and 7 being the largest. Here's the catch: The actual size in points each increment turns out to be when a visitor views your Web page is determined by the visitor's *browser,* not FrontPage.

In FrontPage, for example, the default or Normal text size is 3, which the Editor displays as 12-point type. A visitor's web browser, on the other hand, may be set to display size 3 text as 14-point type. Therefore, you don't have absolute control over the size text appears to your visitors; you control text size only in relation to other text on the page.

Changing text color

Who says that text needs to appear in basic black? With FrontPage, you can apply all sorts of colors to selected text. To do so, follow these steps:

1 **Highlight the words** My Web Site.

2 **On the Format toolbar, click the Text Color button.**

The Color dialog box appears (see Figure 3-4).

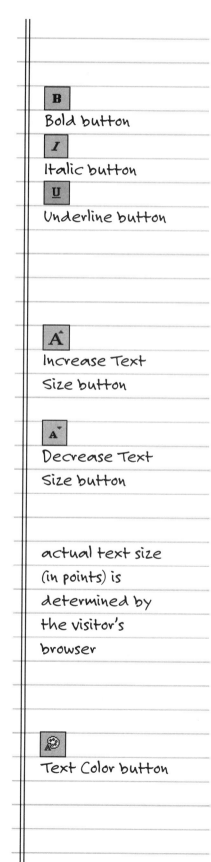

B

Bold button

I

Italic button

U

Underline button

A˄

Increase Text Size button

A˅

Decrease Text Size button

actual text size (in points) is determined by the visitor's browser

Text Color button

Figure 3-4: The Color dialog box.

Notes:

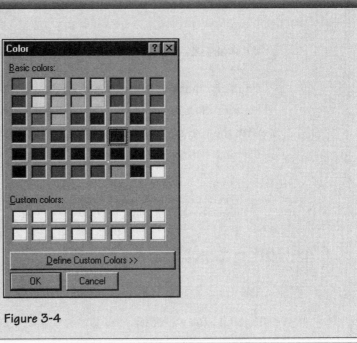

Figure 3-4

3 In the Color dialog box, click the color swatch you want and then click OK.

The dialog box closes and the words change color.

If the colors available in the Color dialog box aren't to your liking, you can define up to 16 custom colors to use in your Web page. To do so, in the Color dialog box, click Define Custom Colors. The dialog box expands to display a colorful palette from which you can choose new colors. For more details about how to use this dialog box, refer to the FrontPage Help system by choosing Help⇨Microsoft FrontPage Help.

The previous steps showed you how to change the color of selected text. You can also set the default color for all the text in a page. I show you how in Unit 5.

✓ Progress Check

If you can do the following you've mastered this lesson:

❏ Add text to a Web page.

❏ Apply boldface or italic formatting to the text.

❏ Change text size.

❏ Change text color.

extra credit

Using Special Styles

The Font dialog box contains a second tab labeled Special Styles. The Special Styles are a collection of HTML text formats that are rarely used or that duplicate more commonly used styles. If you're curious, go ahead and check one or a few of the check boxes on the Special Styles tab; a sample of the resulting format appears in the Sample box, so you know how your text will turn out.

One option in the Special Styles panel may prove handy: the Vertical Position list box. The Vertical Position list box enables you to create superscript or subscript text.

Structuring Your Page with Paragraph Styles

Lesson 3-3

The font styles you put to use in Lesson 3-2 can be used to embellish individual letters and words. *Paragraph styles,* on the other hand, operate on entire paragraphs and are used to structure the text in your Web page.

The FrontPage Editor contains the following paragraph styles: Normal, Formatted, and Address. (Headings and lists are also paragraph styles, but I consider them important enough to merit their own unit: Unit 4.)

> ▶ **Normal.** Normal is the default style for paragraphs. Normal paragraphs are left-aligned and appear in a proportional font. (Times appears in the Editor and in most web browsers.)

> ▶ **Formatted.** The Formatted style creates paragraphs with a monospaced font (in FrontPage and in most browsers, the font is Courier). More importantly, the Formatted style is the only style which exactly preserves the text spacing as you type. For example, text in Normal paragraphs automatically *wraps,* or jumps to a new line, when the text reaches the page margin. Formatted paragraphs do not wrap automatically; you must press Enter (or Shift+Enter) each time you want to create a new line. (I talk about the difference between pressing Enter and Shift+Enter at the end of this lesson.)

> ▶ **Address.** This style isn't used often, because it creates italic paragraphs (just like the Italic button on the toolbar).

To apply a paragraph style to a chunk of text, you click anywhere inside a paragraph, and specify the style you want, like this:

1 **Click anywhere inside the paragraph of text you inserted into the page.**

2 **On the Format toolbar, click the Change Style list box and then select Formatted.**

The Editor applies the Formatted style to the paragraph. Notice how the font changes from Times to Courier, and the text extends in one long line. That's because the Formatted style doesn't know how to automatically wrap text.

3 **Click the Change Style list box and select Address.**

The Editor applies the Address style to the paragraph.

4 **Click the Change Style list box and select Normal.**

The paragraph returns to normal (the Normal paragraph style, that is).

---

font styles = individual characters and words

paragraph styles = entire paragraphs

Normal ▼

Change Style list box

can apply only one paragraph style to a block of text

press Shift+Enter to create a line break

¶

Show/Hide ¶ button

And that's it. As you add text to a page, when you press Enter, FrontPage creates a new paragraph. If you want to move text to a new line but don't want to create a new paragraph, press Shift+Enter. This action creates a line break that, unlike a regular paragraph, isn't preceded by a bit of space and also retains the previous paragraph's style.

To distinguish between paragraphs and line breaks in your page, click Show/Hide ¶ on the Standard toolbar. Paragraphs appear with a ¶ symbol, and line breaks are flagged with left-pointing arrows.

Lesson 3-4   Aligning and Indenting Paragraphs

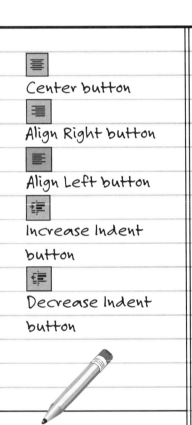

Center button

Align Right button

Align Left button

Increase Indent button

Decrease Indent button

By default, paragraphs appear left-aligned. You can easily align paragraphs with the center of the page or the page's right margin. To do so, follow these steps:

1 **Click anywhere inside the text you inserted into the page.**

2 **Click the Center button.**

The paragraph moves to the center of the page.

3 **Click the Align Right button.**

The paragraph lines up with the right margin.

4 **Click the Align Left button.**

The paragraph returns to its original position.

Indenting paragraphs works the same way:

1 **Click inside the paragraph.**

2 **Click the Increase Indent button.**

The paragraph nudges in from the left and right margins.

3 **Click the Decrease Indent button.**

The paragraph moves back to its original position.

Recess

Ahhhh, a break. Take a moment to let all this text style stuff sink into your brain. If you feel like it, in the first sentence in the home page, replace Asha with your name. Otherwise, press Ctrl+S to save your changes, and look out the window (a real window, not the ones on your computer screen) for a few minutes to give your eyes a rest. Or take a walk. FrontPage will be waiting for you when you return.

Inserting Symbols

At their most basic level, Web pages are nothing more than plain text documents with HTML tags sprinkled throughout. Because the plain text character set doesn't contain fancy characters and symbols (such as ©, &, and @), you need to jump through a few HTML hoops to include these characters in your Web pages. Fortunately, FrontPage does the hoop jumping for you.

In the following steps, you add a sample copyright notice to your home page. Including a copyright notice in your Web pages is always a good idea, just to alert would-be snatchers of text and graphics that you're prepared to protect your intellectual capital.

1 **Place the cursor at the end of the last sentence in the page and press Enter to create a new, blank line.**

2 **Choose Insert⇨Symbol.**

The Symbol dialog box appears. The dialog box contains all sorts of characters, including Latin symbols, fractions, and characters used in words of foreign origin.

3 **In the dialog box, click the copyright symbol (©) and then click Insert.**

The symbol appears in your page at the location of the cursor.

4 **In the dialog box, click Close.**

The Symbol dialog box closes.

5 **To complete the copyright notice, press the spacebar and then type your full name followed by a comma and the current year.**

extra credit

Working with HTML tags

FrontPage protects you from dealing with HTML. If, however, you're curious about how HTML works, or if you like to tinker around at the code level, FrontPage doesn't mind.

To display your page's underlying HTML tags, at the bottom-left corner of the Editor window, click the HTML tab to display the HTML View. The HTML View shows you the HTML tags and text that make up your page. FrontPage even color-codes the HTML tags so that you can easily make them out.

To edit the HTML, click anywhere inside the HTML View and make your desired changes. The Editor's Find and Replace function works in this view — a real time-saver if you want to make sweeping code changes. After you're finished, click the Normal tab to return to the regular Editor view.

If you enter HTML tags the Editor doesn't recognize, an Unknown HTML icon (a little yellow rectangle with a question mark inside) appears inside your page in the regular Editor view . The icon appears if you've made a code mistake or if FrontPage doesn't know how to process that particular tag, even if it's valid. To change the HTML tag, double-click the icon. The HTML Markup dialog box appears, containing the unrecognizable tags. Edit the tags in the dialog box and then click OK to close the dialog box. (The Unknown HTML icon remains in your page even after you correct the offending HTML tag but disappears as soon as you refresh your page's display by clicking the Refresh button on the Editor's Standard toolbar.)

Notes:

☑ **Progress Check**

If you can do the following, you've mastered this lesson:

❏ Insert a special character into your page.

Lesson 3-6

Previewing a Page

Throughout this unit, I've been hinting at why you want to preview your Web page in a browser as you build the page. Here's the full skinny: The Editor closely approximates how your page will look after it's published on the Web, but for the most accurate display, you need to preview your page.

The Editor gives you two easy choices for previewing your page: the Preview View, or a separate web browser such as Microsoft Internet Explorer or Netscape Navigator.

The Editor's Preview View shows you how your page looks when viewed with Microsoft's browser, Internet Explorer. By clicking the Preview tab in the lower-left corner of the Editor window, you can easily and quickly preview your page while staying within the cozy boundaries of FrontPage.

heads up

If you don't see a Preview tab on your screen, it means you don't have Microsoft Internet Explorer 3.0 or later installed on your computer. FrontPage uses Internet Explorer to display what's inside the Preview View. Therefore, if you don't have the program installed, FrontPage has no way of rendering a page preview. The FrontPage program CD comes with Internet Explorer; should you decide you want to give the browser a spin.

If you prefer to preview your pages in another browser, or better yet, more than one browser model and version, you can easily do so. The Preview in Browser command launches the web browser installed on your computer (and if you have more than one browser installed, enables you to choose which program you prefer), and displays the page you're currently working on in the browser window.

heads up

Most web browsers translate HTML tags into slightly different formats, so whereas italic text looks the same in Netscape Navigator and Microsoft Internet Explorer, other less common formats may not look the same. Furthermore, a small percentage of your visitors use older browser versions, or browsers that display only text. For that reason, I advise previewing your pages using a few different browsers (preferably with one being an older version of Navigator or Mosaic) so that you get an accurate idea of how your pages look to all your visitors.

You now preview your home page in a web browser (be sure that you have a web browser installed on your computer before you continue with this lesson).

1 **Save your page.**

If you're not sure how, refer to Lesson 2-6.

2 **Choose File⇨Preview in Browser.**

The Preview in Browser dialog box appears (see Figure 3-5).

for the most accurate display, preview Web pages in a few different web browsers

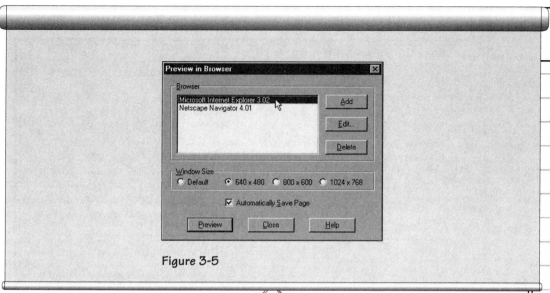

Figure 3-5

Figure 3-5: The Preview in Browser dialog box.

Notes:

3 **In the Browser list box, click the name of the browser you want to use.**

In this example, I chose Internet Explorer 3.02. You can choose whichever browser you like.

4 **In the Window Size section of the dialog box, click the 640 x 480 radio button.**

The numbers listed next to each radio button represent standard monitor resolution values in *pixels*. A monitor's resolution refers to the number of pixels that monitor displays on-screen. The larger that number, the higher the resolution of the picture and the more information a monitor can display. Most Web surfers have 640 x 480 or 800 x 600 resolution monitors, but to be safe, I always preview my pages at 640 x 480.

5 **Mark the Automatically Save Page check box.**

By doing so, you tell the Editor to automatically save any changes each time you preview the page.

6 **Click Preview.**

FrontPage opens your page in the browser of your choice.

Granted, right now, the page doesn't look much different from what you see in the Editor, but you get the point. Previewing your pages becomes more meaningful after you add hyperlinks, graphics, and other interesting effects.

The Standard toolbar contains a shortcut: the Preview in Browser button. Click this button when you want to use the Editor's current settings to preview your page.

Preview in Browser button

If you notice a boo-boo while you're examining your page in the browser win-dow, return to the Editor by clicking the Editor's button on the Windows taskbar. Make any changes to the page you want and then click the Preview in Browser button again. The Editor saves your changes and then switches to your browser and displays the updated version of the page.

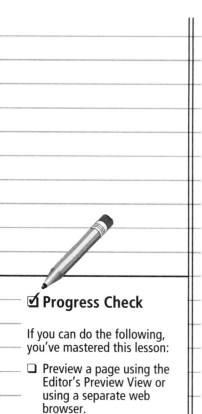

extra credit

Inserting a timestamp

A *timestamp* is the date and/or time the page was last updated. The Editor enables you to insert a timestamp into your page that automatically changes each time the page changes. This feature is a great way to inform frequent visitors that you've added new stuff to the page since the last time they visited.

To use a timestamp in your page, follow these steps:

1. **Place the cursor in your page where you want the timestamp to appear.**

2. **Choose Insert⇨Timestamp.**

   The Timestamp Properties dialog box appears.

3. **In the dialog box, click the radio button next to the display option you prefer.**

   Click the Date This Page Was Last Edited radio button if you want the date to reflect when you last

changed the page by hand. Click the Date This Page Was Last Automatically Updated radio button if you want the date to reflect your edits *and* automatic updates — for example, if a table of contents on the page automatically regenerates (you find out how a table of contents works in Unit 5).

4. **Select a date format from the Date Format list box.**

   If you want to display just the time, select (none) from the list box.

5. **Select a time format from the Time Format list box.**

   If you want to display just the date, select (none) from the list box.

6. **Click OK to close the dialog box.**

   The date and/or time the page was last modified appears in the page.

☑ Progress Check

If you can do the following, you've mastered this lesson:

❏ Preview a page using the Editor's Preview View or using a separate web browser.

Unit 3 Quiz

Quiz time (your favorite time of the day, I know)! For each of the following questions, circle the letter of the correct answer or answers. Remember, I may include more than one right answer for each question.

If you want, you can check your answers in Appendix B.

1. **The font style tools are located in . . .**

   A. The Font dialog box.

   B. The Standard toolbar.

   C. The Format toolbar.

   D. The Explorer.

   E. The tool shed, next to the gardening supplies.

2. **To make a word bold . . .**

   A. Highlight the word and then press Ctrl+B.

   B. Highlight the word and then click the Bold button.

   C. Highlight the word, choose Format⇨Font, and in the Font dialog box, click Bold, and then click OK.

   D. Give the word a rousing pep talk.

   E. Highlight the word, right-click it, and choose Font Properties from the shortcut menu. The Font dialog box appears. In the dialog box, click Bold and then click OK.

3. **In a Web page, text size . . .**

   A. Is relative; the actual text size is determined by the visitor's browser.

   B. Is absolute; if you specify 14-point type, that's what all your visitors will see when they view your page.

   C. Can't be changed.

   D. Is determined by a system of HTML size increments.

   E. Doesn't matter.

4. **The difference between font styles and paragraph styles is . . .**

   A. Font styles add character to the page, and paragraph styles create new paragraphs.

   B. Font styles operate on single characters and words, whereas paragraph styles operate only on entire paragraphs.

   C. Font styles are used to make detail formatting changes, whereas paragraph styles are used to make widespread structure changes.

   D. No difference exists between font and paragraph styles; FrontPage simply didn't have enough room in a single dialog box to hold them all.

5. **Previewing your pages is important, because . . .**

   A. You get a more accurate view of how your page will appear to your visitors.

   B. You can change your page's design to accommodate formatting differences among browsers.

   C. Pfffff. Previewing pages is for perfectionists.

   D. Getting a glimpse of how your page will look after it's "live" is fun.

   E. You can see how your page looks at different screen resolutions.

Notes:

Unit 3 Exercise

1. Launch FrontPage.

2. Open My Web Site.

3. After the Web site is open, launch the FrontPage Editor by opening the home page.

4. Add whatever text you like to the page. Format the text with font and paragraph styles.

5. Press Enter to create a new paragraph, and change the new paragraph's alignment.

6. Insert a special character or two.

7. Preview the page, first using the Editor's Preview tab and then in a web browser.

8. Switch back to the Editor and then exit both the Editor and the Explorer.

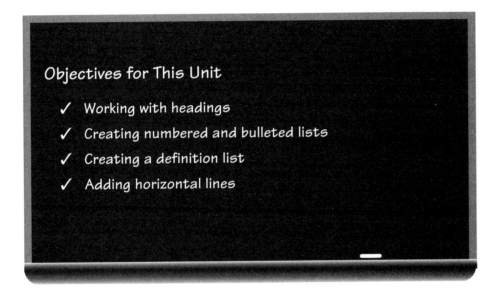

Organizing Your Page with Headings, Lists, and Lines

Objectives for This Unit

✓ Working with headings

✓ Creating numbered and bulleted lists

✓ Creating a definition list

✓ Adding horizontal lines

Prerequisites

▶ Launching FrontPage (Lesson 1-2)

▶ Creating a Web site from scratch (Lesson 1-3)

▶ Opening an existing Web site in the Explorer (Lesson 2-1)

▶ Opening a page from within the Editor (Lesson 2-3)

▶ Saving a page (Lesson 2-6)

▶ Working with the Dummies 101 example files (Lesson 3-1)

▶ unit04.htm

on the CD

U nit 3 introduced you to the font and paragraph styles available in the Editor. Two paragraph styles I didn't discuss in Unit 3 — headings and lists — are special enough to merit their own unit. Headings and lists enable you to group chunks of text into sections, making your page easy to understand at a glance. In fact, you'll probably find that you use these styles more than any other.

In this unit, you create a sample résumé by using headings and three different kinds of lists. You further structure the page with a simple but effective tool: a horizontal line.

Lesson 4-1

Prioritizing Information with Headings

Imagine for a moment what reading the morning paper would be like if the paper didn't have headlines. Everything else is the same — the columns, the ads, the photos — the only items missing are the headlines. Each page would be a wash of tiny words, none of which would stand out and grab your attention. Unless you took time to carefully read each page, you wouldn't be able to discern the important stories from the filler. Extracting information from such a publication would be a major pain, especially if you happened to be smooshed between two other passengers on the commuter train to work.

headings prioritize information in the page

Web surfers can be compared to commuters: They want information fast, and they don't have time to sift through every word on your Web site. In Web pages, *headings* serve the same purpose as newspaper headlines. Thoughtfully placed headings help visitors quickly assess the page's contents. Headings of different sizes indicate which bits of information deserve top priority and which are secondary. Headings can also create a visual break between bunches of text so that visitors know when the subject matter is about to change.

on the test

Using the Editor, you can apply six levels of headings to text in your pages (Heading 1 is the largest, and Heading 6 is the smallest).

on the CD

I supply you with a practice page called unit04.htm (it's waiting patiently for you in the FP101 folder) so you can try headings out for yourself. But first, you must launch FrontPage (if it isn't already open), and set up your workspace so you can proceed with the rest of this unit.

1 **Launch FrontPage, and open My Web Site.**

If you're not sure how to open a Web site, refer to Lesson 2-1.

2 **On the Explorer toolbar, click the Show FrontPage Editor button.**

The Editor launches, and presents you with a new, blank page. (If the Editor is already open, click the New button on the Standard toolbar to create a new page.)

Show FrontPage Editor button

3 **Using the Insert⇨File command, insert the contents of the file named unit04.htm (located in the FP101 folder) into the page.**

For detailed instructions on how to use the Insert⇨File command, see Lesson 3-1.

The contents of the example file appear inside the new page, looking just as if you'd typed all the text yourself (see Figure 4-1).

4 **Save the page as part of your Web site, title the page My Resume, and name the page resume.htm.**

If you can't remember how to save a page, refer to Lesson 2-6.

The sample résumé is far from elegant. The information on the page isn't organized into a clear hierarchy . . . or is it? With the deft application of a few headings, the page's organization soon becomes clear.

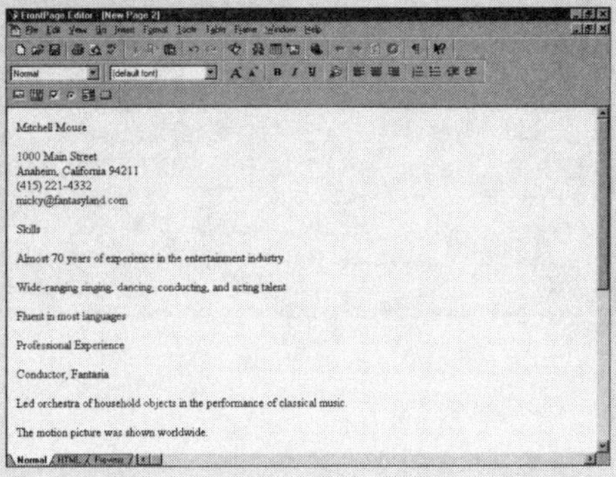

Figure 4-1

Figure 4-1: The beginnings of a résumé.

click the cursor inside a block of text to apply heading; no need to highlight the entire paragraph

1 **Click the cursor inside the line that reads** Mitchell Mouse.

2 **From the Change Style list box on the Format toolbar, select Heading 1.**

The selected text becomes larger and bolder.

3 **Click the cursor inside the word** Skills.

4 **From the Change Style list box, select Heading 2.**

The Heading 2 style is applied to the text. Heading 2 is slightly less prominent than Heading 1, creating a visual hierarchy of information.

5 **Apply the Heading 2 style to the lines that read** Professional Experience **and** Personal Details.

6 **Apply the Heading 3 style to the lines that read** Conductor, Fantasia **and** Founder, Mickey Mouse Club.

There. The information on the page hasn't changed, but the simple application of headings makes the information easier to understand.

☑ **Progress Check**

If you can do the following you've mastered this lesson:

❑ Apply heading styles to text.

Creating a Numbered List or a Bulleted List

Lesson 4-2

Lists corral related bits of information into a single group. Like headings, lists help those scanning your Web page to prioritize and group the information in their minds, making the page easier to understand.

The two most popular types of lists are *numbered lists* and *bulleted lists*. In a numbered list, each item is preceded by a sequential number, and in a bulleted list, each item is preceded by a dot.

Figure 4-2: A numbered list.

Figure 4-3: A bulleted list.

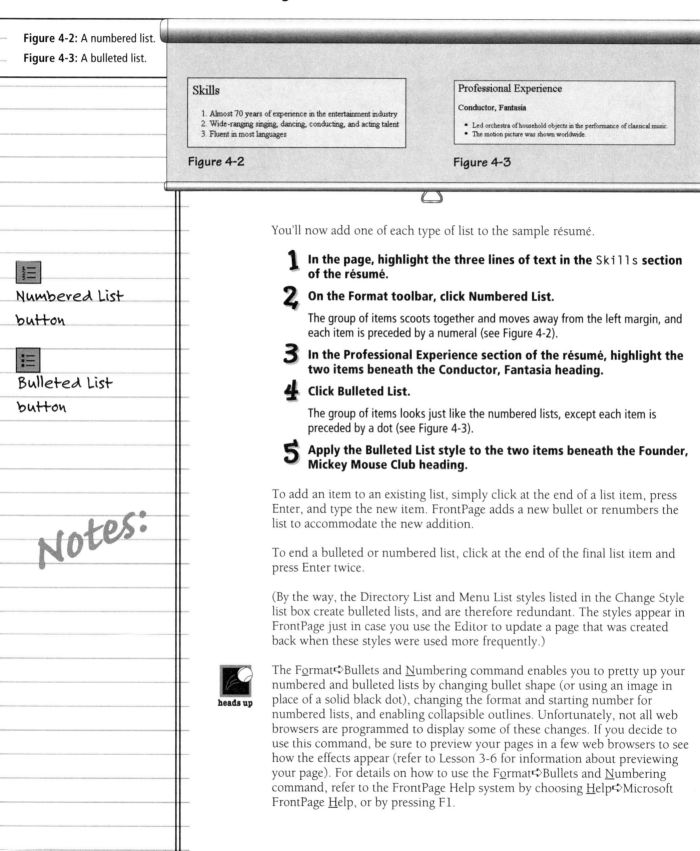

Skills

1. Almost 70 years of experience in the entertainment industry
2. Wide-ranging singing, dancing, conducting, and acting talent
3. Fluent in most languages

Figure 4-2

Professional Experience

Conductor, Fantasia

- Led orchestra of household objects in the performance of classical music.
- The motion picture was shown worldwide.

Figure 4-3

Numbered List button

Bulleted List button

Notes:

You'll now add one of each type of list to the sample résumé.

1 In the page, highlight the three lines of text in the Skills section of the résumé.

2 On the Format toolbar, click Numbered List.

The group of items scoots together and moves away from the left margin, and each item is preceded by a numeral (see Figure 4-2).

3 In the Professional Experience section of the résumé, highlight the two items beneath the Conductor, Fantasia heading.

4 Click Bulleted List.

The group of items looks just like the numbered lists, except each item is preceded by a dot (see Figure 4-3).

5 Apply the Bulleted List style to the two items beneath the Founder, Mickey Mouse Club heading.

To add an item to an existing list, simply click at the end of a list item, press Enter, and type the new item. FrontPage adds a new bullet or renumbers the list to accommodate the new addition.

To end a bulleted or numbered list, click at the end of the final list item and press Enter twice.

(By the way, the Directory List and Menu List styles listed in the Change Style list box create bulleted lists, and are therefore redundant. The styles appear in FrontPage just in case you use the Editor to update a page that was created back when these styles were used more frequently.)

heads up

The Format➪Bullets and Numbering command enables you to pretty up your numbered and bulleted lists by changing bullet shape (or using an image in place of a solid black dot), changing the format and starting number for numbered lists, and enabling collapsible outlines. Unfortunately, not all web browsers are programmed to display some of these changes. If you decide to use this command, be sure to preview your pages in a few web browsers to see how the effects appear (refer to Lesson 3-6 for information about previewing your page). For details on how to use the Format➪Bullets and Numbering command, refer to the FrontPage Help system by choosing Help➪Microsoft FrontPage Help, or by pressing F1.

Creating a list with more than one level

If you want to use a list as an outline, with more than one level of bulleted or numbered items (or both!), you can combine the two styles to create a multilevel, or *nested*, list. To do so, follow these steps:

1. **Create a bulleted or numbered list containing the top-level items.**

2. **Click at the end of the line above where you want to insert the second level of list items, and then press Enter.**

3. **Click the Increase Indent button.**

   The list item turns into a blank line.

4. **Click the Bulleted List or Numbered List button (depending on the type of list you want to insert).**

   Depending on the style you choose, the blank line turns into a bulleted or numbered line.

5. **Type the secondary level of list items, pressing Enter each time to create new lines.**

6. **After you're through, click the cursor anywhere on the page outside the list.**

☑ Progress Check

If you can do the following you've mastered this lesson:

❑ Create a numbered list.

❑ Create a bulleted list.

Creating a Definition List   Lesson 4-3

A *definition list* is handy when you want to present a list of terms or categories followed by their definitions. Definition lists don't appear on Web pages as often as bulleted or numbered lists, but can be useful just the same.

To create a definition list, follow these steps:

1 **In the page, scroll down until the Personal Details section of the résumé is visible.**

2 **Click inside the word** `Family`**.**

3 **From the Change Style list box, select Defined Term.**

The word *Family* doesn't appear to change; however, it is now the first item of a definition list.

4 **Click inside the following line of text (it begins with** `Partner:` `Minnie`**).**

5 **From the Change Style list box, select Definition.**

The definition moves closer to the term and is indented from the left margin.

6 **Repeat steps 2 through 5 for the remaining terms and definitions in the list.**

The finished list looks similar to Figure 4-4. As the figure illustrates, you can apply Bold formatting to the defined terms so they stand out a bit more.

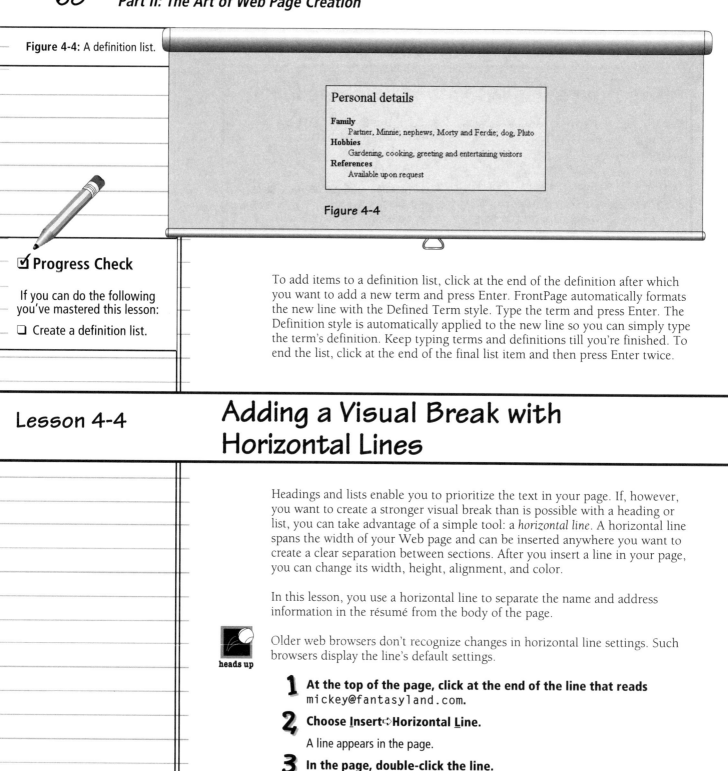

Figure 4-4: A definition list.

Personal details

Family
    Partner, Minnie; nephews, Morty and Ferdie; dog, Pluto
Hobbies
    Gardening, cooking, greeting and entertaining visitors
References
    Available upon request

Figure 4-4

☑ Progress Check

If you can do the following you've mastered this lesson:
❑ Create a definition list.

To add items to a definition list, click at the end of the definition after which you want to add a new term and press Enter. FrontPage automatically formats the new line with the Defined Term style. Type the term and press Enter. The Definition style is automatically applied to the new line so you can simply type the term's definition. Keep typing terms and definitions till you're finished. To end the list, click at the end of the final list item and then press Enter twice.

Lesson 4-4

Adding a Visual Break with Horizontal Lines

Headings and lists enable you to prioritize the text in your page. If, however, you want to create a stronger visual break than is possible with a heading or list, you can take advantage of a simple tool: a *horizontal line*. A horizontal line spans the width of your Web page and can be inserted anywhere you want to create a clear separation between sections. After you insert a line in your page, you can change its width, height, alignment, and color.

In this lesson, you use a horizontal line to separate the name and address information in the résumé from the body of the page.

heads up

Older web browsers don't recognize changes in horizontal line settings. Such browsers display the line's default settings.

1 At the top of the page, click at the end of the line that reads mickey@fantasyland.com.

2 Choose Insert⇨Horizontal Line.

A line appears in the page.

3 In the page, double-click the line.

The Horizontal Line Properties dialog box appears (see Figure 4-5).

4 In the dialog box's Width text box, enter 75.

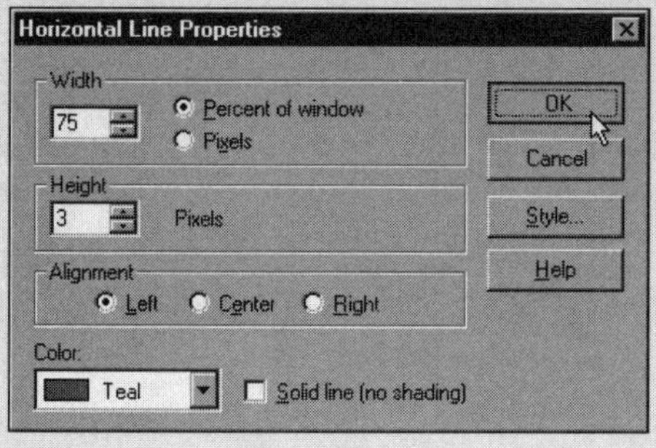

Figure 4-5

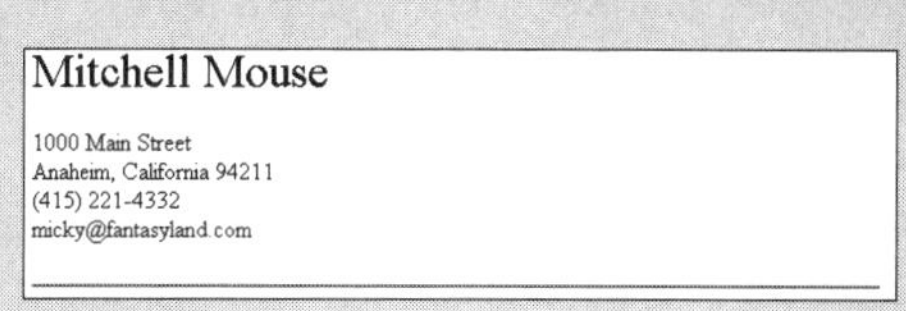

Figure 4-6

Notes:

By doing so, you restrict the line's width to 75 percent of the width of the
browser window. For more precise control over the line's width, click the Pixels
radio button and enter an absolute number of pixels in the Width box.

5 In the Height text box, enter 3.

The Height text box controls the line's thickness.

6 In the Alignment section of the dialog box, click the Left radio button.

The Alignment options control the alignment of the line in the page.

7 From the Color list box, select Teal.

8 Click OK to close the Horizontal Line Properties dialog box.

The dialog box closes, and the newly embellished line appears on the page (see
Figure 4-6).

---

extra credit

Inserting invisible comments

Comments are notes that appear in the
Editor but are invisible when the page is
viewed with a web browser. Use comments to insert explanatory text and reminders into the body of your page.

To insert a comment, do the following:

**1. Place the cursor where you
want the comment to appear
and choose Insert⇨FrontPage
Component.**

The Insert FrontPage Component
dialog box appears.

**2. In the dialog box, click Com-
ment and then click OK.**

The Insert FrontPage Component
dialog box closes and the Comment
dialog box appears.

**3. In the Comment text box, type
your comment and click OK.**

The comment appears on your page
as colorful text preceded by the
word Comment.

To edit a comment, double-click the comment to display the Comment dialog box.
To delete a comment, click the comment
and press the Backspace key.

☑ Progress Check

If you can do the following
you've mastered this lesson:

❏ Insert a horizontal line
   into your page, and alter
   its appearance.

The sample résumé looks much cleaner now that you have used headings, lists, and lines to prioritize its contents. If you want, replace the generic information contained in the résumé with information about your own professional life (I provide a few guidelines in the Exercise at the end of this unit). Then save your changes. If you feel like a break before moving on, exit FrontPage.

Unit 4 Quiz

Here are a few quiz questions to recap what you've learned in this unit. Remember, I may include more than one right answer for each question.

1. **How many levels of headings does FrontPage have?**

   A. 7

   B. 6

   C. 10

   D. 5

   E. You can't apply headings to text in a Web page.

2. **To apply Heading 1 to a paragraph . . .**

   A. Click inside the paragraph and then press Ctrl+H+1.

   B. Right-click the paragraph, select Font Properties from the shortcut menu, select Heading 1 from the dialog box that appears, and click OK.

   C. Right-click the paragraph, select Paragraph Properties from the shortcut menu, select Heading 1 from the dialog box that appears, and click OK.

   D. Click inside the paragraph and select Heading 1 from the Change Style list box.

   E. Click the Heading 1 button on the Format toolbar.

3. **Bulleted and numbered lists . . .**

    A. Group related items together.

    B. Are difficult to create.

    C. Can be changed using the Format⇨Bullets and Numbering command.

    D. Don't like each other.

    E. Can be combined into a single multilevel list.

4. **Definition lists . . .**

    A. Can be used to display terms and their definitions in Web pages.

    B. Define the types of lists available in the FrontPage Editor.

    C. Are not as commonly used as bulleted and numbered lists.

    D. Can be created by clicking the Definition List button on the Format toolbar.

5. **A horizontal line . . .**

    A. Is another tool you can use to categorize and break up text in a Web page.

    B. Is inserted into a page when you choose Insert⇨Horizontal Line.

    C. Can vary in width, height, and color.

    D. Creates a page break when you print the Web page.

    E. Is the shortest distance between two points.

Notes:

Unit 4 Exercise

1. Launch FrontPage, open My Web Site, and then open the sample résumé page (resume.htm).

2. In the page, replace Mitchell Mouse's professional history with your own. Add new sections as you see fit.

3. Use headings to clearly demarcate each section.

4. Use bulleted, numbered, and definition lists to group together chunks of information in your résumé.

5. If you want, separate each section with a horizontal line.

6. Preview the page by clicking the Preview tab in the lower-left corner of the Editor window.

7. Save the page, and exit both the Editor and the Explorer.

Unit 5

• • • • • • • • • • •

Hopping around
the World with Hyperlinks

Objectives for This Unit

✓ Creating hyperlinks

✓ Creating and linking to bookmarks

✓ Changing link colors

✓ Building a navigational structure

✓ Inserting a navigation bar into a page

Prerequisites

▶ Launching FrontPage
(Lesson 1-2)

▶ Creating a Web site from
scratch (Lesson 1-3)

▶ Opening an existing Web
site in the Explorer
(Lesson 2-1)

▶ Opening a page from
within the Editor
(Lesson 2-3)

▶ Saving a page (Lesson 2-6)

▶ Working with the *Dummies
101: FrontPage 98* example
files (Lesson 3-1)

▶ Previewing a page
(Lesson 3-6)

on the CD

▶ unit05.htm

▶ resume.htm

Hyperlinks make the Web go 'round. Links — the words, phrases, or
pictures in a Web page that you click to go elsewhere — are the threads
that tie your Web pages into a neat package called a Web site. In fact, links are
what make surfing the World Wide Web possible in the first place.

You use links in your Web site for two purposes: to fasten the sites' pages
together and to connect the site to other sites on the Web. Using the FrontPage
Editor, you can create either type of link in seconds.

Creating a Hyperlink

Lesson 5-1

A *hyperlink* is a chunk of text or an image that has been endowed with special
powers. Namely, when visitors click a link, they are transported to another
location. That location may be inside the same page they are currently looking

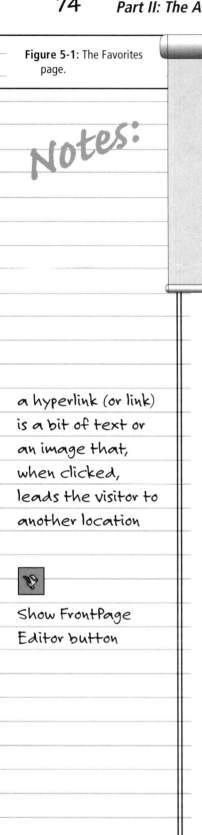

Figure 5-1: The Favorites page.

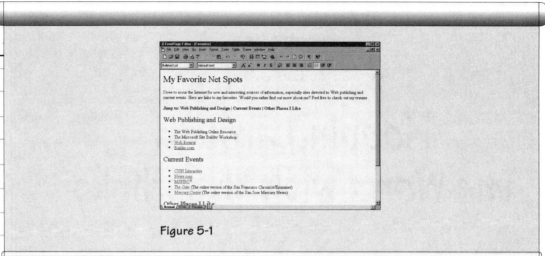

Figure 5-1

a hyperlink (or link) is a bit of text or an image that, when clicked, leads the visitor to another location

Show FrontPage Editor button

at, or it may be in a different page. The page may be part of the current Web site, or it may be part of a site stored on a Web server 1000 miles away. The destination doesn't matter — with the Editor, creating a link to a page inside your Web site is just as easy as creating a link to a page on the other side of the world.

So that you can practice link creation, I have included a Web page called unit05.htm in the FP101 folder. This page contains ready-made links to some of my favorite places on the Web, plus space for you to add your own pet links. I chose this example because many people like to include a Favorites page in their site as a way of bidding visitors a pleasant Web journey.

To follow the examples in the rest of this unit, you must first set up your FrontPage workspace.

1 Launch FrontPage and open My Web Site.

If you're not sure how to open a Web site, refer to Lesson 2-1.

2 On the Explorer toolbar, click Show FrontPage Editor.

The Editor launches, and presents you with a new, blank page. (If the Editor is already open, click the New button on the Standard toolbar to create a new page.)

3 Using the Insert⇨File command, insert the contents of the file named unit05.htm (located in the FP101 folder) into the page.

For detailed instructions on how to use the Insert⇨File command, see Lesson 3-1.

The contents of the example file appear inside the page (see Figure 5-1).

4 Save the page as part of your Web site, title the page Favorites, and name the page favorite.htm.

If you can't remember how to save a page, refer to Lesson 2-6.

You're now ready to begin creating hyperlinks. The Favorites page already contains quite a few hyperlinks; in this unit, you add a few of your own.

Linking to another page in your Web site

The most common type of hyperlink leads to another page inside the current Web site. These links, known as *internal links,* let visitors hop from page to page looking for the information they want.

The following steps take you through creating an internal link from the Favorites page to resume.htm, the sample résumé you created in Unit 4. If you skipped Unit 4, the FP101 folder contains a finished copy of resume.htm. Before you begin this lesson, in the Editor, open resume.htm from within the FP101 folder, and then save the page as part of My Web Site (I explain how to open a Web page stored outside a FrontPage Web site in Lesson 2-3, and I show you how to save that page as part of your Web site in Lesson 2-6).

To create an internal hyperlink, follow these steps:

1 **In the Favorites page, double-click the word *resume* to select it (it's the last word in the page's introductory paragraph).**

In this case, you are about to turn the word **resume** into a hyperlink leading to the page resume.htm. You could just easily have highlighted more than one word (or a single character). Or, if your page contained images, you could have clicked a picture instead of highlighting a word. Both text and images can be transformed into hyperlinks.

2 **On the Format toolbar, click Create or Edit Hyperlink.**

The Create Hyperlink dialog box appears (see Figure 5-2). The dialog box contains a list of the files and folders in My Web Site, plus a number of assorted buttons and options.

When a page is currently open in the Editor, *two* instances of that page appear in the dialog box's file list: One is preceded by a regular page icon, and the other is preceded by a page-and-red-feather icon. The red feather icon is only there to remind you which pages are currently open in the Editor. You can click either icon when you create hyperlinks.

3 **In the file list, click resume.htm and then click OK.**

The dialog box closes, and the word *resume* turns blue and underlined, letting you know that it is now a hyperlink (click elsewhere in the page to deselect the word to better see its new hyperlink markings).

You've just forged your first internal hyperlink. Now, when visitors check out the page, they can easily skirt over to your résumé if they decide they want to know more about you.

To change the link text (without disturbing the link itself), highlight the link and type new text.

To change the link's destination, click the link and then click the Create or Edit Hyperlink button to display the Edit Hyperlink dialog box. Select a new destination (click a different page icon in the file list, for instance), and then click OK to close the dialog box and update the link.

To unlink a link, click the link and choose Edit⇨Unlink.

Margin notes:

internal hyperlinks = links to pages inside the Web site

Create or Edit Hyperlink button

it's easy to change a link's text or destination or unlink links that are obsolete

Figure 5-2: The Create Hyperlink dialog box.

Notes:

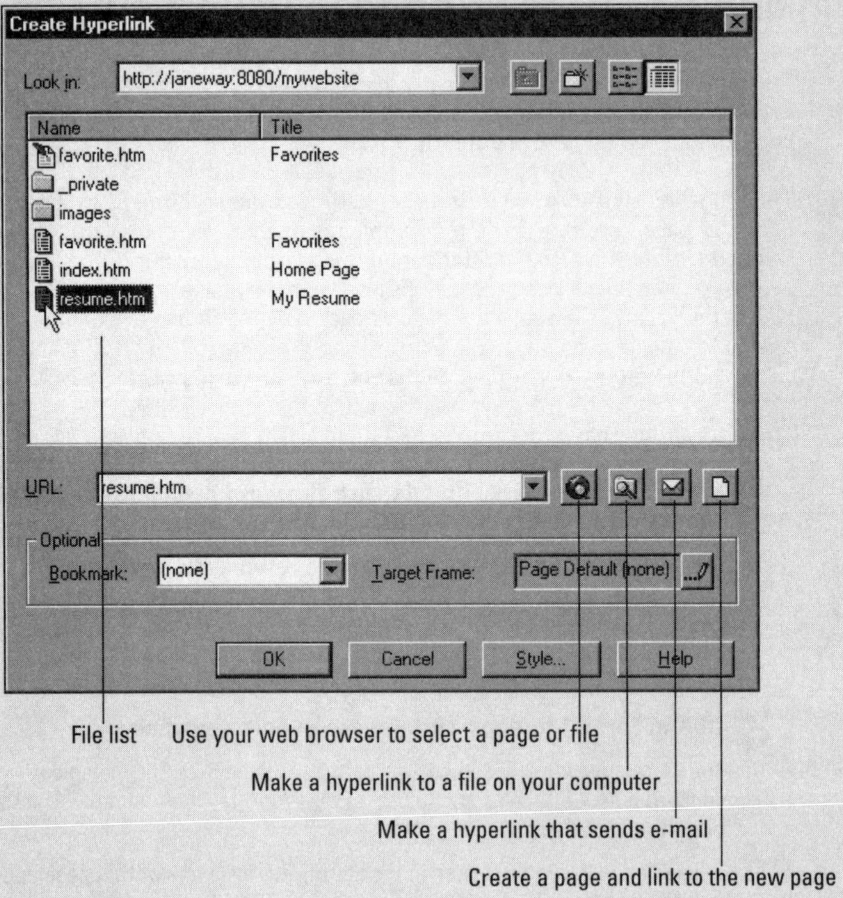

Create Hyperlink

Look in: http://janeway:8080/mywebsite

Name	Title
favorite.htm	Favorites
_private	
images	
favorite.htm	Favorites
index.htm	Home Page
resume.htm	My Resume

URL: resume.htm

Optional
Bookmark: (none)   Target Frame: Page Default (none)

OK   Cancel   Style...   Help

File list   Use your web browser to select a page or file

Make a hyperlink to a file on your computer

Make a hyperlink that sends e-mail

Create a page and link to the new page

Figure 5-2

external
hyperlinks = links to
locations outside
the Web site

Create or Edit
Hyperlink button

Linking to a site on the Web

By publishing a Web site, you pour your own perspective into the World Wide Web's immense data pot. But in order to weave your site into the Web's collective community, you must create links between your site and other sites on the Web. These links are called *external links* because they point to locations outside your own site.

In the following steps, you link My Web Site to a site on the Web:

1 **In the Favorites page, highlight the words** The Web Publishing Online Resource **(the first item in the Web Publishing and Design section of the page).**

2 **Click the Create or Edit Hyperlink button.**

The Create Hyperlink dialog box appears.

3 **In the URL text box, type** `http://www.ashaland.com/webpub.`

Now, instead of connecting the selected text to a page inside your Web site as you did in the previous section, you are creating a link to a Web site URL.

I happen to know the URL of the Web Publishing Online Resource by heart. If you can't remember a URL, click the Use Your Web Browser to Select a Page or File button in the dialog box to launch your web browser. Browse to your destination and then switch back to the FrontPage Editor by clicking the Editor's button on the Windows 95 taskbar, and the URL automatically appears in the URL text box.

4 **Click OK.**

The dialog box closes, and the words `The Web Publishing Online Resource` turn into a hyperlink to the specified URL.

on the test

In this example, you created a hyperlink to a Web site. You can just as easily create a link to other Internet resources such as downloadable programs (many of which are stored on FTP sites) and Usenet newsgroups. To do so, in Step 3 in the previous set of steps, enter a URL for a file on an FTP site (for example, `ftp://ftp.server.com/program.exe`) or a newsgroup (for example, `news:comp.infosystems.www`). Assuming the visitor's browser understands such hyperlinks (most do), the resulting hyperlinks initiate downloads and display newsgroup postings.

extra credit

Inserting a table of contents

A table of contents displays the titles of all your site's pages in a hierarchical list, with links to each page. Many site designers include a separate table of contents page so visitors can get a bird's-eye view of the entire site's contents.

As you can imagine, maintaining a table of contents — especially for a large, dynamic Web site — is a big job.

Fortunately, the Editor's Insert⇨Table of Contents command spits out a fully linked table of contents and keeps the contents list up-to-date as pages change.

For detailed instructions on how to create a table of contents, refer to the FrontPage help system by choosing Help⇨ Microsoft FrontPage Help or pressing F1.

Linking to an e-mail address

A special type of hyperlink called a *mailto link* enables visitors to send you e-mail. When clicked, this link spurs the visitor's Web browser to launch its e-mail component (or in some cases, the visitor's separate e-mail program) and create a new message addressed to the link's recipient. Mailto links are a good way to shout to the world: "I want contact!"

Use your Web Browser to select a page or file button

shortcut: in the page, type a Web URL (like http://www.microsoft.com), and then press the spacebar or Enter; the Editor automatically turns the address into a hyperlink to that location

mailto link = link to an e-mail address

Progress Check

If you can do the following, you've mastered this lesson:

❑ Create a hyperlink that leads to another page inside the site.

❑ Create a hyperlink that leads to another site on the Web.

❑ Create a hyperlink that sends e-mail.

Here is the quick and easy way to create a mailto link:

1 Scroll down to the bottom of the Favorites page and click your cursor at the end of the page (directly after the line that reads `Like this page? Send me e-mail!`).

2 Type your e-mail address and then press the spacebar (if you don't have an e-mail address, use mine: webpub@ashaland.com).

Boom! The address turns into a mailto link — no fuss, no muss.

Wanna see how your newly created link works? Save and preview your page (follow the steps in Lesson 3-6 if you don't remember how). After your page is visible inside the browser, click the mailto link. If your Web browser is able to send e-mail, the browser creates a new message addressed to the e-mail address you specified in Step 2 above.

Lesson 5-2 Working with Bookmarks

A *bookmark* is an invisible spot inside a Web page that is defined as the destination of a link. After you sprinkle bookmarks throughout your page, you can create links (inside the same page or inside other pages) that jump straight to the location of the bookmarks instead of to the top of the page (as a regular link would).

heads up

Don't confuse FrontPage bookmarks with Web browser bookmarks. Using your browser to "bookmark" a favorite Web site so you can easily return there is different than creating a bookmark in FrontPage, as you are about to find out.

Creating a bookmark

on the test

A bookmark can be a location in a Web page (the current location of the cursor) or a selected bit of text. After you create a bookmark, a dotted line appears underneath the bookmark text. (If you create a bookmark without first selecting text, a flag icon appears at the location of the bookmark.) These markers are only visible in the Editor. When the page is viewed with a Web browser, the bookmarks are invisible.

heads up

Keep in mind that bookmarks demarcate the *destination* of the hyperlink (the spot visitors eventually end up after clicking the link). Because you haven't yet created the link, this process may seem turned around. Bear with me — you're on the right track.

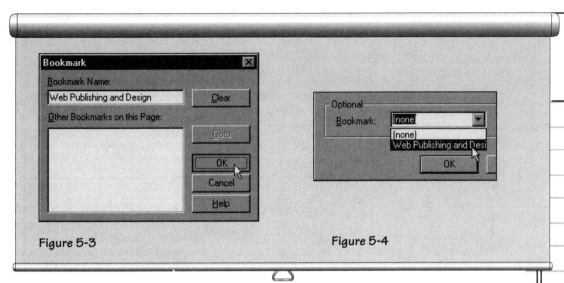

Figure 5-3   Figure 5-4

You now add bookmarks to the Favorites page by following these steps:

1 In the Favorites page, highlight the category heading Web Publishing and Design.

2 Choose Edit⇨Bookmark.

The Bookmark dialog box appears (see Figure 5-3). The Editor assumes that you want to give the bookmark the same name as the text it's made of, and therefore, Web Publishing and Design appears in the Bookmark Name text box.

3 Click OK.

The dialog box closes, and a dotted line appears underneath the selected text (indicating that it is now a bookmark).

Linking to a bookmark

Now you must create a hyperlink that leads to the bookmark you just created. In the following steps, you create a row of hyperlinks inside the Favorites page that allow visitors to jump to the category of information they find most interesting.

To create a link to a bookmark, do the following:

1 In the line that begins with the words Jump to, **highlight the words** Web Publishing and Design.

2 Click the Create or Edit Hyperlink button to open the Hyperlink dialog box.

3 From the Bookmark list box, select Web Publishing and Design.

Figure 5-4 illustrates how this works.

4 Click OK.

The dialog box closes, and the selected text transforms into a hyperlink leading to the Web Publishing and Design bookmark inside the Favorites page.

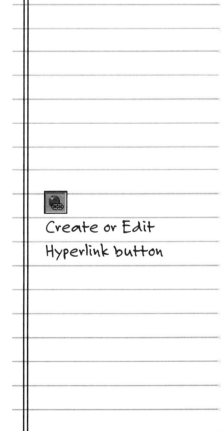

Create or Edit Hyperlink button

☑ Progress Check

If you can do the following,
you've mastered this lesson:

❑ Create a bookmark.

❑ Create a hyperlink that
leads to a bookmark.

To test the new hyperlink, preview your page and then click the link.

In this example, you created a hyperlink that leads to a bookmark inside the same page. To create a hyperlink that leads to a bookmark sitting in a *different* page, click the page that contains the bookmark to which you want to link , in the file list of the Create Hyperlink dialog box after Step 2 in the previous steps and then continue with the steps as listed.

extra credit

Creating a push-button hyperlink

To really impress your techie friends, insert a push-button hyperlink into your page. Also known as a *hover button*, this FrontPage Active Element enables you to create a colorful button visitors can press to jump to a new location. For details, consult the FrontPage Help system by choosing Help⇨Microsoft FrontPage Help or pressing F1.

Recess

The power of hyperlinks may leave your brain a bit fuzzy. If you like, save your page and then get up and take a jog around your living room or down the office corridors. You'll return refreshed and ready for more fun with hyperlinks.

Lesson 5-3   Setting Link Colors

Color (and in some Web browsers, underlining) sets hyperlinks apart from regular text. In most Web browsers, the default hyperlink color is blue, but if you have a snazzy color scheme in mind for your Web site, you can change the color of your links.

Hyperlinks actually have three distinct colors, each of which appears when a visitor views the page in a Web browser. The color of the hyperlink indicates the link's state, as follows:

▶ **The default color** is the link's color before the visitor clicks the hyperlink.

▶ **The active color** is the color the link becomes as the visitor clicks the hyperlink (this color appears only mid-click).

▶ **The visited color** is the color the link changes to after the visitor follows the link and (hopefully) returns to your page. The visited color helps visitors keep track of links they've already followed.

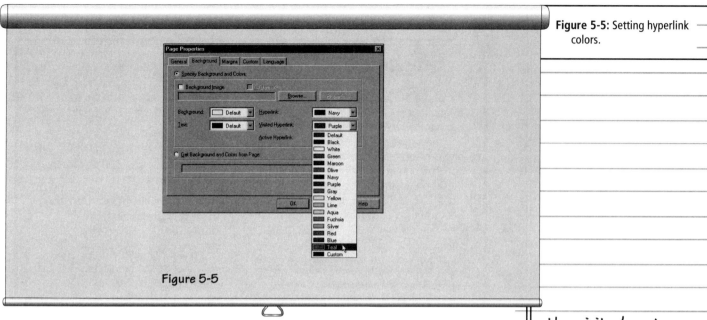

Figure 5-5: Setting hyperlink colors.

Figure 5-5

Right now, the Favorites page uses FrontPage's default link color settings. In the following set of steps, you change the hyperlink colors.

1 With the Favorites page visible in the Editor, choose Format⇨Background.

The Page Properties dialog box appears, with the Background tab visible (see Figure 5-5). The current link colors are visible in the Hyperlink, Visited Hyperlink, and Active Hyperlink list boxes.

2 In the Hyperlink list box, select Navy.

3 In the Visited Hyperlink list box, select Teal.

Because Red is a good color choice for Active hyperlinks, leave that list box alone.

4 Click OK.

The dialog box closes, and the page's links change color.

Aren't sure which colors look good together? No problem. Each FrontPage theme contains a collection of expertly designed colors, backgrounds, and graphics you can slap on top of your site. You apply a theme to My Web Site in Unit 6.

the visitor's web browser records which links the visitor follows, and changes the hyperlink color display accordingly

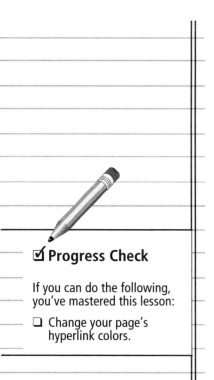

☑ **Progress Check**

If you can do the following, you've mastered this lesson:

❑ Change your page's hyperlink colors.

extra credit

Basing link colors on another page

If you intend to use a standard color scheme throughout your Web site, you can base hyperlink colors (as well as body text color and the page background color or image) on the colors of another page in your Web site. This option saves time in the long run because, should you decide to change the site's color scheme, you need to make background changes only to a single page (the one on which all the other pages' colors are based) to have the change reflected throughout the site.

To base background colors on those of another page, follow these steps:

1. **In the Editor, choose** **F̲ormat⇨Background.**

The Page Properties dialog box appears, with the Background tab visible.

2. **In the dialog box, click the G̲et Background and Colors from Page radio button.**

3. **In the corresponding text box, type the filename of the background color page.**

If you can't remember the filename, click Browse to choose from a list of files in your Web site.

4. **Click OK.**

The dialog box closes and the page's background and hyperlink colors change accordingly.

Lesson 5-4

Creating a Navigation Bar

A *navigation bar* is a special set of internal hyperlinks that help your visitors find their way around your site. Typical navigation bars sit at the top or bottom (or both) of each page in your site and contain hyperlinks to the other site pages and, often, the home page. Depending on the setup of your site, however, you may choose a different navigation bar setup; for example, you may want the navigation bar to display forward and back buttons instead of the standard list o' links. Whatever you decide, FrontPage can save you time by automatically generating and updating navigation bars.

Creating a navigational structure using the Navigation View in the Explorer

To insert a navigation bar, you must first create a *navigational structure* using the Explorer Navigation View. A navigational structure is a visual representation of the levels of pages in your Web site — similar to how a company's organization chart illustrates the leadership structure within the organization (Figure 5-6 illustrates a navigational structure for a typical business Web site).

on the test

The FrontPage Editor relies on information contained in the navigational structure to generate navigation bars. Based on the navigational structure's layout, the navigation bar contains links to pages in the levels you specify.

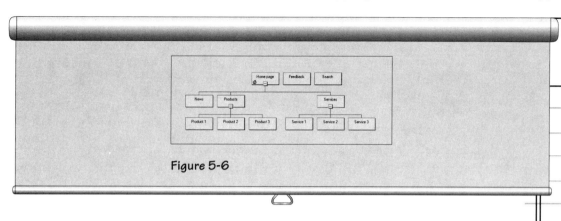

Figure 5-6

Figure 5-6: A navigational
structure for a business
Web site.

As your Web site grows, you can add the new pages to the navigational structure so links to the pages will automatically appear inside your site's navigation bars — sparing you the tedious job of editing the navigation bars in every page in your site. You can also remove pages from the navigational structure (or never add those pages in the first place) if you don't want links to those pages to appear in the site's navigation bars.

In the steps that follow, you build a navigational structure for My Web Site.

Show FrontPage
Explorer button

1 **On the Standard toolbar, click the Show Explorer button.**

The Explorer becomes visible.

2 **If the Navigation View isn't already visible, in the Views bar, click Navigation.**

The Navigation View becomes visible. The navigational structure sits in the top pane, and the site's home page is already represented there. From here, you build the navigational structure by dragging pages from the view's bottom pane and dropping them into place in the top pane.

Navigation button

3 **In the bottom pane, click resume.htm and then, while holding down the mouse button, drag the page into the top pane beneath the HomePage rectangle.**

As you drag the page into the top pane, a line appears connecting the page with the home page.

4 **Release the mouse button.**

The FrontPage Explorer dialog box appears, offering to insert navigation bars into each page that's represented in the navigational structure.

(This dialog box only appears the first time you add a page to the navigational structure.)

5 **In the dialog box, click <u>N</u>o.**

The dialog box closes, the My Resume page appears in the navigational structure beneath the Home Page, and the page's title appears on the chart label. The My Resume page constitutes the first page in the second level of the pages in the site.

(If you had clicked Yes in the FrontPage Explorer dialog box, FrontPage would have created *shared borders* that display a navigation bar inside the margins of each page. I talk about shared borders in the upcoming Extra Credit sidebar called "Using shared borders.")

Figure 5-7: My Web Site's navigational structure.

Figure 5-8: The Navigation Bar Properties dialog box.

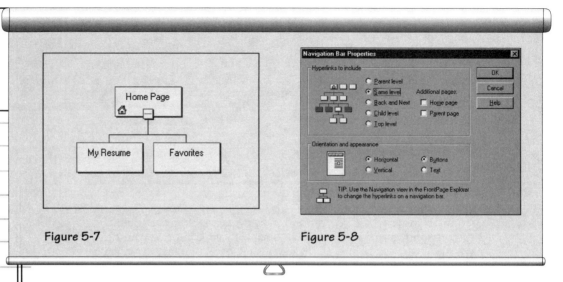

Figure 5-7   Figure 5-8

to make a text
label other than
the page title
appear inside the
navigation bar,
click the label and
type new

the navigational
structure doesn't
illustrate existing
hyperlinks in the
pages (that job is
for the Hyperlinks
View); build the
navigational
structure based on
how you want
visitors to navigate
the site

Rotate button

Size to Fit button

6 **Repeat Steps 3 and 4, this time clicking favorite.htm and dragging it into the chart, and then dropping the page to the right of the My Resume page.**

The resulting navigational structure looks like Figure 5-7.

You can rearrange the navigational structure by clicking any of the rectangles and dragging them to a new spot.

To remove a page from the navigational structure, click the page's rectangle in the chart and then press the Delete key. The Delete Pages dialog box appears, asking whether you want to remove the page from the chart or delete the file from the Web site altogether (the dialog box's default setting is to remove the page from the chart). Click OK to close the dialog box and remove the page from the navigational structure.

extra credit

Changing how the navigational structure looks

You have some control over how the navigational structure looks:

▶ **Contracting and expanding the map.** In the navigational structure, click the minus and plus icons to contract and expand the chart. To expand the entire map in one go, choose View⇨Expand All.

▶ **Rotate.** To change the orientation of the navigational structure, click Rotate on the Explorer toolbar.

▶ **Size to Fit.** To fit the entire chart into the Navigation View's top pane, click Size to Fit.

Inserting a navigation bar into the page

Now that your navigational structure is finished, you're ready to reap the fruits of your labor: a shiny new navigation bar. This is a job for the Editor, which creates navigation bars based on the navigational structure's layout.

The Editor cranks out navigation bars using choices you make using the Navigation Bar Properties dialog box, shown in Figure 5-8. I introduce you to the dialog box now, and then you take this dialog box for a spin in the steps that follow. First, you decide which links you want to appear in the navigation bar. Here are your choices:

- ▶ **Parent level.** This option lists hyperlinks leading to the pages in the level above the current page.

- ▶ **Same level.** This option lists hyperlinks leading to the pages in the same level as the current page.

- ▶ **Back and Next.** This option lists hyperlinks to the previous page and the next page, both of which are on the same level as the current page. (Use this option if you want your Web site to flow like a slide show presentation.)

- ▶ **Child level.** This option lists hyperlinks leading to the pages in the level below the current page.

- ▶ **Top level.** This option lists hyperlinks leading to pages that sit at the topmost level of the site.

You also can include links to the home page (the site's entry page) and the parent page (this page sits in the level above the current page and contains a link to the current page).

on the test

Here's where the layout of the navigational structure comes into play, because the layout determines which pages appear in each level. (Don't worry — you can shuffle the navigational structure around anytime you want, and the navigation bar automatically reflects the change.)

After you specify which links to include, you choose how you want the navigation bar to look. You can choose a Horizontal or Vertical navigation bar, and you can specify text hyperlinks or image buttons.

heads up

Image buttons only appear if you apply a FrontPage theme to the page or site (I show you how in Unit 6). Each theme contains a button image, and the Editor creates a button by superimposing the page title on top of the image.

And now for the navigation bar. Please follow me . . .

1 **On the Explorer toolbar, click the Show FrontPage Editor button.**

The Editor appears, with the Favorites page visible.

2 **Place the cursor at the top of the page (directly before the page heading) and then press Enter to create a new line.**

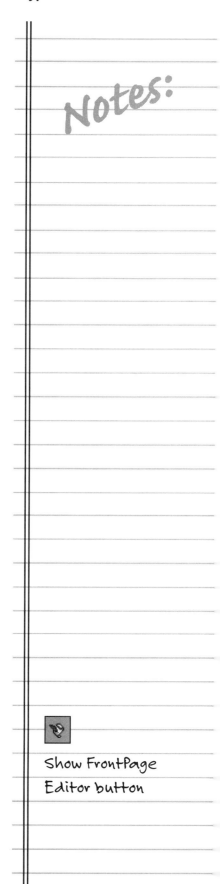

Notes:

Show FrontPage
Editor button

Figure 5-9: A navigation bar.

[Home] [My Resume] [Favorites]

Figure 5-9

3 **Click the cursor in the new empty line at the top of the page, and choose Normal from the Change Style list box.**

4 **Choose Insert⇨Navigation Bar.**

The Navigation Bar Properties dialog box appears.

5 **In the Hyperlinks to Include section of the dialog box, click the Same Level radio button and the Home Page check box.**

The corresponding hyperlinks appear in red in the dialog box's navigational structure diagram.

6 **In the Orientation and Appearance section of the dialog box, click the Horizontal and Buttons radio buttons.**

7 **Click OK.**

The dialog box closes, and the navigation bar appears in the page. Figure 5-9 illustrates what the navigation bar looks like.

heads up

The navigation bar appears as text even though you chose Buttons in Step 6 above because the site is not yet decorated with a theme. You apply a theme to My Web Site in Unit 6.

To change the configuration of the navigation bar, double-click it to display the Navigation Bar Properties dialog box, choose new options, and then click OK. If you want to change the order or level of pages as they appear in the navigation bar, switch to the Explorer to rearrange the layout of the navigational structure.

When you switch back to the Editor after making changes in the navigational structure, click the Refresh button to display the changes inside your page.

Notes:

☑ Progress Check

If you can do the following, you've mastered this lesson:

❑ Build a navigational structure using the Navigation View in the Explorer.

❑ Insert a navigation bar into a page.

Refresh button

extra credit

Using shared borders

Instead of opening each page in your site to add a navigation bar, you can instead create *shared borders* that appear in every page in your Web site. Shared borders enable you to place standard items such as navigation bars, copyright notices, and logos in the margins of your pages and have those items automatically appear in every page in your Web site.

If you later want to change the contents of the borders throughout your site, you simply change the contents of the border in any page and the change is reflected throughout the site. You can also change shared border settings inside individual pages. For information on how to use shared borders, refer to the FrontPage Help systems by choosing Help⇨Microsoft FrontPage Help or by pressing F1.

Good job — you accomplished a lot in this unit. Go ahead and save the Favorites page to preserve all your hard work.

Unit 5 Quiz

Here are a few quiz questions to keep you on your toes.

1. **The following items can be transformed into a hyperlink . . .**

    A. A word.

    B. A sentence.

    C. A navigational structure.

    D. An image.

    E. A single letter.

2. **What's the difference between an internal and an external hyperlink?**

    A. Internal hyperlinks are hidden from view, and external hyperlinks are visible to Web surfers.

    B. Internal hyperlinks are easy to create, and external hyperlinks are difficult to create.

    C. Internal hyperlinks lead to other locations in the same Web site, and external hyperlinks lead to locations outside the Web site.

    D. Internal hyperlinks lead to Web pages stored on the same Web server, and external hyperlinks lead to pages stored on other Web servers.

    E. No difference exists.

3. **A hyperlink can lead to a(n) . . .**

    A. Bookmark.

    B. E-mail address.

    C. Web page.

    D. FTP site.

    E. Usenet newsgroup.

4. **In the context of FrontPage Web page creation, what is a bookmark?**

    A. A piece of text or a picture you click to go somewhere else.

    B. A flashing message that says "Link to me!"

    C. An invisible location in a Web page that is defined as the destination of a hyperlink.

    D. A cocktail napkin stuck between the pages of a novel.

5. **What is a navigation bar?**

    A. A vertical row of image buttons you click to go to a different page in the site.

    B. A collection of text hyperlinks that help visitors find their way around the Web site.

    C. The road map display at the local convenience store.

    D. A list of external hyperlinks that lead to favorite World Wide Web destinations.

    E. An invisible location in a Web page that is defined as the destination of a hyperlink.

6. **What is the relationship between a site's navigational structure and a navigation bar?**

    A. None of your business.

    B. You use the navigational structure in conjunction with Netscape Navigator to find your way around the World Wide Web.

    C. No relationship exists between the two.

    D. The Explorer constructs a navigational structure based on the hyperlinks you insert into your navigation bar.

    E. The Editor uses the layout of the navigational structure to generate a navigation bar.

Unit 5 Exercise

1. In the Favorites page open in the Editor, link the text The Microsoft Site Builder Workshop to the following URL: http://www.microsoft.com/workshop/default.asp.

2. Add three hyperlinks to your own favorite places.

3. Create bookmarks for the two other categories in the page: Current Events and Other Places I Like.

4. In the line that begins with the words Jump to, link the phrases Current events and Other Places I Like to their corresponding bookmarks.

5. Change the page's hyperlink colors.

6. In the page, double-click the navigation bar to display the Navigation Bar Properties dialog box. Experiment with the dialog box's settings to see how the navigation bar changes.

7. Preview the page.

8. Save the page, and exit both the Editor and the Explorer.

Adding Zing with Images

Objectives for This Unit

✓ Inserting an image

✓ Changing the image display

✓ Editing the image file

✓ Creating a background image

✓ Saving a page containing images

✓ Using FrontPage themes

Compelling, timely content separates truly great Web sites from the mediocre masses — but an attractive image certainly doesn't hurt. Pictures help you construct that image. Whether you want your site to project professional legitimacy or fun-loving zaniness, pictures help you say everything you can't say with text.

In this unit, you find out just what pictures can do for your site.

on the CD

▶ unit06.htm

▶ favorite.htm

▶ resume.htm

▶ fish.gif

▶ painter.gif

▶ backgrnd.gif

Inserting an Image

Lesson 6-1

on the test

When you see pictures in a Web page, you are actually looking at distinct graphic files that are separate from the Web page itself. Where each graphic appears in the page, the page contains a reference that points to the graphic file. The visitor's web browser sees this reference and uses it to locate the graphic file and display the file at that location inside the page.

pictures in Web pages are actually distinct graphic files

The steps involved when you insert graphics into your page are not unlike those involved when you create a hyperlink — you connect two files (the Web page and the graphic), and the graphic file can be stored inside your Web site, elsewhere on your computer, or out on the Web.

In Web pages, you have your choice of two graphic formats: GIF (I pronounce it with a hard G; others say "jif") and JPEG. The GIF format is the most commonly used format on the Web, but the JPEG format is preferable for photographs or other images with a wide range of colors.

What if your favorite piece of clip art or your company logo is saved in another file format? Not a problem. The FrontPage Editor automatically converts BMP (Windows and OS/2), TIFF, WMF, RAS, EPS, PCX, and TGA graphic file formats to GIF and JPEG. Images with 256 or fewer colors are converted to GIF, and images with more than 256 colors are converted to JPEG.

heads up

Graphics do come with a price — they take a long time to download. When you visit a Web page that's full of graphics, the page often takes several minutes to appear on-screen. Those minutes drag on and on for visitors who are in search of a quick bit of information. For this reason, be judicious in your use of graphics. Use only those pictures that pack a visual punch and save the random clip art for another project.

I could go on for several more pages about the particulars of Web graphics, but I expect that you want to get your hands on the keyboard. If you're interested in finding out more about how graphics in Web pages work, check out my book *FrontPage 98 For Dummies* (published by IDG Books Worldwide, Inc.). In it, I offer more information and tips on how to beautify your pages with graphics and keep pages loading quickly.

on the CD

In this lesson, you transform the example file named unit06.htm into an Art Gallery, and you add the Art Gallery to My Web Site (the Web site that you created in Lesson 1-3). In the process of creating the Art Gallery page, you work with many of the Editor's graphic tools.

Before you begin, you must set up your FrontPage workspace so that you are ready to move on with the lessons in this unit. To do so, follow these steps:

1 Launch FrontPage, and open My Web Site.

If you're not sure how to open a Web site, refer to Lesson 2-1.

2 Import the graphic files named fish.gif and backgrnd.gif from the FP101 folder on your hard drive into the Web site.

If you didn't create the My Resume page in Unit 4 and the Favorites page in Unit 5, import these pages into your Web site as well (the pages are named resume.htm and favorite.htm). If you can't remember how to import files, refer to Lesson 1-5.

3 On the Explorer toolbar, click Show FrontPage Editor.

The Editor launches, and presents you with a new, blank page. (If the Editor is already open, click the New button on the Standard toolbar to create a new page.)

graphics in Web pages = GIF and JPEG

the Editor can convert other graphic formats into GIF and JPEG

Show FrontPage Editor button

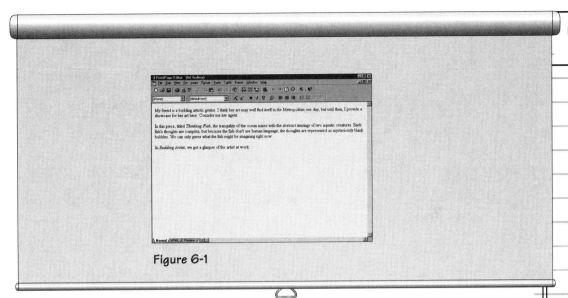

Figure 6-1

Figure 6-1: The Art Gallery page, sans images.

Notes:

4 Using the Insert⇨File command, insert the contents of the file named unit06.htm (located in the FP101 folder) into the page.

For detailed instructions on how to use the Insert⇨File command, see Lesson 3-1.

The contents of the example file appear inside the page (see Figure 6-1).

5 Save the new page as part of your Web site, title the page Art Gallery, and name the page art.htm.

The Art Gallery page is quite plain at the moment, but that will soon change in the lessons that follow.

Inserting a graphic stored in your Web site

If the graphic you want to insert already lives inside your Web site, inserting the graphic into a page is a snap. In the steps that follow, you insert a graphic called fish.gif into the Art Gallery page.

1 In the Art Gallery page, place the cursor at the beginning of the second paragraph.

2 Click Insert Image.

The Image dialog box appears (see Figure 6-2).

The dialog box displays the image files stored inside My Web Site. (In this example, the images are stored inside the Web site's main folder, but you may choose to store your images inside the images folder. If so, double-click the images folder to display its contents.)

3 Click fish.gif.

A preview of the graphic appears in the Preview area.

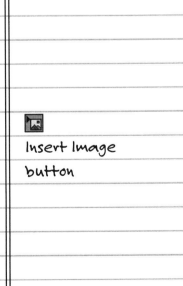

Insert Image button

Figure 6-2: The Image
dialog box.

Notes:

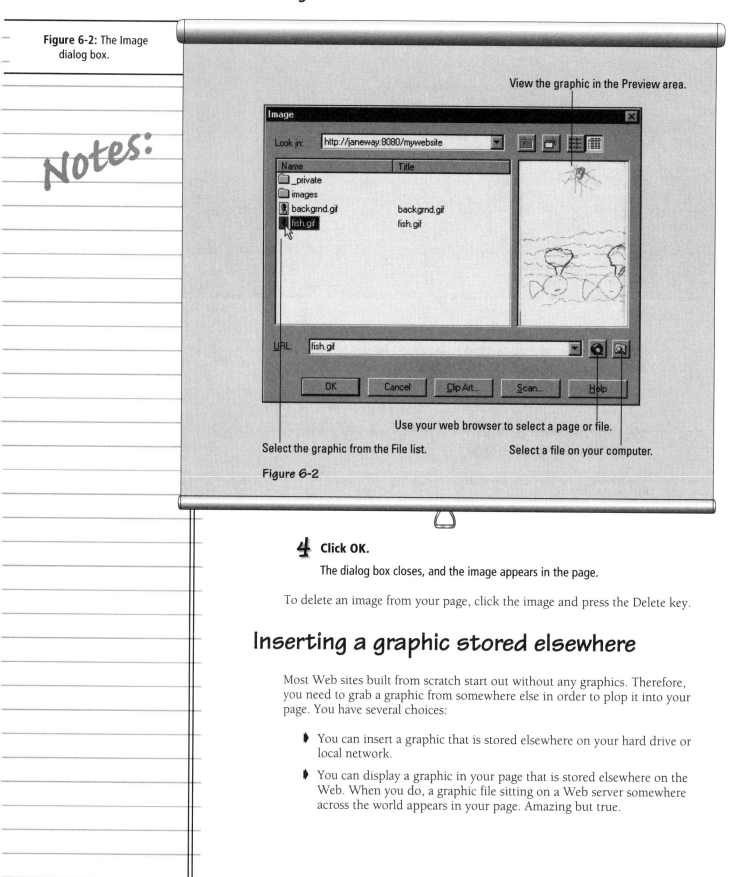

View the graphic in the Preview area.

Select the graphic from the File list.

Use your web browser to select a page or file.

Select a file on your computer.

Figure 6-2

4 **Click OK.**

The dialog box closes, and the image appears in the page.

To delete an image from your page, click the image and press the Delete key.

Inserting a graphic stored elsewhere

Most Web sites built from scratch start out without any graphics. Therefore, you need to grab a graphic from somewhere else in order to plop it into your page. You have several choices:

- ◗ You can insert a graphic that is stored elsewhere on your hard drive or local network.

- ◗ You can display a graphic in your page that is stored elsewhere on the Web. When you do, a graphic file sitting on a Web server somewhere across the world appears in your page. Amazing but true.

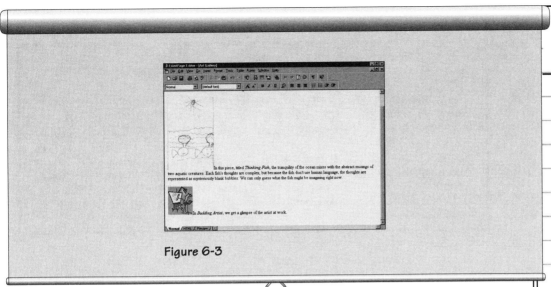

Figure 6-3

Figure 6-3: The Art Gallery page now contains some art!

▶ You can cut and paste a graphic from another program into an open Web page.

▶ You can grab an image from a digital camera or scanner.

▶ You can use clip art stored in the Microsoft Clip Gallery (a cool program that was installed on your computer along with FrontPage).

In the following steps, I demonstrate how to insert a graphic that's stored elsewhere on your computer into your page, because that's the most common scenario (in this case, the graphic is named painter.gif and it's currently stored in the FP101 folder). For instructions on how to insert graphics using one of the other methods described in the preceding list, refer to the FrontPage Help system by choosing Help⇨Microsoft FrontPage Help or by pressing F1.

Insert Image button

1 **In the Art Gallery page, place the cursor at the beginning of the third paragraph.**

2 **Click Insert Image.**

The Image dialog box appears.

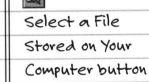

Select a File Stored on Your Computer button

3 **In the dialog box, click the Select a File Stored on Your Computer button.**

The Select File dialog box appears. The dialog box lists the folders and files on your computer.

4 **Navigate to the FP101 folder, click painter.gif, and then click OK.**

Both dialog boxes close, and the image appears in the document (see Figure 6-3).

extra credit

The Microsoft Clip Gallery

The colorful image you just inserted into your page is one example of the collection of pictures, buttons, and icons housed in the Microsoft Clip Gallery. You access the Clip Gallery by choosing Insert⇨Clipart or by clicking the Clip Art button at the bottom of the Image dialog box. The Clip Gallery is a separate program that works like a graphic repository. You can store images there, search for images by keyword, and even download new images from the Microsoft Web site. The Clip Gallery has its own Help system, which tells you everything you need to know about how the program works (in the Clip Gallery dialog box, click the Help button).

☑ **Progress Check**

If you can do the following, you've mastered this lesson:

❑ Insert an image that is currently stored inside your Web site.

❑ Insert an image that is currently stored elsewhere on your hard drive.

Lesson 6-2

Changing How the Image Is Displayed in the Page

After an image is safely ensconced in your page, chances are that you want to adjust how it's positioned there. The Editor gives you plenty of flexibility.

Aligning an image with surrounding text

When you insert an image into a Web page, by default, the image is aligned with the left page margin. The situation becomes a little more interesting when you place the image in the same line as text (as you did in the preceding two sets of steps). The default image alignment setting causes surrounding text to line up along the bottom edge of the graphic, and then continue to flow underneath the image. You can change the image's alignment by using the Alignment list box in the Image Properties dialog box (I introduce you to this dialog box in a moment).

The alignment options are as follows:

Left and Right alignment options cause surrounding text to wrap around the image

▶ **Left** aligns the image with the left margin and wraps surrounding text around the right side of the image.

▶ **Right** aligns the image with the right margin and wraps surrounding text around the left side of the image.

▶ **Top** aligns the top of the image with the text.

▶ **Texttop** aligns the top of the image with the top of the tallest text in the line.

➧ **Middle** aligns the middle of the image with the text.

➧ **Absmiddle** aligns the middle of the image with the middle of the tallest text in the line.

➧ **Baseline** aligns the image with the text baseline. (The *baseline* is the invisible line that runs beneath your text to keep it straight.)

➧ **Bottom** aligns the bottom of the image with the text.

➧ **Absbottom** aligns the image with the bottom of the text in the line.

➧ **Center** works just like the Middle option.

In the following set of steps, you use the Left alignment option. This setting causes text to wrap around the image, similar to how text in newspaper columns wraps around the accompanying pictures. Many Web designers use this effect, so I figured you would enjoy trying it out in your Web site.

1 **In the Art Gallery page, right-click fish.gif and, from the shortcut menu that appears, choose Image Properties.**

The Image Properties dialog box appears. The dialog box contains three tabs along the top that separate the properties into related groups (General, Video, and Appearance).

2 **Click the Appearance tab (see Figure 6-4).**

3 **In the Alignment list box, select Left.**

4 **Click OK.**

The dialog box closes, and the rest of the page content scoots around to the right side of fish.gif. A left-pointing arrow appears at the beginning of the paragraph next to the graphic to remind you that the Left alignment option is in effect (the arrow is invisible when the page is viewed with a web browser).

on the test

When you use the Left and Right alignment options, you can control how much text wraps around the image. You can stop text wrapping by inserting a special kind of line break where you want the wrapping to end. A line break moves all the subsequent text underneath the image, where the text flows along as usual.

To see how line breaks work, follow these steps:

1 **Click the cursor at the end of the paragraph that describes *Thinking Fish*.**

2 **Choose Insert⇨Line Break.**

The Break Properties dialog box appears (see Figure 6-5).

The type of line break you choose depends on how the image is aligned, as follows:

• **Clear Left Margin.** If the image is left-aligned, select this option to cause text after the line break to shift to the first empty space along the left margin below the image.

• **Clear Right Margin.** If the image is right-aligned, select this option to cause text after the line break to shift to the first empty space along the right margin below the image.

Notes:

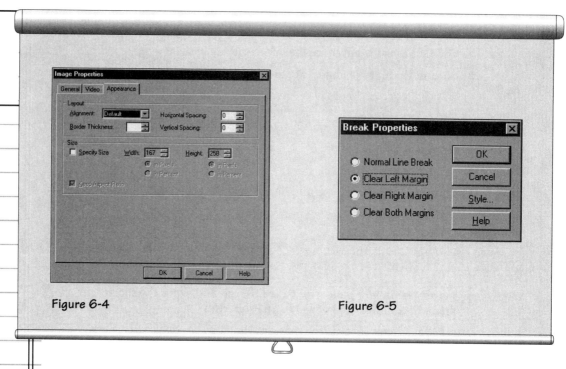

Figure 6-4   Figure 6-5

heads up

- **Clear Both Margins.** If the page contains images along both the left
  and right margins, select this option to cause text to shift to the first
  empty space where both margins are clear.

The Normal Line Break option creates a regular line break. In Unit 3, I showed
you how to insert regular line breaks by pressing Shift+Enter. When used
together with images aligned using the Left and Right alignment options,
regular line breaks have no effect on text wrapping.

3 Click the Clear Left Margin radio button, and then click OK.

The dialog box closes, and the Editor inserts a line break. All the stuff after the
line break moves beneath fish.gif.

Setting how much space
surrounds the image

The Art Gallery page is starting to shape up, but still needs fine tuning. For
example, the text wrapping around fish.gif butts up against the graphic,
making the page appear claustrophobic. The Editor enables you to open the
page up by increasing the amount of space surrounding the image.

To do so, follow these steps:

**1 Right-click fish.gif and, from the shortcut menu that appears,
choose Image Properties.**

The Image Properties dialog box appears.

2 **Click the Appearance tab.**

3 **In the Horizontal Spacing text box, type** 20.

By doing so, you tell the Editor to insert 20 pixels of space between the image and the text next to the image.

4 **Leave the Vertical Spacing text box alone.**

Because the space above and below the image looks just fine, you leave this setting as it is.

5 **Click OK.**

The dialog box closes, and the Editor inserts 20 pixels of space between the image and the text.

Ahhhh. That's better. All the image needed was breathing room.

extra credit

Giving graphic hyperlinks a border

Images that double as hyperlinks can sometimes cause confusion among newbie Web surfers because they don't necessarily recognize which images are clickable and which are purely decorative. By adding borders to graphic hyperlinks, you let visitors know which graphics they can click. Graphic hyperlink borders are the same color as the page's text link colors.

To give a linked image a border, follow these steps:

1. **Right-click the image and, from the shortcut menu that appears, choose Image Properties.**

The Image Properties dialog box appears.

2. **Click the Appearance tab.**

3. **In the Border Thickness text box, type the thickness (in pixels) of the image border.**

Most Web designers, if they use image borders at all, stick to a border thickness of 1 or 2 pixels.

4. **Click OK to close the dialog box and apply the border.**

Setting image display dimensions

The FrontPage Editor enables you to magnify or compress the display size of an image in your Web page. This option doesn't affect the size of the graphic file itself; it controls only the image dimensions as they appear when viewed with a web browser.

To see how this option works, shrink down fish.gif in the steps that follow:

1 **Right-click fish.gif and, from the shortcut menu that appears, choose Image Properties.**

The Image Properties dialog box appears.

resizing shortcut: click graphic and drag its size handles

corner handles maintain the image's proportions

Notes:

dimensions can be
specified in pixels
or as percentage
of the browser
window

Resample button

alternative text
appears in place of
graphics when
visitors turn off
their browsers'
image loading
function

2 **Click the Appearance tab.**

3 **Mark the Specify Size check box.**

The Width and Height text boxes come into view. The text boxes contain the image's original dimensions in pixels.

4 **In the Width text box, type** 150.

Because the Keep Aspect Ration check box is marked, the value in the Height text box changes accordingly.

In this example, you specified dimensions using an absolute number of pixels. You can also specify a percentage of the browser window. To do so, click the In Percent radio button and then type a percentage value in the Width and/or Height text box (for example, a Width value of 50% tells the Editor to give the image a width of half the browser window). To make sure that the image maintains the correct proportion, be sure the Keep Aspect Ratio check box is marked.

5 **Click OK.**

The dialog box closes, and the image shrinks accordingly.

If you decide that you prefer the image's new size, or you notice that resizing the image reduces the image's quality, you can *resample* the image. Resampling changes the image file by filling in colors and smoothing out rough spots to match its new dimensions. To resample an image, click the image, and on the Image toolbar, click Resample. (The Image toolbar comes into view whenever you click an image.)

heads up Whenever possible, use graphics in their original dimensions to keep them looking sharp and clean. Only resort to resampling as a quick fix. If you do decide to resample an image, remember that you change the image file itself.

Providing an alternative text label

Most web browsers let surfers turn off automatic loading of images while browsing. What Web sites minus their graphics lack in visual flair, they make up with download speed — a text-only site loads much faster than a site cluttered with graphics. For this reason, you should give each of your Web images an *alternative text label*. When viewed with a browser (with image loading turned off), alternative text appears inside a blank placeholder where the original graphic would have appeared if image loading were turned on.

Alternative text provides an extra bonus for visitors who view Web pages with pictures intact: In some web browsers (including Microsoft Internet Explorer), visitors can pass the cursor over the image to see the alternative text label pop up, similar to how a descriptive label pops up when you pass your cursor over a toolbar button in FrontPage.

The Editor automatically applies a generic text label to your images. The generic label contains the image's filename and size (the file size gives visitors an idea of how long the image would take to download). I recommend adjusting the label to make it more meaningful for your visitors. You can also place a descriptive text overlay on an image. I show you how in the Unit 7 Extra Credit sidebar called "Adding a descriptive text label to hotspots and graphics."

In these steps, you use alternative text to supply information about the graphic so visitors can decide whether they want to download the image.

1 Right-click fish.gif and, from the shortcut menu that appears, choose Image Properties.

The Image Properties dialog box appears, with the General tab visible.

2 In the Text text box, highlight fish.gif **and type** "Thinking Fish".

The new text replaces the text you highlighted, so the alternative text label now reads "Thinking Fish" (8421 bytes).

3 Click OK.

The dialog box closes.

Although nothing appears to have changed, the Editor added the text label information to your page.

extra credit

Using the Banner Ad Manager

One of the most popular uses for images in Web pages is advertising. Many Web sites keep themselves financially afloat by selling space to companies who wish to hawk products and services to the Web site's readership. No doubt you've already seen the rectangular banner ads sitting inside the home pages of popular Web sites such as Yahoo! (www.yahoo.com) and CNET (www.cnet.com).

If you want to use banner ads in your site, avail yourself of the Banner Ad Manager.

This Active Element enables you to create a rotating display of banner graphics, each of which can be linked to a different location. The Banner Ad Manager also lets you choose the transition effect and the amount of time each ad is visible.

To use the Banner Ad Manager, choose Insert⇨Active Element⇨Banner Ad Manager. For instructions on how to put the Banner Ad Manager to work, in the Banner Ad Manager dialog box, click Help.

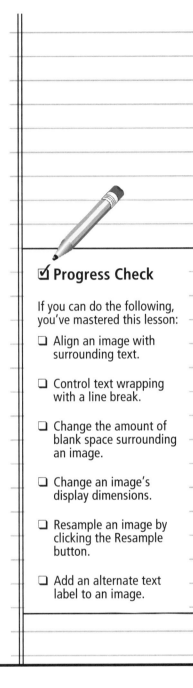

☑ Progress Check

If you can do the following, you've mastered this lesson:

❑ Align an image with surrounding text.

❑ Control text wrapping with a line break.

❑ Change the amount of blank space surrounding an image.

❑ Change an image's display dimensions.

❑ Resample an image by clicking the Resample button.

❑ Add an alternate text label to an image.

Editing the Image File

Lesson 6-3

The Editor's talent lies in building Web pages, not tinkering with graphic files. Even so, the program can take care of simple image editing tasks that pop up from time to time.

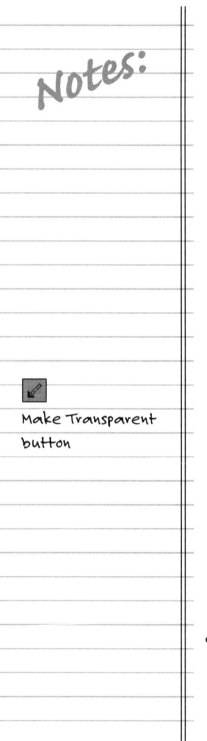

Notes:

Make Transparent
button

Most of the tools you use in this lesson live on the Image toolbar, shown in Figure 6-6. This toolbar appears whenever you click an image in your page, or when you choose View➪Image Toolbar.

heads up

The options in this lesson change the graphic file itself. After you save the changed file, the changes are irreversible. You do have the option of saving the changed graphic as a second file (keeping the original file aside in case you goof) — I show you how in Lesson 6-5.

Making a GIF transparent

Among the GIF graphic format's virtues is a very special effect: *transparency.*

A *transparent GIF* has had one of its colors made invisible so the color of the page shows through. Generally, this feature is used to erase the graphic's background color when the color is different from the page's background color.

To better understand what I mean, in the following steps you turn one of the images you inserted earlier, painter.gif, into a transparent GIF.

1 **In the page, click painter.gif.**

The image is selected, and the Image toolbar comes into view.

2 **In the Image toolbar, click Make Transparent.**

As you move the pointer over the image, the pointer turns into a pencil with an arrow sticking out of the eraser.

3 **Position the arrow so it points to the gray background color inside the image, and then click once.**

The color disappears, and the white background color of the page shows through (see Figure 6-7).

heads up

A GIF can have only one transparent color. When you make a color transparent, that color disappears throughout the image. Therefore, choose a unique color as a candidate for transparency.

extra credit

To interlace or not?

On the surface, an *interlaced GIF* looks no different from a regular GIF. The difference becomes apparent only when the page is viewed with a web browser. An interlaced GIF appears gradually on the screen as it downloads, beginning as a blurry glob and ending in full clarity. A regular GIF downloads in full form from top to bottom. Although the two types download at the same speed, interlacing creates the illusion that the image is loading more quickly than a regular GIF. So the choice to apply interlacing to your GIFs is up to you (I happened to like the interlacing effect). To do so, right-click the image, and from the shortcut menu that appears, choose Image Properties. In the Image Properties dialog box, click the Interlaced checkbox, and then click OK.

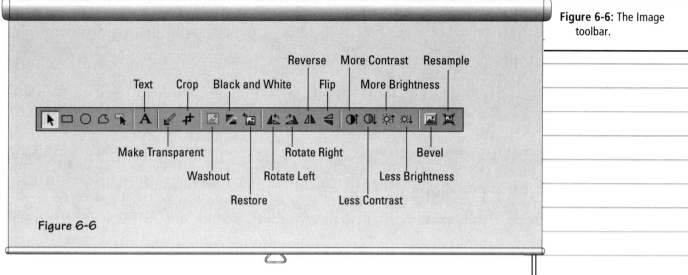

Figure 6-6: The Image toolbar.

Figure 6-6

Cropping an image

Cropping an image is like getting your hair trimmed: You cut off only the stuff you don't like. Cropping is handy when an image in its original form is a little bit too big. Take fish.gif, for example. The bottom edge of the graphic — the blank white space — doesn't add much to the picture. Why not trim it off?

To do so, follow these steps:

1 Click fish.gif.

2 On the Image toolbar, click Crop.

A border appears inside the selected image — all the stuff outside this border will disappear after the image is cropped.

3 Reshape the border by dragging its shape handles until only the bottom portion of the image hangs outside the border (see Figure 6-8).

4 Click the Crop button.

The extra stuff disappears.

Ack! You mean you cropped too much? Unlike with a haircut, you can click a magic button on the Image toolbar and the image reverts to its original state. Okay, maybe the Restore button isn't magic, but it certainly does wonders when you really need it. If only hairdressers could do the same.

Applying an effect

The rest of the Editor's image editing features let you play with the image's color, orientation, and border, as follows:

♦ **Washout:** This effect fades the image.

♦ **Black and White:** This effect turns a color image black and white.

Crop button

Restore button

Figure 6-7: Creating a transparent GIF.

Figure 6-8: Cropping an image.

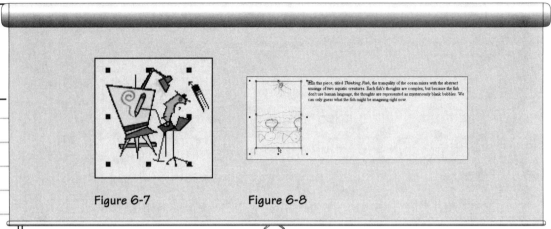

Figure 6-7 Figure 6-8

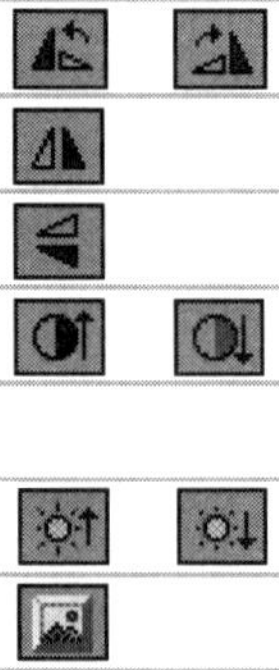

more Contrast button

undo button

☑ **Progress Check**

If you can do the following, you've mastered this lesson:

❑ Make a GIF transparent.

❑ Crop an image.

❑ Apply an effect to an image.

▶ **Rotate Left and Rotate Right:** These effects rotate the image a quarter turn to the left or right.

▶ **Reverse:** This effect flips the image horizontally.

▶ **Flip:** This effect flips the image vertically.

▶ **More Contrast and Less Contrast:** These effects increase or decrease the image's contrast.

▶ **More Brightness and Less Brightness:** These effects increase or decrease the image's brightness.

▶ **Bevel:** This effect places the image on a raised platform.

All the tools described here work the same way: First click the image, and then click the tool of your choice, as follows:

1 In the page, click fish.gif.

2 On the Image toolbar, click More Contrast.

The contrast in the image increases, and the colors in the image appear more clearly against the image background.

To undo an effect, click the Undo button.

Recess

You have covered a lot of ground so far. Take a quick break to refill your coffee cup or stretch your legs.

Inserting a Background Image   Lesson 6-4

In the previous lessons, you decorated your page's foreground with pictures. In this lesson, you pay attention to the page's background.

on the test

When you use an image as the page background, the page's text sits on top of a *tiled* version of the image (the image repeats over and over until it fills the window, creating a uniform background for the text). Tiling makes it possible to use a small image as the background for an entire page.

In the following steps, you use the file backgrnd.gif as the Art Gallery page's background image.

1 Choose Format⇨Background.

The Page Properties dialog box appears, with the Background tab visible. Look familiar? This is the same dialog box you used to change hyperlink color in Lesson 5-3.

2 In the Specify Background and Colors area of the dialog box, click Browse.

The Select Background Image dialog box appears. The dialog box works exactly like the regular Image dialog box that you used in Lesson 6-1.

3 In the dialog box, click backgrnd.gif, and then click OK.

The dialog box closes, and the Page Properties dialog box becomes visible again.

heads up

Look again at the Page Properties dialog box. See the Watermark checkbox? A *watermark* is the same as a regular background, except that a watermark appears fixed in place when viewed with a web browser — when a visitor scrolls around the screen, the text appears to move over the fixed background. (With regular background images, the background and text move together when a visitor scrolls around the page.) As of this writing, Microsoft Internet Explorer is the only browser that can display watermarks (other browsers display watermarks as regular backgrounds). Therefore, checking this box is optional.

4 Click OK to close the dialog box.

The background image appears in your page (see Figure 6-9).

If a background image makes the page look too cluttered, you can fill the background with a solid color instead. To specify a background color instead of a graphic, choose Format⇨Background to display the Page Properties dialog box. Select a color from the Background list box and click OK. Or you can base the page's background color or image on that of another page in your Web site. For instructions, refer to the Extra Credit sidebar "Basing link colors on another page" in Lesson 5-3.

make sure that
background image
colors don't
obscure the page
text

Notes:

☑ **Progress Check**

If you can do the following, you've mastered this lesson:

❑ Use an image as a page's background.

❑ Use a solid color as a page's background.

Lesson 6-5   Saving a Page Containing Images

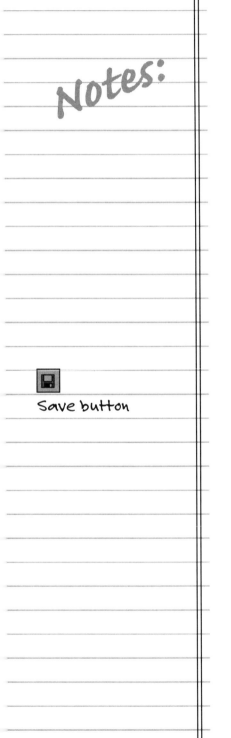

Notes:

Save button

When you save a Web page into which you have inserted or which contains edited images, a new variable is added to the mix: the Save Embedded Files dialog box. This dialog box appears when you attempt to save a page after doing one (or both) of the following things:

▶ You insert an image that is currently stored elsewhere on your computer or local network (including images from the Clip Gallery).

▶ You edit an image using the Resample button or one of the tools described in Lesson 6-3.

The Save Embedded Files dialog box serves two important purposes. First, it is the Editor's way of asking where in your Web site you want to save graphics that are currently stored elsewhere on your computer. The reason for this step lies in the way graphics work in Web pages. Because Web graphics are really HTML references to graphic files, the Editor must know the location of the graphic file in order to create the correct reference. By automatically importing the graphic into the Web site, the Editor can keep track of the file's where-abouts and can therefore create and maintain a valid reference.

The dialog box's second purpose is to alert you when you are about to save an edited version of the image file and overwrite the original graphic.

In the following steps, you save the changes you have made to the Art Gallery page and, in the process, get to know the Save Embedded Files dialog box.

1 **On the Standard toolbar, click Save.**

The Save Embedded Files dialog box appears (see Figure 6-10). The Embedded Files to Save area contains a list of the images that are about to be imported into the Web site from another location or that are about to overwrite the original version of the graphic file.

In this example, the edited version of fish.gif is about to overwrite the original graphic (you edited the original file by cropping it and changing its contrast, remember?). The action associated with painter.gif is Save, because the file is currently stored inside the FP101 folder, and it is about to be imported into My Web Site.

By clicking one of the files, you can perform different operations on each file before saving them and the page.

2 **In the Embedded Files to Save area, click fish.gif.**

A preview of the file appears in the Image Preview box.

In order to preserve the original graphic file, you rename the changed file, thereby saving the changes in a second graphic file, which is displayed in the page. (The original graphic file remains untouched.)

3 **Click Rename.**

The filename becomes highlighted.

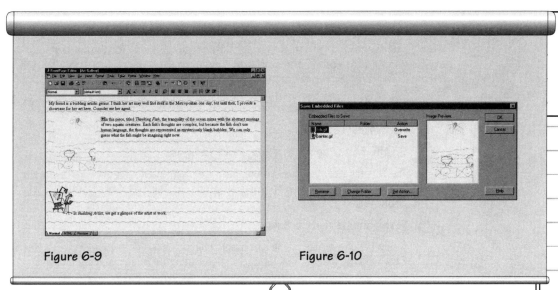

Figure 6-9

Figure 6-10

 Type fish2.gif **and then press Enter.**

The filename changes, and the action changes from Overwrite to Save (because you are no longer overwriting the original file).

5 **Click OK.**

The dialog box closes, and the Editor saves the newly renamed fish2.gif, imports painter.gif into the Web site, and saves the Art Gallery page.

To save the graphics inside one of the Web site's folders, in the Save Embedded Files dialog box, click Change Folder, and select the destination folder. If you click Set Action, the Set Action dialog box appears, enabling you to specify how you want the Editor to save the file.

The Art Gallery page now displays fish2.gif, painter.gif, and backgrnd.gif, and the original version of fish.gif sits unchanged inside the Web site.

☑ **Progress Check**

If you can do the following, you've mastered this lesson:

❏ Save a page that contains images.

❏ Save a second copy of an edited image.

Applying a Theme to a Web Site

Lesson 6-6

If you're like me, you can't simply fire up an image editing program and whip out dazzling pictures, background images, and little graphic accessories for your Web site. Most people don't have the time or expertise to make the graphics look truly professional, or the money to pay a *real* graphic designer.

Luckily, the FrontPage programmers understand this situation and included a bunch of *themes* in the FrontPage Explorer. Themes are sets of matching banner graphics, backgrounds, text and link colors, fonts, and doodads (buttons, horizontal lines, and bullets) that you can throw over your Web site to transform — as advertising and marketing folks would say — the site's look and feel. Do you want your site to project a cool, professional image? Use the Global Marketing theme. How about something more whimsical? Try on the Arcs theme. Whatever your mood, chances are that you can find a theme to match.

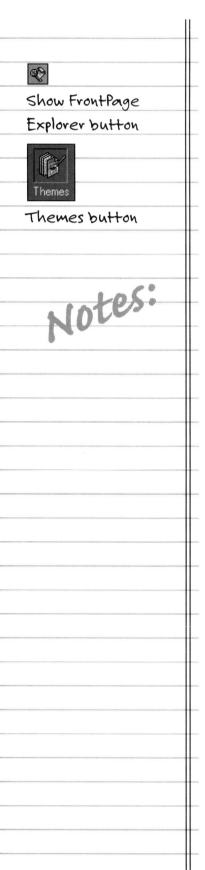

Show FrontPage
Explorer button

Themes button

Notes:

heads up

Themes help smooth out your page's rough graphic edges. You can apply a theme to an entire Web site or to a single page. In this lesson, you apply a theme to My Web Site to see how your pages change.

1 **On the FrontPage Standard toolbar, click Show FrontPage Explorer.**

The Explorer becomes visible.

2 **On the FrontPage Views bar, click Themes.**

The Themes View becomes visible. Because My Web Site doesn't currently use a theme, the Theme Preview box is empty, and the This Web Does Not Use Themes radio button is selected.

3 **In the theme list, click Arcs.**

A sampler of the Arcs theme's elements appears in the Theme Preview area (see Figure 6-11). The elements include a page banner (with the page's site map label stuck on top), navigation bar buttons, text colors and fonts, link colors, bullet shapes (each theme contains three different bullets for multilevel lists), a graphical horizontal line, and a background graphic.

The Themes View also gives you some control over theme variations by offering three check boxes, as follows:

- **Vivid Colors:** By checking this option, you choose a brighter set of theme text and link colors.

- **Active Graphics:** This option adds movement to your page. Instead of using plain graphics as navigation bar buttons, FrontPage substitutes a *Java applet* (an embedded program written in the Java language) that creates buttons that change color or shape when the visitor clicks them. Some themes also contain animated bullets instead of static graphic bullets.

  Not all web browsers are able to display Java applets, so if you use this feature, some of your visitors may not be able to use your navigation bars.

- **Background Image:** This option lets you decide whether you want to use the theme's background image.

4 **Click the Vivid Colors, Active Graphics, and Background Image check boxes to mark them.**

I want you to see how your pages look with all the theme goodies included. You can always remove them later.

5 **Click Apply.**

The FrontPage Explorer dialog box appears reminding you that themes change many of the Web site's formatting choices.

6 **In the dialog box, click Yes.**

The Explorer applies the theme to the site (this process takes a few moments).

Now for the fun part: opening your pages to see how they have changed.

1 **On the FrontPage toolbar, click Show FrontPage Editor.**

The Editor appears, with the Art Gallery page visible. The page contains new fonts, colors, and a background graphic.

2 **Open the My Resume page.**

The page opens. Here, you can see newfangled bullets and a horizontal line.

3 **Open the Favorites page.**

The page opens, showing off its new link colors and graphical navigation bar buttons.

heads up

If, in place of the navigation bar, you see labels that read [Button], it means that you haven't yet created a navigational structure for My Web Site. Go back and follow Lesson 5-4 for directions showing you how.

To see the new navigation bar in action, preview the page using a web browser — preferably a recent version of Internet Explorer or Netscape Navigator.

If the navigation bar's text labels are too long to fit on the graphic buttons, shorten the text labels by switching to the Explorer's Navigation View and typing new labels in the navigational structure.

Also, because you have added a new page to My Web Site — the Art Gallery page — be sure to add the page to the navigational structure so the page is represented in the site's navigation bars. (If you need a navigation bar refresher, refer to Lesson 5-4.)

Feeling wowed by themes? The fun's not over yet. My favorite theme trick is the *page banner*. This FrontPage Component uses the site's theme to create an attractive banner graphic that you can use in your pages.

In the following steps, you insert a page banner in the Favorites page.

1 **In the page, position the cursor at the top of the page, right before the navigation bar.**

2 **Click Insert FrontPage Component.**

The Insert FrontPage Component dialog box appears.

3 **In the dialog box, double-click** Page Banner.

The dialog box closes, and the Page Banner Properties dialog box appears. This dialog box lets you choose a text- or image-based banner.

4 **Click the Image radio button and then click OK.**

The dialog box closes, and the banner appears in the page. (Press Enter to move the navigation bar onto its own line.)

Figure 6-13 shows how the newly festooned Favorites page looks when previewed in Internet Explorer.

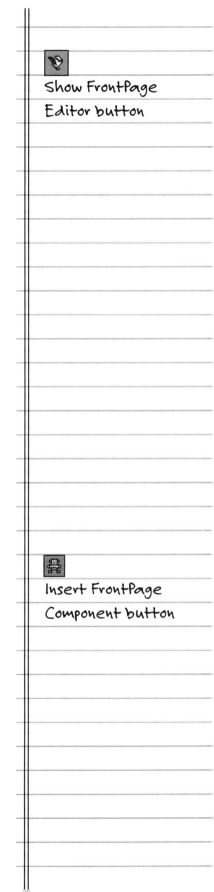

Show FrontPage
Editor button

Insert FrontPage
Component button

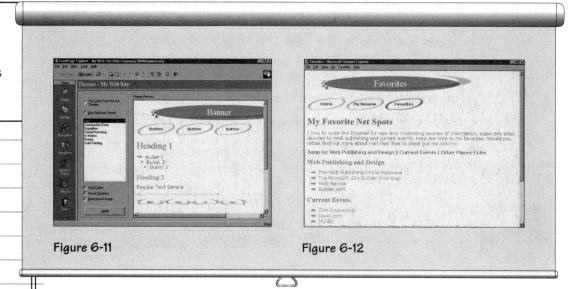

Figure 6-11   Figure 6-12

heads up

Progress Check

If you can do the following, you've mastered this lesson:

❑ Apply a theme to a Web site.

❑ Insert a page banner.

❑ Adjust the theme settings in a single page.

If, in place of the page banner, you see a graphic with the label [Banner] on top, it means you haven't yet created a navigational structure for My Web Site. Go back and follow Lesson 5-4 for directions showing you how.

You can change theme settings for individual pages in the site. For example, you can turn on or off a theme option, or use a different theme (or turn off themes altogether) for a particular page. To do so, with the page you want to change open in the Editor, choose Format➪Theme. The Choose Theme dialog box appears. The dialog box looks like a miniversion of the Explorer's Themes View. Select the option you want, and then click OK to close the dialog box and apply the new effect.

When you apply a theme to your Web site, you don't need to save the pages in order to save the theme settings; the Explorer automatically saves the settings. Just to make sure you've saved any other changes in your pages, in the Editor, choose File➪Save All. You can leave the pages open in order to do the Exercise at the end of the unit, or you can exit FrontPage if you feel like a break.

Unit 6 Quiz

Congratulations — you just finished an especially information-packed unit. Take this quiz for a quick review of the material you picked up.

1. **When you insert a graphic into a Web page . . .**

    A. You are actually inserting a reference into the page to a separate graphic file.

    B. You are combining the graphic file and the Web page into a single file.

C. The graphic must be stored in EPS or PICT format.

D. The graphic must be stored in GIF or JPEG format.

E. You increase the page's total download time.

2. **What happens when you use the Editor to insert a TIFF graphic into a Web page?**

A. The Editor crashes, and your Web page is wiped from your hard drive.

B. The graphic appears, unchanged, in the page.

C. If the image contains fewer than 256 colors, the Editor converts the image to JPEG and inserts the converted file into the page.

D. If the image contains fewer than 256 colors, the Editor converts the image to GIF and inserts the converted file into the page.

E. Nothing.

3. **When you align a graphic using the Left alignment option . . .**

A. The graphic moves to the left margin, and surrounding text moves beneath the graphic.

B. The graphic moves to the right margin, and surrounding text wraps around the graphic to the left.

C. The graphic moves to the left margin, and surrounding text wraps around the graphic to the left.

D. You have no control over how much text wraps around the image.

E. You can control how much text wraps around the image by inserting a line break.

4. **What image editing tasks can the Editor perform?**

A. Crop an image.

B. Apply transparency to a GIF.

C. Change an image's contrast and brightness levels.

D. Apply a color palette to an image.

E. Resize an image.

5. **In the context of Web graphics, what does *tiling* mean?**

A. The background graphic increases in size until it fills the page's background area.

B. The background graphic repeats over and over (in its original size) until it fills the page's background area.

C. When you apply a theme to a Web site, the site's navigation bars turn into individual tiles, hence the term *tiling*.

D. A kitchen refurbishing project.

Notes:

6. **When you apply a theme to a Web site . . .**

    A. FrontPage lets you choose from a list of catchy jingles that play upon entry to your site.

    B. Every page in the site must conform to that theme's settings.

    C. FrontPage applies a predetermined set of fonts, colors, and graphics to the pages in the site.

    D. You can then insert a graphical page banner.

    E. You can no longer use a text navigation bar.

Unit 6 Exercise

1. In the Art Gallery page, click painter.gif and align the image with surrounding text using the Right option.

2. Increase the amount of horizontal space surrounding the image to 10 pixels.

3. Stretch the image to any size you want, and then resample the image.

4. Flip the image upside down.

5. Save the page, and save the edited graphic as a different file named painter2.gif.

6. Apply a different theme to the Web site.

7. Preview one or a few of the site's pages in a web browser.

8. Exit both the Editor and the Explorer.

Creating an Image Map

Objectives for This Unit

✓ Understanding what an image map is

✓ Choosing an image map style

✓ Creating and working with hotspots

✓ Setting the default link

Prerequisites

▶ Launching FrontPage (Lesson 1-2)

▶ Creating a new Web Site from scratch (Lesson 1-3)

▶ Adding existing files to a FrontPage Web Site (Lesson 1-5)

▶ Opening an existing Web site in the Explorer (Lesson 2-1)

▶ Launching the FrontPage Editor (Lesson 2-2)

▶ Inserting an image (Lesson 6-1)

▶ Saving a page that contains images (Lesson 6-5)

Image maps are the five-star versions of graphic hyperlinks. Unlike a regular linked image, which leads to only one destination, an image map can lead to several places. To go to a particular destination, visitors click different areas inside the graphic.

Image maps are popular because they offer a creative alternative to button-based navigation bars and lists of links. In this unit, you call on the Editor's image map talents to transform a regular graphic into an attractive navigation bar.

on the CD

▶ imagemap.gif

▶ resume.htm

▶ art.htm

▶ fish2.gif

▶ painter2.gif

Choosing an Image Map Style

Creating an image map involves two steps:

▶ Inserting the image map graphic into a page

▶ Defining the areas inside the graphic where visitors can click to activate a link

on the test

If you intend to publish your finished Web site on a Web server that doesn't support FrontPage Server Extensions, you have an additional task: choosing an image map style. (I discuss the different publishing options in detail in Chapter 13.) If you will be publishing your site on a Web server that *does* support FrontPage Server Extensions, FrontPage's default image map settings are already set, and you can skip the following discussion and move on to the first set of numbered steps in this lesson. If you're not sure whether your host server supports FrontPage Server Extensions, ask your system administrator or Internet service provider (ISP).

Most image maps operate with the help of a server-based program called a *map program*. Because different companies and ISPs use different types of server programs, plenty of variation exists among map programs as well. Before you create an image map, ask your company system administrator or your ISP what type of map program the host server uses. All servers use one of three types of map programs: NCSA, CERN, or Netscape.

This person can also tell you the map program's *path*, or its location in the server's system of files. You need this information to create a working image map.

extra credit

Client-side image maps

A *client-side* image map ignores the server-based map program and instead communicates directly with the visitor's web browser. This is a boon for Web surfers, because without the clunky map program acting as go-between, the image map works more quickly. On the down side, older web browsers don't know how to process client-side image maps. FrontPage solves this problem by generating matching client- and server-side image maps in your pages so everybody is satisfied.

Before you continue, you must get your FrontPage setup in order. To do so, follow these steps:

1 **Launch FrontPage and open My Web Site.**

If you're not sure how to open a Web site, refer to Lesson 2-1.

on the CD

If you didn't create the My Resume page in Unit 4 and the Art Gallery page in Unit 6, import the following pages and files from the FP101 folder into your Web site: resume.htm, art.htm, fish2.gif, and painter2.gif. If you can't remember how to import files, refer to Lesson 1-5.

2 **On the Explorer toolbar, click Show Editor.**

The Editor launches and presents you with a new page. (If the Editor is already open, click the New button on the Standard toolbar to create a new page.)

3 **Save the new page, title the page Image Map Page, and name the page imagemap.htm.**

If you don't remember how to save a page that contains images, refer to Lesson 6-5.

if host server doesn't support FrontPage Server Extensions, need to choose an image map style

Notes:

Show FrontPage Editor button

(In this lesson, you place the image map in its own page, because you will use the page in an upcoming lesson. You could just as easily insert an image map into a page that contains text or other graphics.)

You're now ready to continue.

heads up

You need to go through the following steps only if you are publishing your Web site on a server that *doesn't* support FrontPage Server Extensions. (If your Web server supports FrontPage Server Extensions, skip merrily to the next lesson.) Note that because this task is specific to your individual situation, the steps are written in general terms.

To choose an image map style for your Web site, follow these steps:

1 **On the FrontPage Standard toolbar, click Show Explorer.**

2 **In the Explorer, choose Tools⇔Web Settings.**

The FrontPage Web Settings dialog box appears.

3 **Click the Advanced tab.**

4 **In the Style list box, select the image map style that's specific to your host Web server.**

5 **In the Prefix text box, enter the path to your host server's map program.**

heads up

FrontPage automatically fills in the common path for each type of image map style. You need to talk to your system administrator or ISP, however, because each system has its own setup.

6 **Mark the Generate Client-Side Image Maps check box to have FrontPage generate a client-side image map in addition to a server-side image map.**

If someone visits your site using a browser that can't process client-side image maps, that browser will use the corresponding server-side image map.

7 **Click OK to close the FrontPage Web Settings dialog box.**

A FrontPage Explorer dialog box pops up, telling you that the Explorer needs to *recalculate* the Web site (that is, update the Web site's settings) to put the new settings into effect.

8 **Click Yes.**

FrontPage recalculates the Web site, and you're ready to go.

heads up

If your image map is server-side; NCSA-, CERN-, or Netscape-style; and part of a *per-user* Web site, FrontPage can't set up your image map correctly. A quirk in the program causes FrontPage to mess up image maps for Web sites with URLs that look like this: www.domain.com/~username.

A solution exists, but it involves some legwork on your part. For details, visit the Microsoft Knowledge Base at www.microsoft.com/kb/default.asp and search for article number Q154598. This article describes the problem in detail and shows you how to adjust your FrontPage settings to fix the problem.

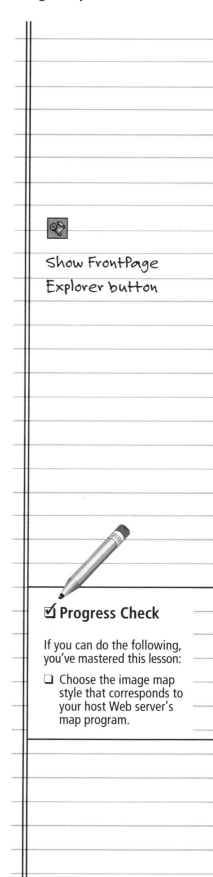

Show FrontPage Explorer button

☑ **Progress Check**

If you can do the following, you've mastered this lesson:

❏ Choose the image map style that corresponds to your host Web server's map program.

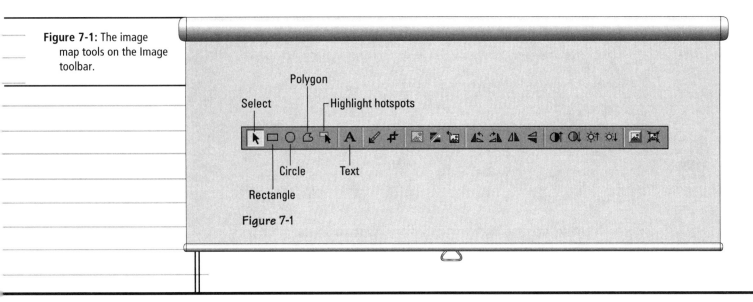

Figure 7-1: The image map tools on the Image toolbar.

Polygon

Select — Highlight hotspots

Circle   Text

Rectangle

Figure 7-1

Lesson 7-2

Drawing Hotspots

on the test

The clickable areas inside an image map are called *hotspots*. Hotspots work just like regular hyperlinks — click a hotspot and you find yourself in a new location.

The Editor's Image toolbar contains hotspot drawing tools that enable you to "draw" rectangles, circles, and polygons around the areas you want to turn into hotspots (see Figure 7-1). You don't really draw on the image — you simply define the areas inside the image that are clickable. Although hotspots are visible in the Editor, when viewed with a web browser, image map hotspots are invisible: All visitors see is the image. After you're finished, you can move and reshape your hotspots until the image map works the way you want.

on the CD

In the steps that follow, you insert an image named imagemap.gif into the empty page visible in the Editor. You then draw hotspots on the image. Imagemap.gif is a regular graphic, just like the ones you worked with in Unit 6.

1 **On the Explorer toolbar, click Show FrontPage Editor.**

The Editor, with the empty page open, becomes visible.

2 **Click Insert Image.**

The Image dialog box appears.

3 **Insert imagemap.gif, which is currently located on your hard drive in the FP101 folder, into the page.**

If you can't remember how to insert an image that is stored in another location on your computer, refer to Lesson 6-1.

The image map graphic appears in the page (see Figure 7-2).

The graphic will eventually work like a navigation bar, with hyperlinks leading to each page in the site. This particular graphic is especially well suited to

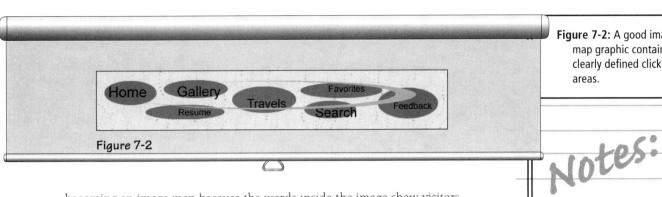

Figure 7-2

Figure 7-2: A good image map graphic contains clearly defined clickable areas.

becoming an image map because the words inside the image show visitors where to click. (Of course, if one were to click the image right now, nothing would happen because the image doesn't yet have any hotspots.)

Now that the image is in place, you're ready to draw hotspots. To do so, follow these steps:

1 Click the image map graphic.

The Image toolbar comes into view.

2 On the Image toolbar, click Rectangle.

A rectangular hotspot is the best choice in this case because each word is roughly rectangular.

3 Move the pointer inside the image map graphic over the word Resume.

The pointer turns into a pencil.

4 Click and drag the pointer diagonally across the word until a rectangular border surrounds the word.

Don't worry if the hotspot isn't perfectly shaped — you can reshape it later or delete the hotspot and start over.

5 Release the mouse button.

The Create Hyperlink dialog box appears, enabling you to choose the hotspot's destination.

6 In the file list, click resume.htm, and then click OK.

The dialog box closes, and the hotspot is now a link to the My Resume page. In addition, a colorful border appears around the image map graphic, indicating the graphic is clickable. (In Lesson 6-2, I talk about how borders can enhance a graphic hyperlink or an image map.)

If you don't like how the hotspot looks, click the hotspot and then press the Delete key. The hotspot disappears, and you can try again.

In the next set of steps, you draw another hotspot. This time you practice using the Polygon tool.

1 Click Polygon.

2 Click the area inside the image directly above the word Gallery, **and then move the pointer to the left.**

A line extends from the hotspot's starting point.

Notes:

Rectangle button

Polygon button

Figure 7-3: The image map contains rectangular and polygonal hotspots.

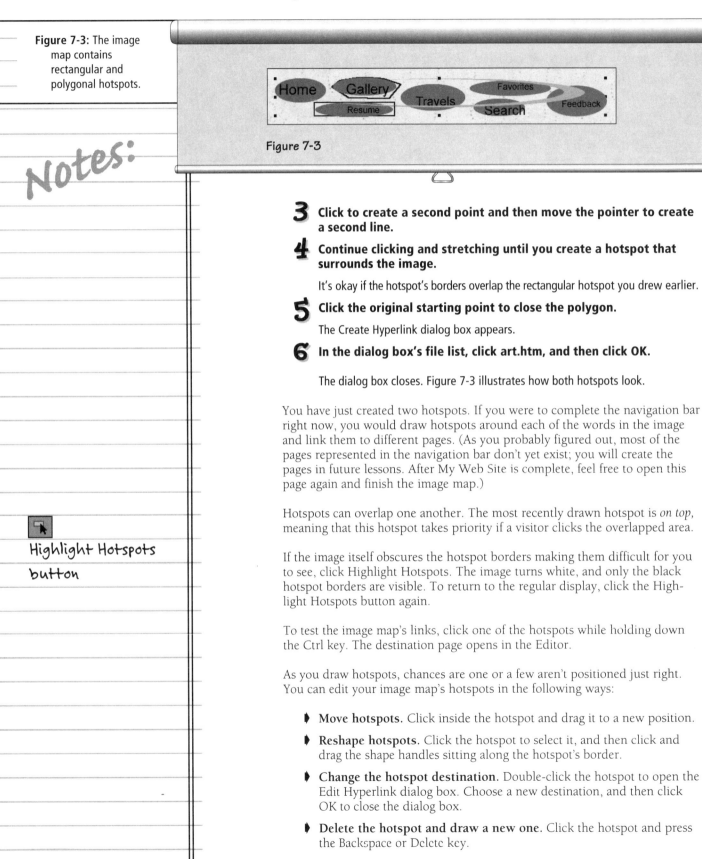

Figure 7-3

Notes:

Highlight Hotspots button

3 **Click to create a second point and then move the pointer to create a second line.**

4 **Continue clicking and stretching until you create a hotspot that surrounds the image.**

It's okay if the hotspot's borders overlap the rectangular hotspot you drew earlier.

5 **Click the original starting point to close the polygon.**

The Create Hyperlink dialog box appears.

6 **In the dialog box's file list, click art.htm, and then click OK.**

The dialog box closes. Figure 7-3 illustrates how both hotspots look.

You have just created two hotspots. If you were to complete the navigation bar right now, you would draw hotspots around each of the words in the image and link them to different pages. (As you probably figured out, most of the pages represented in the navigation bar don't yet exist; you will create the pages in future lessons. After My Web Site is complete, feel free to open this page again and finish the image map.)

Hotspots can overlap one another. The most recently drawn hotspot is *on top*, meaning that this hotspot takes priority if a visitor clicks the overlapped area.

If the image itself obscures the hotspot borders making them difficult for you to see, click Highlight Hotspots. The image turns white, and only the black hotspot borders are visible. To return to the regular display, click the Highlight Hotspots button again.

To test the image map's links, click one of the hotspots while holding down the Ctrl key. The destination page opens in the Editor.

As you draw hotspots, chances are one or a few aren't positioned just right. You can edit your image map's hotspots in the following ways:

- **Move hotspots.** Click inside the hotspot and drag it to a new position.
- **Reshape hotspots.** Click the hotspot to select it, and then click and drag the shape handles sitting along the hotspot's border.
- **Change the hotspot destination.** Double-click the hotspot to open the Edit Hyperlink dialog box. Choose a new destination, and then click OK to close the dialog box.
- **Delete the hotspot and draw a new one.** Click the hotspot and press the Backspace or Delete key.

Adding a descriptive text label to hotspots and graphics

Whereas regular hotspots are invisible, *labeled hotspots* contain a descriptive text label visitors see when they view the image map. Text labels are ideal when the graphic you use as the basis of your image map doesn't cue visitors where to click. The image map graphic you use in this unit already contains words that show visitors where to click inside the graphic, so you don't need additional text labels. Even so, this feature may come in handy later on, so I show you how it works.

To draw a labeled hotspot, follow these steps:

1. **Click the image map image.**

2. **On the Image toolbar, click the Text button.**

   A rectangular area with a flashing insertion point appears in the center of the image.

3. **Type a descriptive text label, and then click anywhere outside the label (but inside the graphic) to deselect the label.**

If you want the label to sit in a different location inside the graphic, drag the label where you want it to appear.

Now you need to transform the label into a working hotspot.

4. **Right-click the label, and from the shortcut menu that appears, choose Image Hotspot Properties.**

   The Create Hyperlink dialog box appears.

5. **Select a link destination, and then click OK to close the dialog box.**

To change the text label, click the hotspot and then click inside the text label, and enter new text. You can also format the text inside the label using the Editor's font styles (refer to Lesson 3-2 for a refresher).

You can also use the Text button to add a caption to any graphic in your page, even if that graphic is not the basis of an image map. To do so, follow the steps listed above, but skip Steps 4 and 5.

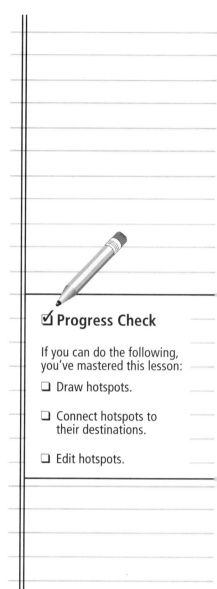

☑ Progress Check

If you can do the following, you've mastered this lesson:

❑ Draw hotspots.

❑ Connect hotspots to their destinations.

❑ Edit hotspots.

Setting the Default Link

Lesson 7-3

Right now, if a visitor were to click an area in the image that falls outside a hotspot, nothing would happen. You can change this behavior by giving the image map a *default link*. Visitors jump to the default link destination when they click anywhere on the image map that's not already defined by a hotspot.

In the steps that follow, you specify the My Web Site home page as the image map's default link.

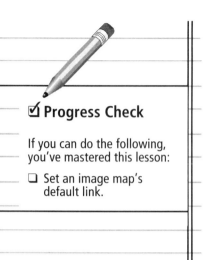

1 **Right-click the image map and choose Image Properties from the shortcut menu that appears.**

The Image Properties dialog box appears, with the General tab visible.

2 **In the Location text box, type** index.htm **(or, if you use the Microsoft Personal Web Server, type** Default.htm**).**

If you're not sure which version of the Personal Web Server you're using, see the Extra Credit sidebar called "How to tell which Personal Web Server you're using" in Unit 1.

3 **Click OK.**

The dialog box closes, and the Editor applies the default hyperlink to the image map.

Good job — you now know how to create an image map! Be sure to save the page before you move on to the next unit.

Unit 7 Quiz

Take this quiz to review the material you covered in this unit.

1. **An image map is . . .**

    A. A graphical representation of the Web site.

    B. An image that contains several clickable areas linked to different destinations.

    C. An image that, when clicked, leads to a single destination.

    D. A regular GIF or JPEG graphic to which hotspots are added.

    E. A special type of image file that is different from regular Web graphics.

2. **If you publish your Web site on a Web server that doesn't support FrontPage Server Extensions . . .**

    A. You can't use FrontPage to create image maps.

    B. The Web design gods will look unfavorably upon your Web site.

    C. You must choose an image map style that corresponds to your host Web server program.

    D. You need to talk to your system administrator or ISP to get information about the host Web server.

    E. You must create a client-side image map.

3. **What are the clickable areas inside an image map called?**

    A. Hyperlinks.

    B. Hotspots.

    C. Age spots.

    D. Polka dots.

    E. Hot potatoes.

4. **How does a visitor activate an image map's default link?**

    A. By clicking a hotspot.

    B. By right-clicking the image map and choosing Default Link from the shortcut menu.

    C. By clicking a spot inside the image map that isn't contained within a hotspot.

    D. By clicking a text hyperlink.

    E. By saying "Wonder Twin powers — activate!"

Notes:

Unit 7 Exercise

1. In the image map page open in the Editor, delete the image map's hotspots.

2. Draw new hotspots around the words `Resume` and `Gallery`, choosing whichever shape you want.

3. Change the shape of the Resume hotspot.

4. Move the Gallery hotspot to a new position.

5. Remove the image map's default hyperlink.

6. Save the page, and exit both the Editor and the Explorer.

Building Sturdy Tables

Objectives for This Unit

✓ Finding out how tables can enhance your site's design

✓ Creating a table

✓ Handling cells, columns, and rows

✓ Adjusting a table size, shape, and layout

✓ Adding color to a table

Prerequisites

◗ Launching FrontPage (Lesson 1-2)

◗ Creating a Web Site from scratch (Lesson 1-3)

◗ Opening an existing Web site in the Explorer (Lesson 2-1)

◗ Launching the FrontPage Editor (Lesson 2-2)

◗ Saving a page (Lesson 2-6)

◗ Working with the *Dummies 101: FrontPage 98* example files (Lesson 3-1)

◗ Previewing a page (Lesson 3-6)

◗ unit08.htm

on the CD

Of all the HTML loopholes Web designers use to bully their Web pages into shape, *tables* are probably the most popular. Tables provide an alternative to plain vanilla paragraphs by creating a framework of rows and columns into which you can plug your page's content. By fiddling with the table's attributes, you can crank out just about any layout you want.

Fascinated? Good, because in the course of this unit, you get lots of hands-on experience with tables.

Creating a Table   Lesson 8-1

Tables are useful both for creating grids of information (similar in appearance to spreadsheet worksheets) and as the basis for the page's layout. Figures 8-1 and 8-2 illustrate each case.

Figure 8-1 shows a simple three-row, two-column table filled with a price list. Each table *cell* contains a bit of text, and the cells are lined up in rows and columns, making the whole thing easy to read at a glance.

Figure 8-1: A traditional grid table with visible borders.

Figure 8-2: An invisible table structures the layout of this page.

Item	Price
Double-dip ice cream cone	$1.00
Super huge, gooey hot fudge sundae	$2.50

Figure 8-1

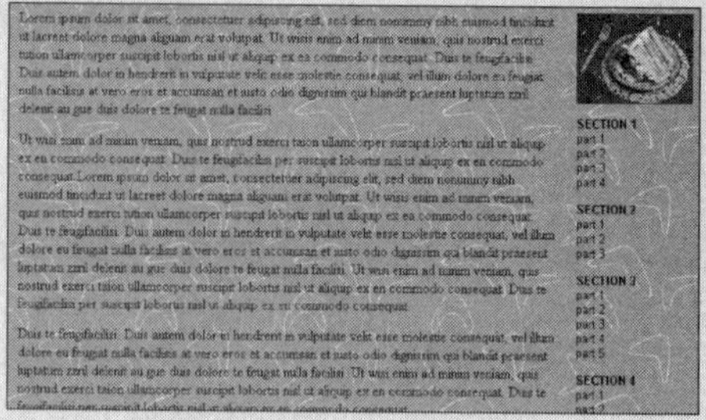

Figure 8-2

tables = grids of visible rows and columns

tables = invisible framework to structure page layout

on the CD

Show FrontPage Editor button

In Figure 8-2, the table acts as a container for the page's content. In fact, the page in Figure 8-2 is one of the Editor's page templates, most of which use tables to structure layout. The major difference between this table and the one shown in Figure 8-1 (besides the obvious layout differences) is that this table contains no visible borders between its cells. The result is a table that *acts* like a table but that, when viewed with a web browser, is invisible.

In this unit, you practice working with tables by adding a new page called My Travels to My Web Site, the scratch-pad Web site you first created in Unit 3. Many people use their Web sites to share travel experiences and connect with other globetrotters. The My Travels page looks very much like a travel diary, complete with destinations, dates, and comments. The basis of this page is sitting in the FP101 folder in the form of a file named unit08.htm, which you add to My Web Site in the steps that follow.

1 **Launch FrontPage, and open My Web Site.**

If you're not sure how to open a Web site, refer to Lesson 2-1.

2 **On the Explorer toolbar, click Show FrontPage Editor.**

The Editor launches, and presents you with a new page. (If the Editor is already open, click the New button on the Standard toolbar to create a new page.)

3 **Using the Insert⇨File command, insert the contents of the file named unit08.htm (located in the FP101 folder) into the page.**

For detailed instructions on how to use the Insert⇨File command, see Lesson 3-1.

The contents of the example file appear inside the page (see Figure 8-3). The page contains a background graphic and a nice color scheme because of the Arcs theme you applied to My Web Site in Unit 6.

4 **Save the new page as part of your Web site, title the page My Travels, and name the page travel.htm.**

And now, back to our regularly scheduled lesson on tables.

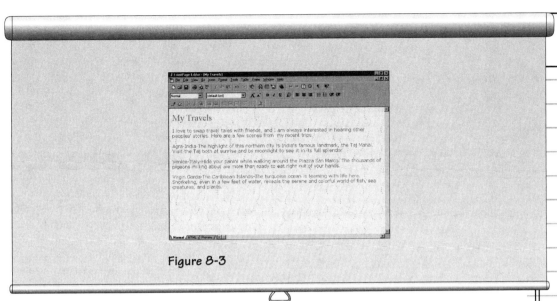

Figure 8-3

Figure 8-3: The My Travels page.

Notes:

Creating an empty table

Because tables appear in Web pages so often, the FrontPage Editor takes special pains to make tables easy to use and customize. The Editor's Table toolbar (made visible by choosing View⇨Table Toolbar) contains many of the tools that you use regularly (see Figure 8-4).

You can create a new table in any of four ways, as follows:

▶ Click Insert Table.
▶ Choose Table⇨Insert Table.
▶ Click Draw Table and then sketch the table's borders.
▶ Convert regular text into a table.

The first three operations accomplish the same goal: creating an empty table. In the following steps, you use the easiest of the three tools, the Insert Table button.

1 **In the My Travels page, place the cursor at the beginning of the first descriptive paragraph (the paragraph begins with the words** I love to swap**).**

2 **On the toolbar, click Insert Table.**

A grid of white boxes representing rows and columns appears underneath the button on the toolbar.

3 **Click and drag your Standard pointer on the grid until you highlight the boxes representing a 2-by-2 table (see Figure 8-5).**

As you highlight boxes, the table dimensions appear at the bottom of the grid.

4 **Release the mouse button.**

An empty two-row, two-column table appears in your page (see Figure 8-6).

Insert Table button

Figure 8-4: The Table toolbar.

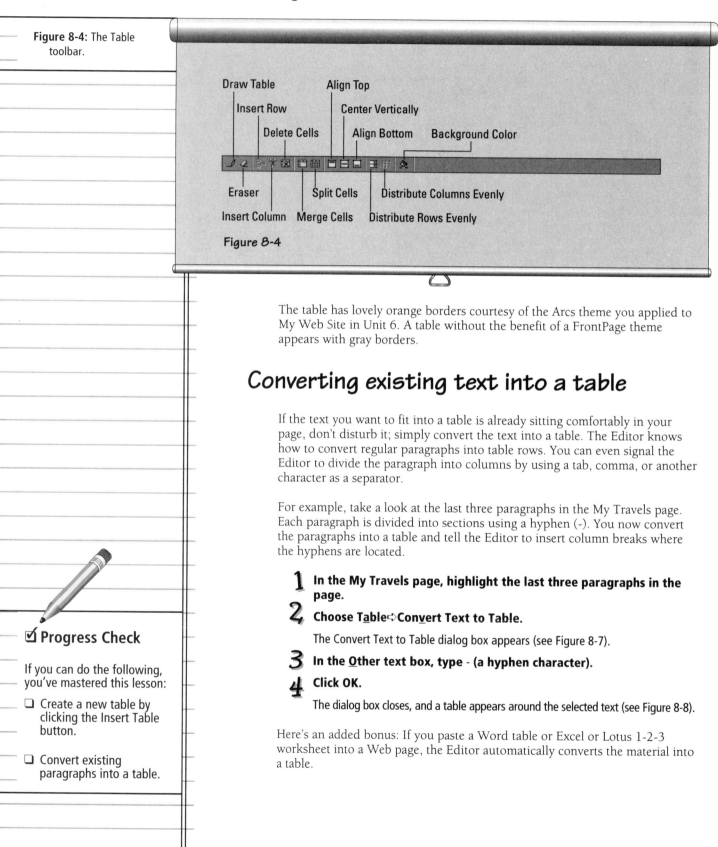

Figure 8-4

The table has lovely orange borders courtesy of the Arcs theme you applied to My Web Site in Unit 6. A table without the benefit of a FrontPage theme appears with gray borders.

Converting existing text into a table

If the text you want to fit into a table is already sitting comfortably in your page, don't disturb it; simply convert the text into a table. The Editor knows how to convert regular paragraphs into table rows. You can even signal the Editor to divide the paragraph into columns by using a tab, comma, or another character as a separator.

For example, take a look at the last three paragraphs in the My Travels page. Each paragraph is divided into sections using a hyphen (-). You now convert the paragraphs into a table and tell the Editor to insert column breaks where the hyphens are located.

1 **In the My Travels page, highlight the last three paragraphs in the page.**

2 **Choose Table⇨Convert Text to Table.**

The Convert Text to Table dialog box appears (see Figure 8-7).

3 **In the Other text box, type - (a hyphen character).**

4 **Click OK.**

The dialog box closes, and a table appears around the selected text (see Figure 8-8).

Here's an added bonus: If you paste a Word table or Excel or Lotus 1-2-3 worksheet into a Web page, the Editor automatically converts the material into a table.

☑ **Progress Check**

If you can do the following, you've mastered this lesson:

❑ Create a new table by clicking the Insert Table button.

❑ Convert existing paragraphs into a table.

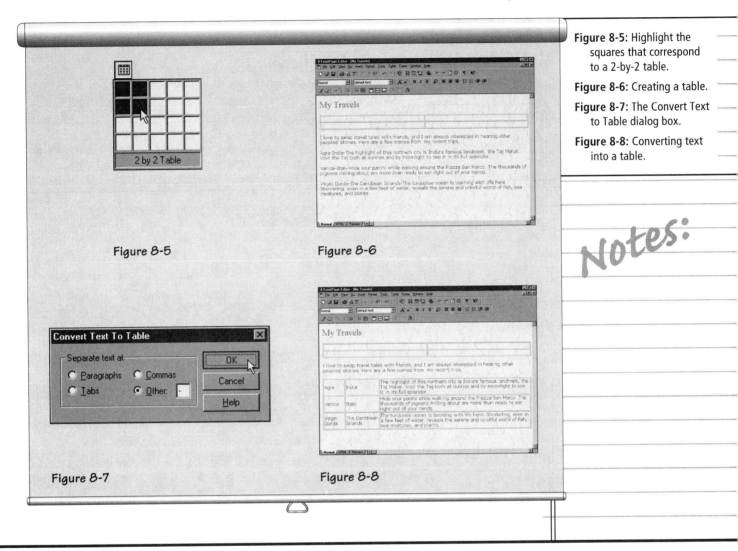

Figure 8-5

Figure 8-6

Figure 8-7

Figure 8-8

Figure 8-5: Highlight the squares that correspond to a 2-by-2 table.

Figure 8-6: Creating a table.

Figure 8-7: The Convert Text to Table dialog box.

Figure 8-8: Converting text into a table.

Notes:

Setting the Table's Attributes

Lesson 8-2

After you create a table, you can adjust its size, alignment, and layout in any number of ways. In this lesson, I show you how to tinker with attributes that affect the entire table. (In Lesson 8-3, you concentrate on individual cells, rows, and columns.)

For the rest of this unit, you will work with the second table you created in Lesson 8-1 (the one full of text). You have a chance to revisit your original table during the Exercise at the end of this unit.

Changing table dimensions

By default, FrontPage creates new tables that span the width of the page. The height of the table is determined by the number of rows it contains and the amount of stuff packed inside each cell. If this default size doesn't match how you want your table to look, you can change both the table's height and width. There is more to table dimensions than meets the eye, however, and the reason lies in the way the Web works.

When viewed with a web browser, the placement of text, graphics, and other elements in a Web page is determined by the size of the browser window. When you shrink the window, the page contents rearrange themselves (or *wrap*) to fit inside the smaller space. When you expand the browser window, the page contents spread out to fill the extra space.

What does browser window behavior have to do with tables? A lot! Depending on how you specify your table's dimensions, the table will act differently in various browser window sizes.

▶ If you give your table *proportional dimensions,* or dimensions based on a percentage of the browser window, the table will expand and contract to fit inside differently sized browser windows. For example, if you specify that you want the width of your table to fill 50 percent of the width of the browser window, all your visitors (even those with small monitors and a correspondingly smaller amount of browser real estate) will be able to see the entire table on their screens.

▶ On the other hand, if you give your table fixed or *absolute dimensions,* the table will remain the same size regardless of browser window size. This option is fine for small tables, but large tables (those with a width of more than 600 pixels) will run beyond the edge of the browser window when viewed with smaller monitors, causing visitors to scroll (while grumbling under their breath) to see the entire thing.

▶ The third option is to turn off dimension settings and leave the decision entirely up to the size of the cell contents. The size of the table will stretch just enough to fit around the stuff inside its cells.

Which option do you choose? The answer is different for table width versus table height, and it also depends on the table's job. Generally, for small tables, absolute widths are fine. For large tables, or for tables in which the overall structure is less important than the specific dimensions, consider using proportional widths. For most tables, I recommend not specifying a height and letting the height expand to fit the table contents, or setting the height of individual rows (you find out how in Lesson 8-3).

The simplest way to change the size of your table is to drag the right or bottom table border to a new position (try it now — don't worry about how your table ends up). This method works if you want your table to use absolute dimensions.

To use proportional dimensions, or to control absolute dimensions down to the pixel, you need to use the Table Properties dialog box. In the following steps, you use this dialog box to set the dimensions of your table.

proportional
dimensions =
tables change size
to fit browser
window

absolute
dimensions =
tables stay size
regardless of
browser window
size

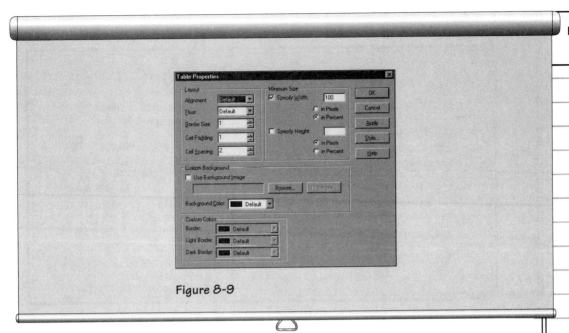

Figure 8-9: The Table Properties dialog box.

Figure 8-9

Notes:

1 **Click inside the table and choose Table⇨Table Properties.**

The Table Properties dialog box appears (see Figure 8-9).

2 **In the Specify Width text box, type** 75, **and then click the In Percent radio button.**

By doing so, you tell the Editor to set the width of your table to 75 percent of the width of the browser window.

3 **Click the Specify Height check box to unmark it. (If the check box is already unmarked, leave it that way.)**

In this table, the contents determine the table's height.

4 **Click OK.**

The dialog box closes, and the table size changes accordingly.

To see how your table looks in a small window size, save the page and then preview your page using a web browser. Adjust the size of the browser window to see how the table layout changes.

Aligning a table on the page

By default, tables hug the left page margin. If you prefer, you can push your table to the middle or the right side of the page instead.

To see how this adjustment works, center your table by following these steps:

1 **Click inside the table and choose Table⇨Table Properties.**

The Table Properties dialog box appears.

2 **From the Alignment list box, select Center, and then click OK.**

The dialog box closes, and the table moves to the center of the page.

extra credit

Making your table float

A recent HTML addition enables you to wrap text around the left or right side of a table, similar to how text can wrap around an image. This effect is called a *floating table*.

To create a floating table, follow these steps:

1. **Click in the table and choose Table⇨Table Properties.**

   The Table Properties dialog box appears.

2. **Choose an option from the Float list box.**

   The Left option causes the table to float over to the left margin, with text wrapping around its right side. The Right option causes the table to float over to the right margin, with text wrapping around its left side.

3. **Click OK.**

   The table changes position.

Setting border thickness

The presence of borders in a table determines whether the table looks like a classic rows-and-columns operation, or whether the table itself is invisible and only the table contents appear on the page.

In this set of steps, you adjust the table's border thickness to see how the table looks, both without borders and with.

1 **Click inside the table and choose Table⇨Table Properties.**

The Table Properties dialog box appears.

2 **In the Border Size text box, type** 0.

3 **Click OK.**

The dialog box closes, and the borders turn into dotted lines. The dotted lines surrounding each table cell let you know that the table is now invisible. To get a better idea of how the table looks to your visitors, preview the page.

4 **Preview your page (if you don't know how, refer to Lesson 3-6).**

When viewed in a web browser or in the Editor's Preview View, the table is invisible; only its structure remains (see Figure 8-10).

5 **Return to the Editor's Normal View.**

If you are currently looking at your web browser, click the FrontPage Editor button on the Windows taskbar to return to FrontPage.

6 **Click inside the table and choose Table⇨Table Properties.**

The Table Properties dialog box appears.

7 **In the Border Size text box, type** 5, **and then click OK.**

The dialog box closes, and the borders reappear. The table's outer border is now 5 pixels thick (see Figure 8-11).

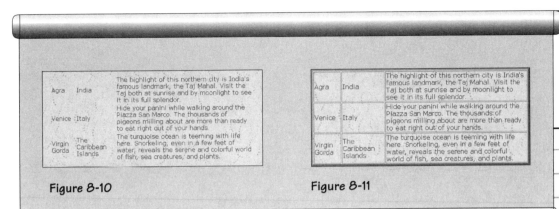

Figure 8-10   Figure 8-11

Padding cells

When you turned off your table's borders, you may have noticed that the contents of the table cells appeared to be jammed together. Without the borders separating the cells, the table appeared crowded. Here's where *cell padding* enters the picture. By increasing cell padding, you add space between the contents of table cells and the cell borders.

To see how table padding works, you now increase your table's padding.

1 Click inside the table and choose Table⇨Table Properties.

The Table Properties dialog box appears.

2 In the Cell Padding text box, type 5, and then click OK.

The dialog box closes, and 5 pixels of space appear between the cell borders and contents.

Adding space between cells

Cell spacing refers to the amount of space sitting between table cells. By adjusting the cell spacing, you affect how thick the borders between cells look. Technically, borders between cells are always 1 pixel thick, but by increasing cell spacing, you can make the borders appear thicker.

By default, FrontPage creates tables with 2 pixels of cell spacing. In the following steps, you increase and then decrease cell spacing to see how the change affects your table.

1 Click inside the table and choose Table⇨Table Properties.

The Table Properties dialog box appears.

2 In the Cell Spacing text box, enter 5, and then click OK.

The dialog box closes, and the table's cell spacing increases to 5 pixels (see Figure 8-12).

3 Click inside the table and choose Table⇨Table Properties.

The Table Properties dialog box appears.

add cell spacing to make borders appear thicker

Figure 8-12: See how 5 pixels of cell spacing make the cell borders look thicker?

Figure 8-13: By eliminating cell spacing, the cell borders now appear thinner.

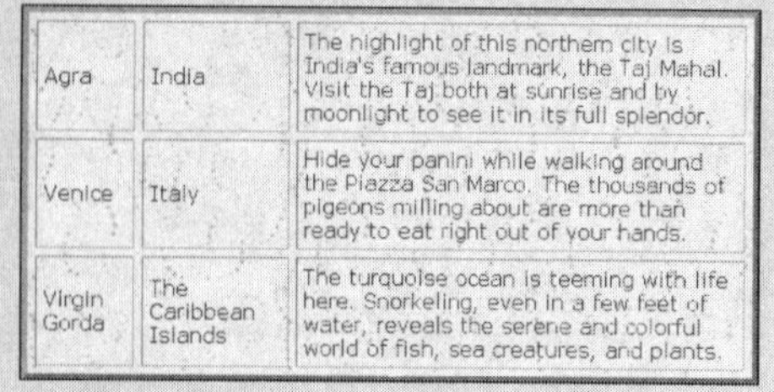

Agra	India	The highlight of this northern city is India's famous landmark, the Taj Mahal. Visit the Taj both at sunrise and by moonlight to see it in its full splendor.
Venice	Italy	Hide your panini while walking around the Piazza San Marco. The thousands of pigeons milling about are more than ready to eat right out of your hands.
Virgin Gorda	The Caribbean Islands	The turquoise ocean is teeming with life here. Snorkeling, even in a few feet of water, reveals the serene and colorful world of fish, sea creatures, and plants.

Figure 8-12

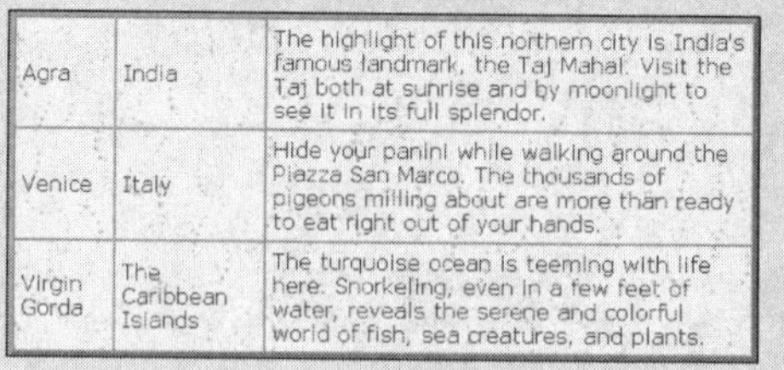

Agra	India	The highlight of this northern city is India's famous landmark, the Taj Mahal. Visit the Taj both at sunrise and by moonlight to see it in its full splendor.
Venice	Italy	Hide your panini while walking around the Piazza San Marco. The thousands of pigeons milling about are more than ready to eat right out of your hands.
Virgin Gorda	The Caribbean Islands	The turquoise ocean is teeming with life here. Snorkeling, even in a few feet of water, reveals the serene and colorful world of fish, sea creatures, and plants.

Figure 8-13

4 **In the Cell Spacing text box, enter 0, and then click OK.**

The dialog box closes, and the cell spacing goes away, leaving behind slender, elegant borders (see Figure 8-13).

extra credit

Adding a caption

Every now and then, tables benefit from a title or an extra bit of explanation. For those occasions, give your table a caption.

To add a caption, follow these steps:

1. **Click in the table and choose Table⇨Insert Caption.**

   The cursor hops to an empty space above the table.

2. **Type the caption text.**

To move the caption underneath the table, follow these steps:

1. **Click in the caption and choose Table⇨Caption Properties.**

   The Caption Properties dialog box appears.

2. **Click the Bottom of Table radio button and click OK.**

   The caption moves underneath the table.

☑ Progress Check

If you can do the following, you've mastered this lesson:

❑ Understand the difference between absolute and proportional table dimensions.

❑ Change the dimensions of a table.

❑ Align a table in a page.

❑ Change the table's border setting.

❑ Increase and decrease cell padding (the amount of space between the cell border and the cell content).

❑ Increase and decrease cell spacing (the amount of space between cells).

Recess

Tired of tables? Save your page, and take a break. Flip through your favorite magazine (a great way to pick up design ideas for your Web site!), or listen to some music.

Adjusting Table Layout   Lesson 8-3

As you customize your table, you don't necessarily want every change to apply to the entire table. In this lesson, I show you how to adjust the settings of the individual table parts: cells, rows, and tables.

Adding and deleting rows and columns

Let's face it — few of us can create a perfectly engineered table on the first try. At some point, you want to add a few rows and columns to hold new data, or erase rows or columns you don't need.

Right now, your table contains plenty of information but lacks category headers. Headers sit at the beginning of a row or column and define the contents of the row or column. Headers aren't mandatory, but they are a nice touch, especially when your table displays a grid of related information. Now practice adding a new row by creating text headers for your new table.

1 **If the Table toolbar isn't already visible, choose View⇨Table Toolbar.**

2 **Click inside the first row of the table and choose Table⇨Select Row.**

Alternatively, you can select a row by moving the pointer over the row's left margin until the pointer turns into an arrow pointing to the right. Click once to select the row.

3 **Click Insert Rows.**

A new empty row appears above the selected row.

4 **Click inside the first cell in the new row and type** Destination.

5 **Press the Tab key twice.**

The cursor advances to the third cell in the row (for now, leave the second cell empty).

6 **In the third cell, type** What it was like.

The headers are now complete, but they don't look much like headers — without formatting, the headers blend into the table's body text.

7 **Choose Table⇨Select Row.**

8 **Click Bold.**

The selected text turns bold.

9 **Click Increase Text Size.**

The selected text becomes one size bigger, and the headers' text now stands apart from the body text.

Adding a new column to a table involves the same process: Select the column to the left of where you want the new column to appear, and click Insert Column.

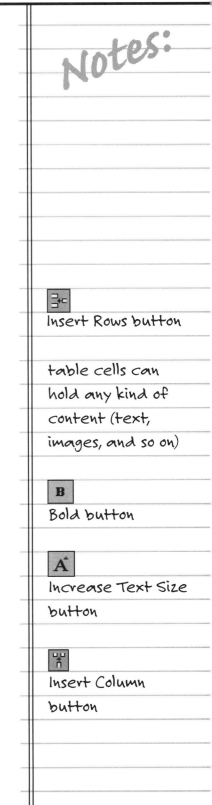

Insert Rows button

table cells can hold any kind of content (text, images, and so on)

Bold button

Increase Text Size button

Insert Column button

For more control over the placement of new rows and columns (or to add more than one row or column at a time), choose Table⇨Insert Rows or Columns. The Insert Rows or Columns dialog box enables you to choose the number of rows you want to add, as well as their location in the table.

Inserting a single table cell

If you want to add a single cell rather than an entire row or column, you can do that, too. The result is a lopsided table, but this effect may be just what you're after. To add a cell, do the following:

1. **Click in the cell to the right of where you want the new cell to appear.**

2. **Choose Table⇨Insert Cell.**

   A new cell appears.

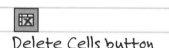

Delete Cells button

To delete a cell, row, or column, select the cells you want to delete (choose Table⇨Select Cell, Table⇨Select Row, or Table⇨Select Column), and click Delete Cells. To delete the contents of the cells instead of the cells themselves, press the Backspace or Delete key.

Changing the dimensions of cells, rows, and columns

In the preceding lesson, you discovered that you can size your table using absolute or proportional measurements (or you can forgo size specifications altogether). The same goes for cells, columns, and rows. You can control row height and column width using absolute pixel measurements or proportional measurements based on the size of the table. You can also let the cell's contents determine its height and width. You can even combine the three options in a single table — for example, giving some columns an absolute width and others a proportional or undefined width.

To use absolute measurements, the easiest way to adjust the dimensions of rows and columns is to drag them into shape with your mouse, as follows:

1. **In the table, move the pointer over the column border between the first and second columns.**

   The pointer turns into a double-facing arrow.

2. **Click and, while holding down the mouse button, drag the border to the left. Then release the mouse button.**

   The border moves to the left.

3. **Do the same thing with the row border separating the first and second table rows.**

See how easy?

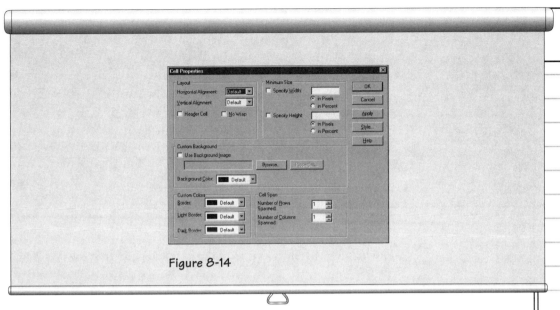

Figure 8-14

Figure 8-14: The Cell Properties dialog box.

Notes:

If you prefer to use proportional measurements, or you want to set the precise height and/or width for a cell, column, or row, you need to turn to the Cell Properties dialog box (shown in Figure 8-14). This dialog box works just like the Table Properties dialog box, except that its settings apply only to selected cells.

To change cell, column, or row dimensions using the Cell Properties dialog box, select the table part you want to format (choose Table➪Select Cell, Table➪Select Row, or Table➪Select Column), and then choose Table➪Cell Properties. The Cell Properties dialog box appears. Make whatever adjustments you want to the selected part's dimensions, and then click OK to close the dialog box. (For details on how to specify dimensions, refer to the Lesson 8-2 section called "Changing table dimensions.")

Distribute Rows Evenly button

If you simply want to even out the dimensions of your rows and columns (distributing the rows and/or columns equally in the table), choose Table➪Select Table, and then, on the Table toolbar, click Distribute Rows Evenly or Distribute Columns Evenly.

Distribute Columns Evenly button

Merging and splitting cells

Designwise, sometimes symmetrical rows and columns don't do the trick. Your table is a good example: Notice the first two cells in the table's top row. The header `Destination` applies to the information in both the first and second columns, but right now, the header only tops the first column, and an empty cell tops the second column.

The solution is to *merge* the two cells so the header — now sitting inside a single cell — covers both columns. To do so, follow these steps:

1 **Click in the cell that contains the header** `Destination` **and choose Table➪Select Cell.**

Figure 8-15: The Split Cells dialog box.

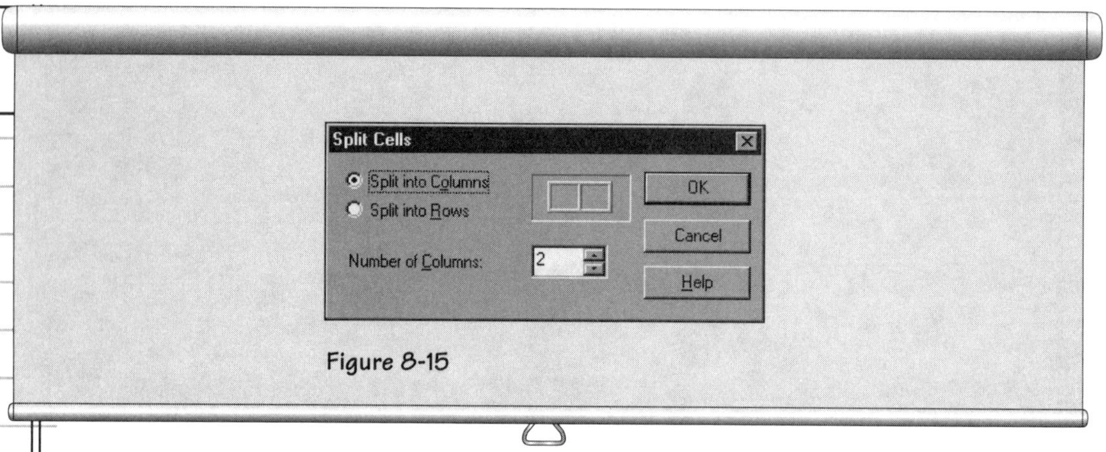

Figure 8-15

Notes:

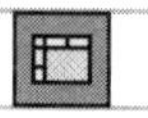

Merge Cells button

Eraser button

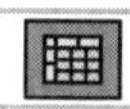

Split Cells button

2 **While holding the Shift key, click the second cell in the row (the empty cell).**

Both cells are now selected.

3 **Click Merge Cells.**

The cells merge into a single cell, and the `Destination` header tops both the first and second table columns.

If you prefer to use table drawing tools, click Eraser and drag the pointer over the borders you want to erase.

Splitting cells means dividing single cells into more than one cell. To do so, follow these steps:

1 **Click in the first cell in the third row, so the cursor sits after the words** `Virgin Gorda.`

2 **Click Split Cells.**

The Split Cells dialog box appears (see Figure 8-15).

3 **Click the Split into Columns radio button.**

By selecting this option, you choose to divide the cell vertically. If you would rather divide the cells horizontally (so they appear one on top of the other), click Split into Rows.

4 **Click OK.**

The dialog box closes, and the cell splits into two cells.

5 **Press the Tab key to move the cursor into the new cell, and then type** British Virgin Islands.

Aligning cell contents

The Editor also lets you determine where inside the cell you want the text (or other contents) to sit. You can vertically and horizontally align the contents of selected cells.

In the following steps, you first change the table body's vertical alignment, and then the table headers' horizontal alignment.

1 **Move the pointer over the left table border, next to the cell that contains the word** Agra.

The pointer turns into a right-pointing arrow.

2 **Click, and while holding down the mouse button, drag the cursor down to the third row until all three rows are selected.**

3 **Click Align Top.**

The text in the selected cells aligns with the top cell borders.

4 **Select the table's top row.**

5 **Click Center.**

The selected text moves to the center of the cell. By the way, this Center button is the same one you used to center a regular paragraph in Unit 3.

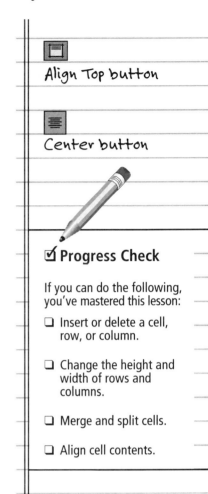

Align Top button

Center button

☑ **Progress Check**

If you can do the following, you've mastered this lesson:

❑ Insert or delete a cell, row, or column.

❑ Change the height and width of rows and columns.

❑ Merge and split cells.

❑ Align cell contents.

Coloring a Table   Lesson 8-4

After your table is in good working order, you can dress it up with color. Selected table cells — or the entire table — can be embellished with a background color or image. This effect looks great, especially when paired with a complementary border color.

heads up

Unfortunately, advanced browsers such as Internet Explorer (3.0 or greater) or Netscape Navigator (4.0 or greater) are the only ones capable of displaying changes in table color.

Adding background color

Background color in tables works just like the background color of a page; the color creates a backdrop for the stuff inside the table. In the following steps, you change the background color of the header cells so they frame the rest of the table.

Figure 8-16: Your finished table.

Destination			What it was like
Agra		India	The highlight of this northern city is India's famous landmark, the Taj Mahal. Visit the Taj both at sunrise and by moonlight to see it in its full splendor.
Venice		Italy	Hide your panini while walking around the Piazza San Marco. The thousands of pigeons milling about are more than ready to eat right out of your hands.
Virgin Gorda	British Virgin Islands	The Caribbean Islands	The turquoise ocean is teeming with life here. Snorkeling, even in a few feet of water, reveals the serene and colorful world of fish, sea creatures, and plants

Figure 8-16

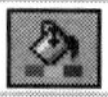

Background Color button

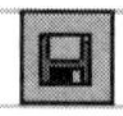

Save button

1. **Click inside the first row of the table and choose Table⇨Select Row.**
2. **Click Background Color.**

   The Color dialog box appears.
3. **In the dialog box, click the Gray swatch.**

   If you don't like gray, choose any color you like.
4. **Click OK.**

   The dialog box closes, and the selected cells turn gray (click anywhere outside the table to deselect the cells so you can see the color change). Figure 8-16 shows how your finished table looks.
5. **Click Save to save the changes you have made to the My Travels page.**

extra credit

Adding a background image

If you'd rather use an image as a table background, so be it. To add a background image to a table or cell, follow these steps:

1. **If you're changing the background of the entire table, click in the table and choose Table⇨Table Properties. If you're changing the background of selected cells, choose Table⇨Cell Properties.**

   Depending on your choice, the Table Properties or Cell Properties dialog box appears.
2. **In the dialog box, click the Use Background Image check box.**
3. **Type the URL of the background image in the accompanying text box.**

   If you don't remember the URL, click the Browse button to choose an image using the Select Background Image dialog box. (This dialog box works just like the Image dialog box; refer to Lesson 6-1 if you're not sure how to use this dialog box.)
4. **Click OK.**

   The dialog box closes, and the background image appears in the table or selected cells.

Changing border color

Border colors are another way to spice up a table. You can use color to create two different visual effects: a flat table with solid borders; or a raised table, where you use light and dark colors to simulate shadows. The border colors adorning the table in the My Travels page come as part of the Arcs theme and can't be changed unless you remove the theme. In this section, therefore, I offer generic instructions for changing border color.

heads up

As with table background colors and images, only advanced browsers such as Internet Explorer (3.0 or greater) or Netscape Navigator (4.0 or greater) are able to display table border color.

heads up

Heads Up No. 2: Internet Explorer and Netscape Navigator interpret border colors differently, so be sure to preview your page in each browser for the closest approximation of how the table will look after it's live.

To change border color, follow these steps:

1 **If you're changing the border color of the entire table, click in the table and choose T̲able⇨Table P̲roperties. If you're changing the border color for selected cells, choose T̲able⇨Cell Properties.**

Depending on your choice, the Table Properties or Cell Properties dialog box appears.

2 **In the dialog box, choose colors from the list boxes in the Custom Color area.**

The Border list box applies a flat color to the entire table border. The Light Border and Dark Border list boxes enable you to create a shadow effect by choosing separate colors for the top and left borders, and the right and bottom borders (similar to how your table looks now).

3 **Click OK.**

The dialog box closes, and the border color changes accordingly.

Notes:

☑ **Progress Check**

If you can do the following, you've mastered this lesson:

❑ Add background color to a table.

❑ Change the color of the table's borders.

Unit 8 Quiz

Take this quiz to review the material you covered in this unit.

1. **Why would someone use a table in a Web page?**

   A. Because they need a place to put down their cocktail.

   B. Because they want their Web page to automatically calculate mathematical formulae, like an Excel worksheet.

   C. Because they want to present a grid of information, such as a price list or a timetable.

Notes:

D. Because they want to arrange the page's text and pictures into columns.

E. Because they want to control the shape of a single paragraph.

2. **How do you create a new table?**

   A. You click the Insert Table button.

   B. You choose Table⇨Insert Table.

   C. You cut and paste a table from a Word document.

   D. You draw the table's borders using table drawing tools.

   E. You convert existing text into a table.

3. **How do you make a table invisible?**

   A. You choose Table⇨Hide Table.

   B. You click the Invisible Table button on the Table toolbar.

   C. You set the table's border width to 0 pixels.

   D. You wave a wand over the table and recite an incantation.

   E. You make the table transparent.

4. **When you increase a table's cell padding . . .**

   A. You increase the space between the table cells.

   B. You increase the amount of space separating the table from surrounding text.

   C. You increase the amount of space between the cell contents and the cell borders.

   D. You increase the size of the cells' contents.

   E. You make the table more comfortable.

5. **Name the factors that can influence the dimensions of a table when someone views it with a web browser.**

   A. The size of the table's contents.

   B. The size of the visitor's browser window.

   C. The fixed pixel values you specify for the table's width and height.

   D. The number of hyperlinks inside the table.

   E. The size of the visitor's monitor.

Unit 8 Exercise

1. In the My Travels page open in the Editor, highlight the paragraph of descriptive text that begins with the words I love to swap.

2. Cut the highlighted text, and paste it into the top-right cell of the empty table at the top of the page (or if you prefer, drag and drop the text into the table cell).

3. Delete the table's empty second column. The resulting table contains two cells arranged in a single column.

4. Delete the empty bottom cell. The resulting table contains a single cell.

5. Set the width of the table to 450 pixels.

6. Turn off the table's borders.

7. Save and preview the page. Notice how the invisible table compacts the paragraph into an attractive block of text.

8. Return to the Editor's Normal view, and exit both the Editor and the Explorer.

Part II Review

Unit 3 Summary

▶ **Working with text in a Web page:** In the FrontPage Editor, adding text to a Web page feels similar to creating a word processing document.

▶ **Font styles:** Font styles, such as typeface, text color, text size, and formatting, can be applied to selected characters, words, sentences, and blocks of text. To use font styles, highlight the text you want to format, and then click buttons on the Format toolbar, or choose Format⇨Font to display the Font Properties dialog box. Choose the font style you want, and then click OK.

▶ **Paragraph styles:** Paragraph styles apply only to entire blocks of text. Paragraph styles include Normal (the default style; left-aligned, proportional font), Formatted (left-aligned, monospaced font), and Address (left-aligned, italic formatting). To use paragraph styles, click inside the paragraph, and then choose an option from the Change Style list box on the Format toolbar.

▶ **Aligning and indenting paragraphs:** Click inside the paragraph you want to change, and then, on the Format toolbar, click the Align Left, Center, or Align Right button, or the Increase Indent or Decrease Indent button.

▶ **Inserting symbols:** To insert a symbol or special character (such as the © character), choose Insert⇨Symbol to display the Symbol dialog box. Choose the symbol you want, and then click Close.

▶ **Previewing a page:** For the most accurate representation of how your page will appear after it's published on the Web, you must preview your page. You can preview your page in the Editor by clicking the Preview tab in the lower-left corner of the window. You can also preview your page by launching a separate web browser. To do so, on the Standard toolbar, click the Preview in Browser button, or choose File⇨Preview in Browser to display the Preview in Browser dialog box. Choose the browser and screen size you want, and then click Preview.

Unit 4 Summary

▶ **Headings:** Headings are paragraph styles that help you prioritize information in your page. The Editor provides six levels of headings, with Heading 1 being the boldest style and Heading 6 the smallest. To apply a heading to a paragraph, click inside the paragraph and then, from the Change Style list box on the Format toolbar, choose a heading style.

▶ **Numbered and bulleted lists:** The two most popular types of lists in Web pages are numbered and bulleted lists. To create a numbered or bulleted list, highlight the paragraphs you want to turn into a list, and then, on the Format toolbar, click the Numbered List or Bulleted List button.

▶ **Definition lists:** Definition lists are a good way to format lists of terms and their definitions. To create a definition list, type the terms and definitions in the page. Click inside a term, and then, from the Change Style list box on the Format toolbar, choose Defined Term (repeat this task for each term in the list). Next click inside each definition, and then, from the Change Style list box on the Format toolbar, choose Definition.

Part II Review

◆ **Horizontal lines:** Horizontal lines span the width of your Web page, and can be inserted anywhere you want to create a visual separation between sections. To insert a horizontal line, choose Insert⇨Horizontal Line. To change the horizontal line's attributes, double-click the line to display the Horizontal Line Properties dialog box. Choose the options you want, and then click OK.

Unit 5 Summary

◆ **What is a hyperlink?** A hyperlink is a bit of text or a picture that, when clicked, transports the visitor to a new location. The new location may be inside the same page, in a different page, or in a different location on the Internet. If the hyperlink is connected to an e-mail address or a downloadable file, clicking the hyperlink activates the visitor's e-mail program or initiates a download.

◆ **Creating hyperlinks:** To create a hyperlink, highlight the thing you want to turn into a link, and then click the Create or Edit Hyperlink button to display the Edit Hyperlink dialog box. This dialog box enables you to create a link to another page in your Web site, a location on the Web, an e-mail address, a file on your computer, or a new page. Choose the link destination you want, and then click OK.

◆ **What is a bookmark?** A bookmark is an invisible flag you use to define a hyperlink destination. After you create a bookmark, you can create hyperlinks that lead directly to the bookmark instead of to the top of the page.

◆ **Creating a bookmark:** To create a bookmark, highlight text or place the cursor where you want the bookmark to sit, and then choose

Edit⇨Bookmark to display the Bookmark dialog box. Specify a bookmark name, and then click OK.

◆ **Creating a hyperlink that leads to a bookmark:** To create a link to a bookmark, create a regular hyperlink, but before you close the Edit Hyperlink dialog box, choose a bookmark name from the Bookmark list box, and then click OK.

◆ **Choosing hyperlink colors:** Choose Format⇨Background to display the Page Properties dialog box. Choose colors from the Hyperlink, Visited Hyperlink, and Active Hyperlink list boxes, and then click OK.

◆ **What is a navigation bar?** A navigation bar is a group of hyperlinks that lead to other pages in your site, helping visitors find their way around. FrontPage automatically generates navigation bars based on the structure of the site, as represented in a navigational structure. You create a navigational structure by arranging pages in a hierarchical flow chart using the Explorer's Navigation View.

◆ **Creating a navigation bar:** In the Explorer's Navigation View, create a navigational structure. Switch to the Editor, and place the cursor in the page where you want the navigation bar to appear. Choose Insert⇨Navigation Bar to display the Navigation Bar Properties dialog box. Choose the settings you want, and then click OK.

Unit 6 Summary

◆ **Web graphics basics:** You can use two types of graphic formats in Web pages: GIF and JPEG. If you insert another type of graphic into your Web page, the Editor converts a copy of the file into GIF or JPEG format. Graphics add color and interest, but also increase the page's total download time, so use graphics judiciously.

Part II Review

▶ **Inserting a graphic:** To insert an image in your page, on the Standard toolbar, click the Insert Image button to display the Image dialog box. This dialog box enables you to insert into your page a graphic that is stored in your Web site, elsewhere on your computer, on the Web, or in the Microsoft Clip Gallery. Choose the image you want to insert, and then click OK.

▶ **Changing the image display:** You can change how the image is positioned in your page by changing options in the Image Properties dialog box. To access this dialog box, right-click an image, and then, from the shortcut menu that appears, choose Image Properties. This dialog box lets you change how the image is aligned with surrounding text, how much blank space surrounds the image, adjust the image's dimensions, and give the image an alternate text label. Choose the options you want, and then click OK.

▶ **Changing the image file itself:** The Editor can perform simple image-editing tasks, including making GIF images transparent, cropping images, applying a washout, turning color images black and white, rotating and flipping images, changing brightness and contrast levels, and beveling the image's border. To accomplish these tasks, click the image, and then click the corresponding button on the Image toolbar.

▶ **Inserting a background image:** You can use an image as the backdrop of a page. The Editor tiles the image until the image fills the entire page background area. To use an image as the page's background, choose Format➪Background to display the Page Properties dialog box. In Background Image text box, enter the image's filename or location, and then click OK.

▶ **Save Embedded Files dialog box:** If you save a page containing images, the Save Embedded Files dialog box appears when one of the images has been edited or is currently stored elsewhere on your computer. This dialog box enables you to control how and where the image is saved. Choose the settings you want, and then click OK.

▶ **What's a theme?** A theme is a set of coordinated text fonts, colors, background graphics, banner graphics, buttons, bullets, and horizontal lines. You can apply one of over 50 themes to your Web site.

▶ **Applying a theme to a Web site:** In the Explorer's Themes View, click the name of the theme you want to apply to the open Web site.

▶ **Inserting a page banner:** If your Web site uses a theme, you can insert a decorative page banner in your site. To do so, on the Editor's Standard toolbar, click the FrontPage Component button to display the Insert FrontPage Component dialog box. Click Page Banner, and then click OK.

Unit 7 Summary

▶ **What is an image map?** An image map is a graphic hyperlink that leads to different places, depending on where inside the graphic the visitor clicks. The clickable areas inside the image map are called hotspots. Hotspots work just like regular hyperlinks, but are invisible when viewed with a web browser.

▶ **Creating an image map:** Creating an image map involves two steps: 1) inserting the image map graphic into the page, and 2) drawing hotspots on the image. If you publish your Web site on a web server that doesn't support FrontPage Server Extensions, you also must specify the image map's style. The style you choose (NCSA, CERN, or Netscape) depends on the type of web server to which you publish your site.

Part II Review

▶ **Drawing hotspots:** The Editor's Image toolbar contains buttons that activate hotspot drawing tools. You can draw circular, rectangular, or polygonal hotspots, and then attach the hotspots to link destinations.

▶ **Default link:** You can specify a hyperlink destination for the area in the image that lies outside hotspot boundaries. To do so, right-click the image map graphic, and then, from the shortcut menu that appears, choose Image Properties to display the Image Properties dialog box. Enter a location in the Location text box, and then click OK.

Unit 8 Summary

▶ **What is a table?** A table is a grid-like structure of cells, arranged into rows and columns. You can insert text, graphics, and other page elements into a table. By turning off the table's borders, you can use a table as an invisible framework for page layout.

▶ **Creating a table:** The Editor offers four table creation methods: the Insert Table button (on the Standard toolbar), the Table⇨Insert Table command, table drawing tools (on the Table toolbar), and the Table⇨Convert Text to Table command.

▶ **Changing the table's attributes:** The Table Properties dialog box contains options that enable you to adjust the table's dimensions, alignment, border thickness, cell padding, and cell spacing. (Cell padding is the amount of space separating the cell contents from cell borders, and cell spacing is the amount of space between cells.) To access the Table Properties dialog box, click inside the table, and then choose Table⇨Table Properties. Choose the settings you want, and then click OK.

▶ **Resizing tables by hand:** If you prefer to eyeball your table's dimensions, click the top or right border of the table and drag the border to the desired position.

▶ **Adding and deleting rows and columns:** To insert a new table row, highlight an existing row, and then, on the Table toolbar, click the Insert Row button. To insert a new column, highlight an existing column, and then click the Insert Column button. To delete a row or column, highlight the cells you want to delete, and then click the Delete Cells button.

▶ **Resizing cells, rows, and columns:** Click row and cell borders and then drag them to the desired position. Alternatively, select the cell, row, or column you want to resize, and then choose Table⇨Cell Properties to display the Cell Properties dialog box. Enter dimension measurements in the Specify Width and Specify Height text boxes, and then click OK.

▶ **Merging and splitting cells:** To merge multiple cells into a single cell, select the cells you want to merge, and then click the Merge Cells button. Alternatively, click the Eraser button, and then drag the cursor over the cell borders you want to remove. To split a single cell into multiple cells, click the Split Cell button to display the Split Cells dialog box. Choose your desired options, and then click OK.

▶ **Aligning cell contents:** To vertically align cell contents, select the cells you want to align, and then click the Align Top, Center Vertically, or Align Bottom button. To horizontally align cell contents, select the cells you want to align, and then click the Align Left, Center, or Align Right button.

▶ **Adding color to a table:** To give a table background color, select the cells you want to change, and then click the Background Color button. To change the table's border colors, click inside the table, and then choose Table⇨Table Properties to display the Table Properties dialog box. Choose colors from the Border, Light Border, or Dark Border list boxes, and then click OK.

Part II Test

Take this test as a review of the material covered in Part II, Units 3 through 8. You covered a lot of ground in this part, and this test will help you remember the information.

If you'd like to check your answers, refer to Appendix B.

True False

T F 1. Font styles apply to selected text (characters, words, and blocks of text), whereas paragraph styles apply to entire paragraphs.

T F 2. To preview your page, you must launch a separate web browser.

T F 3. How you answer this question doesn't matter, because no one is grading this test.

T F 4. Hyperlinks can lead only to other Web pages.

T F 5. To connect a hyperlink to a specific spot inside a Web page, you must place a bookmark in that spot, and then connect the hyperlink to the bookmark.

T F 6. Inserting lots of graphics into a Web page doesn't affect the page's download speed (and if it did, who cares?).

T F 7. The Editor can convert graphics saved in other file formats into GIF or JPEG.

T F 8. An image map is another name for a graphic hyperlink.

T F 9. If you give a table a proportional width, the table's size is dependent on the size of the visitor's browser window.

T F 10. The Editor's page templates use invisible tables to structure layout.

Multiple Choice

For each of the following questions, circle the correct answer or answers.

11. **What types of lists can you use in a Web page?**

    A. A numbered list.

    B. A laundry list.

    C. A to-do list.

    D. A definition list.

    E. A bulleted list.

12. **How do you create a navigation bar?**

    A. First, you create hyperlinks that connect the site's pages together. Then you choose Insert⇨Navigation Bar and select the links you want to include in the navigation bar.

    B. You click the Navigation Bar button on the Editor's Standard toolbar.

    C. First, you define the site's structure by creating a navigational structure in the Explorer's Navigation View. Then you switch to the Editor and choose Insert⇨Navigation Bar.

    D. You create individual links to the site's pages, and then copy and paste each link into each page in the site.

    E. You follow a recipe.

Part II Test

13. **Which page elements change when you apply a theme to your Web site?**

    A. Page background.

    B. Navigation bars.

    C. Text and hyperlink colors.

    D. Bulleted lists.

    E. Horizontal lines.

14. **How do you turn a traditional grid-like table into an invisible table?**

    A. Say "abracadabra."

    B. Set the table's border width to 0.

    C. Choose Table⇨Hide Table.

    D. Click the Eraser button and erase the table borders.

    E. Change the table border color from Default to Transparent.

Matching

15. **Match each of the following buttons with its name:**

    A. **B**

    B. [table icon]

    C. [preview icon]

    D. [image icon]

    E. [globe icon]

    1. Insert Image

    2. Create or Edit Hyperlink

    3. Bold

    4. Insert Table

    5. Preview in Browser

16. **Match each of the following buttons with its function:**

    A. [pencil icon]

    B. **A**

    C. [palette icon]

    D. [icon]

    E. [icon]

    1. Changes the color of selected text

    2. Inserts a new row in a table

    3. Increases text size

    4. Makes an image transparent

    5. Shows the FrontPage Explorer

17. **Match each of the following Editor commands or tasks with another action that accomplishes the same thing:**

    A. Choose File⇨Preview in Browser.

    B. Choose Table⇨Table Properties.

    C. Click the Insert Image button.

    D. From the Change Style list box on the Format toolbar, choose Bulleted List.

    E. Click the Text Color button.

    1. Choose Format⇨Font. From the Font Properties dialog box that appears, choose a color from the Color list box, and then click OK.

    2. Right-click the table, and then, from the shortcut menu that appears, choose Table Properties.

    3. Click the Bulleted List button.

    4. Click the Preview in Browser button.

    5. Choose Insert⇨Image.

Part II Lab Assignment

This lab assignment continues where the Part I Lab Assignment left off. At the end of Part I, you created a new Web site based on a personal project you want to accomplish. In this lab assignment, you flesh out the Web site by adding and formatting its content. You pull the site together with hyperlinks, navigation bars, and a theme. You add graphics and (if you like) an image map for some color and variety. The specifics are up to you — this project gives you the chance to create whatever site you want.

Don't hesitate to flip back through the units in this part if you can't remember how to do something.

Step 1: Launch FrontPage, and open the Web site you created in the Part I Lab Assignment

Step 2: Open one or more of the site's pages

Step 3: Add text to the pages, and format the text with styles, headings, and lists

Use only those text effects that help make the information easier to understand. If you find your site needs more pages, create new pages and fill them with content.

Step 4: Save all your pages

Step 5: Insert at least three hyperlinks in your site: one to another page inside the Web site, one to another location on the Internet, and one to your e-mail address

Step 6: Apply your favorite theme to the Web site

Step 7: Insert an image button-based navigation bar in each page

In other words, switch to the Explorer's Navigation View and create a navigational structure. After the structure is complete, switch back to the Editor and insert a navigation bar into your page.

Part II Lab Assignment

Step 8: Insert a page banner in each page

Step 9: If you have any graphics available, insert them into your pages

Perhaps, somewhere on your hard drive, you have a company logo, or a photograph of your dog. After you insert the graphic, notice how it adds to — or detracts from — your page's content.

Step 10: Use an invisible table to structure the layout of the site's home page

Try inserting a table in the page, and then cutting and pasting the page's text into the table. Fiddle with the table's layout until you're happy with how the page looks.

Step 11: Preview the page in a web browser

Step 12: Switch back to the Editor and save all your pages

Step 13: Exit FrontPage

This Step means exiting the Editor, the Explorer, and the Personal Web Server.

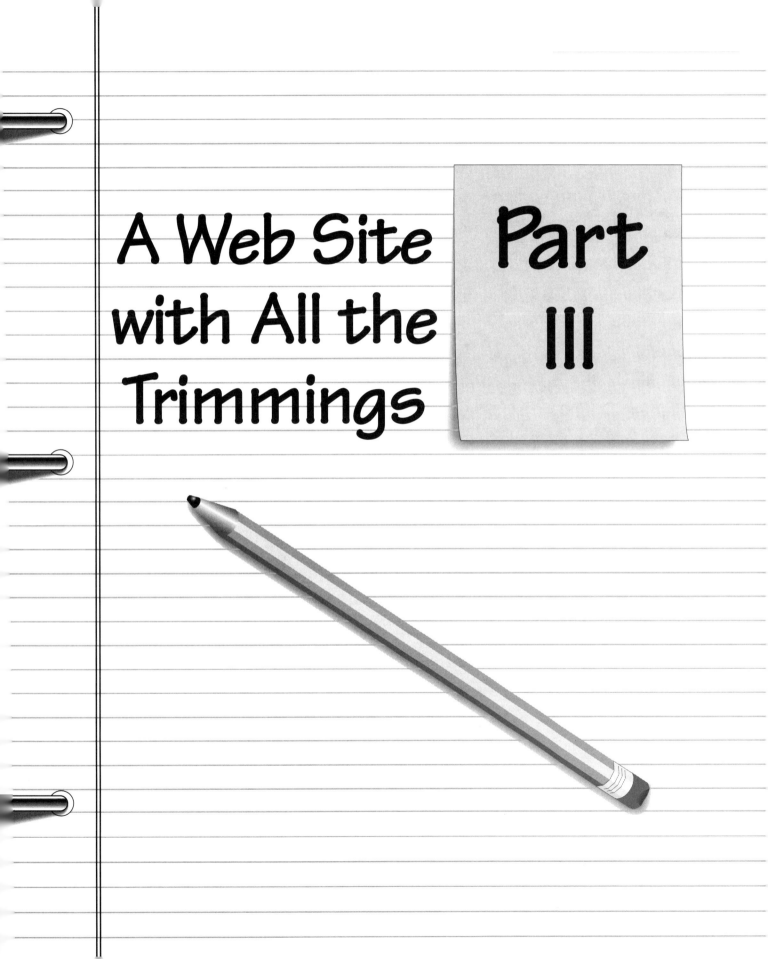

A Web Site with All the Trimmings

Part III

In this part . . .

Basic Web-building stuff such as adding and formatting text, working with pictures, and inserting hyperlinks are the required classes in the Web publishing program.

This part contains the electives — all the effects and additions that aren't mandatory but that give your site sparkle and cutting-edge cachet.

In this part, you add an interactive feedback form to My Web Site, you get familiar with frames, and you sample Active Elements and FrontPage Components.

Keeping in Touch Using Forms

Objectives for This Unit

- ✓ Understanding how forms work
- ✓ Creating a form
- ✓ Working with form fields
- ✓ Choosing how information submitted from forms gets processed
- ✓ Seeing form results

Prerequisites
- ▶ Launching FrontPage (Lesson 1-2)
- ▶ Creating a new Web Site from scratch (Lesson 1-3)
- ▶ Opening an existing Web site in the Explorer (Lesson 2-1)
- ▶ Launching the FrontPage Editor (Lesson 2-2)
- ▶ Saving a page (Lesson 2-6)
- ▶ Working with the *Dummies 101: FrontPage 98* example files (Lesson 3-1)
- ▶ Previewing a page (Lesson 3-6)

on the CD
- ▶ unit09.htm
- ▶ form.htm

Publishing a Web site isn't just about advertising a product or engaging in a one-way conversation — a Web site lets you enter into a dialog with people all over the world. To give your visitors a way to talk back, add an *interactive form* to your Web site.

Not so long ago, forms inhabited the realm of advanced HTML. Only experienced Web publishers knew how to create and work with forms. No more. With FrontPage, you can create a sophisticated form that enables visitors to send feedback, respond to a survey — and even order products — with no experience required.

In this unit, you add a feedback form to My Web Site so visitors can send you their questions and comments.

Lesson 9-1   **Understanding Form Fundamentals**

form fields =
places in a form
where visitors
supply information

form handler =
server-based
program that
processes
information sent
from forms

create a form by
using a page
template, the Form
Page Wizard, or by
building from
scratch

A quick overview of how forms work helps you understand each form-building task. In this lesson, I introduce you to the fundamentals of forms. After you have a sense for the big picture, you can confidently take the next step: building your own form.

on the test

A form is a special set of HTML tags that you add to your Web page to collect information from visitors. These tags create *fields,* or places in which visitors enter information or choose items from a list. Fields come in all shapes and sizes, such as text boxes, radio buttons, check boxes, drop-down menus, and more (you learn about each field type in upcoming lessons). Figure 9-1 illustrates a simple form containing two fields: one for the visitor's name and another that lets visitors specify a preference.

After visitors complete the form, they click the Submit button to send the information. What happens to that information after a visitor submits the completed form depends on the type of *form handler* assigned to the form. A form handler is a program that sits on the web server hosting the Web site. When form information is submitted, the form handler receives the form data and then does something with it. Depending on the type of form handler, the program may save the information in a text file, format the results as a Web page, or even send the information back to the site administrator in an e-mail message.

In this unit, you build a form from scratch by inserting individual form fields into a Web page. This approach is not the only way to build a form, however. The Editor provides two other options: using a form page template and launching the Form Page Wizard.

The Editor comes with four templates that you can use as a starting point for a form, as follows:

- ▶ **Feedback Form:** The Feedback Form template creates a form that visitors use to send comments, questions, or suggestions.

- ▶ **Guest Book:** The Guest Book template also collects comments but, in its case, saves the submissions in a public Web page that other visitors can read.

- ▶ **Search Page:** This template works with the Search Form Active Element to create a searchable keyword index of your Web site. You find out how to create a site search page in Unit 11.

- ▶ **User Registration:** The User Registration template creates a registration page that enables visitors to choose a unique user name and password to gain access to a members-only section of the Web site. For more information about FrontPage registration systems, refer to the FrontPage Help system by choosing Help⇨Microsoft FrontPage Help, or by pressing F1.

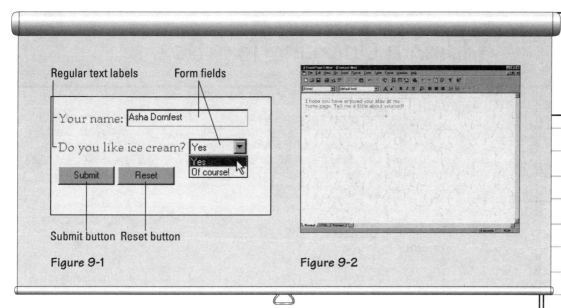

Regular text labels   Form fields

Your name: Asha Dornfest

Do you like ice cream? Yes
Yes
Of course!

Submit   Reset

Submit button   Reset button

Figure 9-1

Figure 9-2

Figure 9-1: A simple, two-field form.

Figure 9-2: This empty Web page is the basis of a feedback form.

Notes:

The Form Page Wizard leads you through the process of creating a sophisticated form by prompting you to choose categories of information, set the page layout, and choose what happens to form results. This Wizard works wonders and saves time, especially if you want to create a long, involved form. To launch the Form Page Wizard, in the Editor, choose File⇨New to display the New dialog box. In the dialog box, double-click Form Page Wizard.

on the CD

In this unit, you use a file named unit09.htm (stored in the FP101 folder) as the basis of a feedback form, which you add to My Web Site in the steps that follow.

1 **Launch FrontPage, and open My Web Site.**

If you're not sure how to open a Web site, refer to Lesson 2-1.

2 **On the Explorer toolbar, click Show FrontPage Editor.**

The Editor launches, and presents you with a new page. (If the Editor is already open, click the New Button on the Standard toolbar to create a new page.)

3 **Using the Insert⇨File command, insert the contents of the file named unit09.htm (located in the FP101 folder) into the page.**

For detailed instructions on how to use the Insert⇨File command, see Lesson 3-1.

The contents of the example file appear inside the page (see Figure 9-2). The page contains a background graphic and a nice color scheme because of the Arcs theme that you applied to My Web Site in Unit 6.

4 **Save the new page as part of your Web site, title the page Contact Me, and name the page feedback.htm.**

The page is empty except for introductory text and a horizontal line. In the lessons that follow, you transform the page into a form.

Show FrontPage Editor button

☑ **Progress Check**

If you can do the following, you've mastered this lesson:

❑ Know what a form is, what it can do, and the basics of how it works.

Lesson 9-2   Adding a One-Line Text Box

To build a form, you add one or more form fields to a page and then customize the fields to work the way you want. The first time you add a form field to a page, the Editor creates a form boundary in the page, inside which you can insert more form fields. The Editor also inserts Submit and Reset buttons at the bottom of the form. Visitors click these buttons to submit form information and to clear form contents.

The Editor simplifies inserting form fields by providing a Forms toolbar (see Figure 9-3). To make the toolbar visible on-screen, choose View⇨Forms Toolbar.

One-line text boxes are a species of form field that appears most often in Web pages. Visitors enter a single line of text into a one-line text box.

In the steps that follow, you begin your form by inserting a one-line text box into the Contact Me page. The purpose of this field is to collect the visitor's name.

1 **In the Contact Me page, place the cursor to the right of the horizontal line and then press Enter to create a new line.**

2 **On the Forms toolbar, click One-Line Text Box.**

A one-line text box appears in your page, along with a form boundary (a rectangular area surrounded by dotted lines) and Submit and Reset buttons (see Figure 9-4). After you insert a field, you must customize the field.

3 **In the page, double-click the one-line text box field.**

The Text Box Properties dialog box appears (see Figure 9-5).

4 **In the dialog box's Name text box, type Name.**

Every form field must have a field name. FrontPage provides a default name for each field you create (in this case, the default field name is *T1*). You should replace the default name with a one-word field name that describes the information that the field collects. In this case, the text box collects the visitor's name; hence the field name *Name*.

5 **In the Width In Characters text box, type 30.**

In this step, you increase the visible width of the text box to 30 characters (if you prefer to resize the field by hand, after you're finished with this set of steps, click the text box field and drag its size handles to a new position).

What about the dialog box's Initial Value text box, you ask? I explain this text box at the end of this lesson, and you get to use the text box later in the unit.

6 **Click OK to close the Text Box Properties dialog box.**

7 **In the page, place the cursor directly before the one-line text box field (but still inside the form boundary), type Your name, and then press Enter.**

This text label tells visitors what information to enter into the field.

one-line text box field = single line of text

One-Line Text Box button

create a new form by inserting a form field into a regular page

Check Box

Scrolling Text Box

One-Line Text Box

Radio Button

Drop-Down Menu

Push Button

Figure 9-3

Form field

Form boundary

Figure 9-4

Figure 9-5

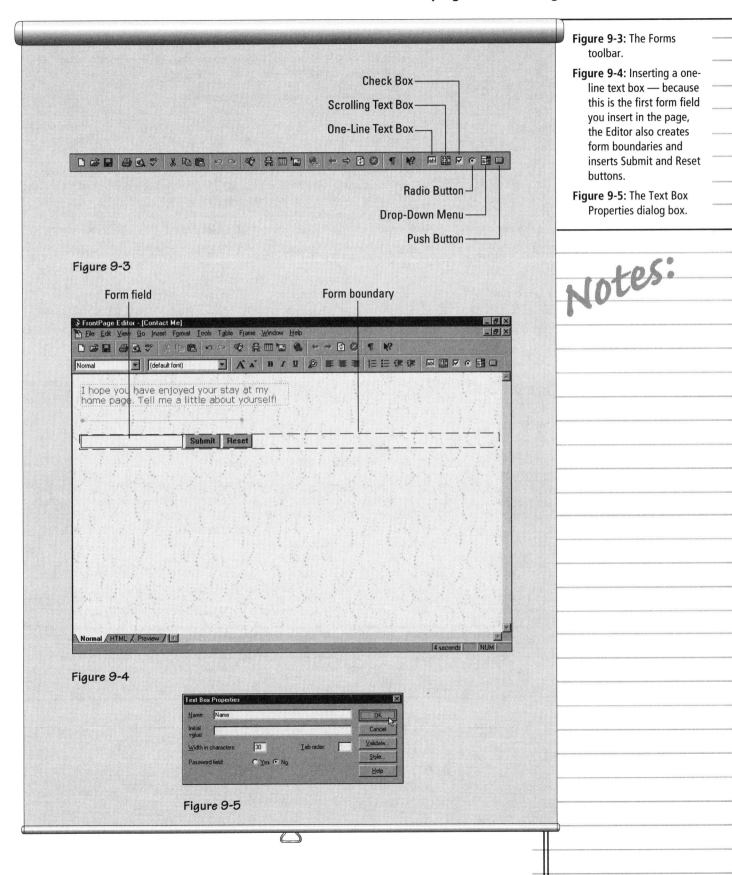

Figure 9-3: The Forms toolbar.

Figure 9-4: Inserting a one-line text box — because this is the first form field you insert in the page, the Editor also creates form boundaries and inserts Submit and Reset buttons.

Figure 9-5: The Text Box Properties dialog box.

Notes:

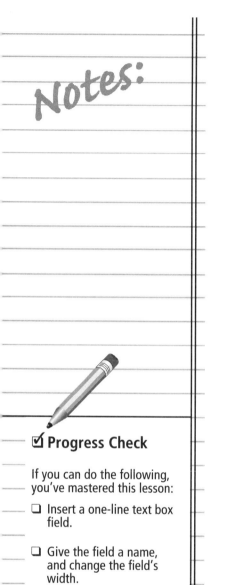

Notes:

☑ Progress Check

If you can do the following, you've mastered this lesson:

❏ Insert a one-line text box field.

❏ Give the field a name, and change the field's width.

8 **Press the → (right arrow) key to move the cursor directly after the one-line text box field, and then press Enter.**

The Submit and Reset buttons move to a new line.

The Text Box Properties dialog box contains a few options you didn't need to use in the preceding steps, so I explain them here:

⬧ **Initial value:** When you create a new one-line text box field, the field appears empty. To have the field appear with text already filled in, enter the text in the Initial Value text box. You can use initial text to provide an example of the data you want visitors to enter, or you can indicate the most common response, saving many of your visitors some typing.

⬧ **Tab order:** The *tab order* is the order in which the cursor jumps between fields when a visitor presses the Tab key. By entering a number in the Tab Order text box, you can control the sequence in which the cursor moves. In this form, the default tab order (in which the cursor moves between fields sequentially) is just fine, so I leave the Tab Order text box alone.

heads up

The tab order control works only for those of your visitors who use the Internet Explorer browser, Version 4.0 or later.

⬧ **Password field:** Password fields are no different from regular text box fields except that, if viewed with a browser, text that someone types into a password field appears on-screen as dots or asterisks.

heads up

Including a password field in your form does *not* automatically provide password protection; doing so requires coordination with your ISP, or using a FrontPage registration system.

⬧ **Data validation:** By clicking the Validate button, you can set up rules to check the information entered into the field. You can specify the format of text or numbers someone enters into a field, or you can make certain fields mandatory — so that visitors cannot submit the form until they fill in all the required fields.

To find out more about registration systems and form validation, refer to the FrontPage Help system by choosing Help⇨Microsoft FrontPage Help, or by pressing F1.

Lesson 9-3

Adding a Scrolling Text Box

scrolling text box
field = more than
one line of text

A *scrolling text box* can hold more than one line of text and is a good choice for collecting comments, questions, and other lengthy responses.

You now add a scrolling text box to your feedback form to collect your visitors' comments. The process is the same as for adding any other type of form field: First insert the field, and then customize the field.

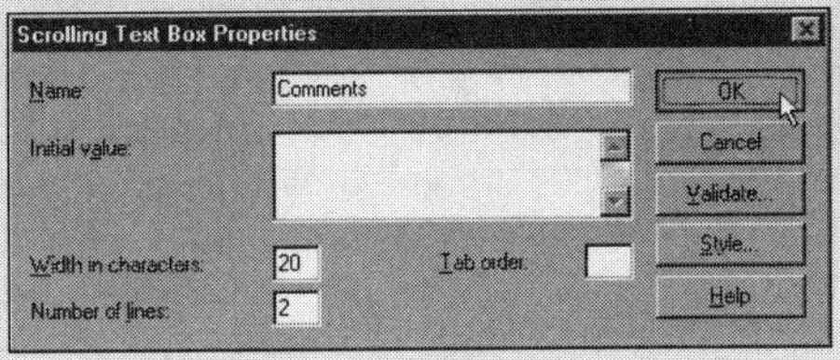

Figure 9-6

Figure 9-6: The Scrolling
Text Box Properties
dialog box.

1 **With the cursor to the left of the Submit button, type** What would you
like to tell me?**, and then press Enter.**

2 **Click Scrolling Text Box.**

A scrolling text box field appears in the page.

3 **Press Enter to move the Submit and Reset buttons to a new line.**

4 **In the page, double-click the scrolling text box field to customize it.**

The Scrolling Text Box Properties dialog box appears (see Figure 9-6). This
dialog box contains many of the same options as the Text Box Properties dialog
box you used in the preceding lesson. The dialog box contains an additional
space for the scrolling text box field's height dimension (the Number of Lines
text box).

5 **In the Name text box, type** Comments.

As with the text box field name, you replace the generic field name supplied by
FrontPage with a more descriptive name.

6 **Click OK to close the dialog box.**

Scrolling Text Box
button

The scrolling text box field looks admittedly puny — especially considering
that it must be able to hold the volumes of praise that visitors are sure to heap
on your site. Instead of changing the field's dimensions by entering pixel
values in the Width in Characters and Number of Lines text boxes, you now
resize the field by hand . . . I mean, by mouse.

1 **In the page, click the size handle (the little black square) sitting on
the lower-right corner of the scrolling text box field and, while
holding down the mouse button, drag the border down and to the
right.**

Stretch the border until you feel that the field is big enough to hold your
visitors' comments.

2 **Release the mouse button.**

The field changes size.

☑ Progress Check

If you can do the following,
you've mastered this lesson:

❏ Insert a scrolling text
box field.

❏ Give the field a name.

❏ Resize the field by
dragging the field's
borders.

Lesson 9-4   Adding a Group of Check Boxes

check box fields =
choose more than
one option (or none)
from a list of
choices

field name =
identifying label

field value =
information
contained in field

Check Box button

Check boxes enable visitors to select as many items from a predefined list as they want. You can include a single check box field in your form, or you can group them together (as you do in this lesson).

on the test

Unlike with the text box fields, you must specify a *value* for each check box field. Where the field name is a label that identifies the field, the field's value is its contents. With text box fields, the field's value is the information that visitors type into the field. With check box fields, you must specify what a marked check box signifies.

To understand what I mean, proceed with the following steps, in which you add two check box fields to your feedback form.

1 **With the cursor to the right of the scrolling text box field, press Enter to create a new line.**

The cursor is now sitting in a blank line between the scrolling text box field and the Submit and Reset buttons.

2 **Type** Type of feedback **and press Enter.**

3 **Click Check Box.**

A check box field appears in your page.

4 **Type** Comment **and press Shift+Enter.**

5 **Click the Check Box button to insert a second check box field.**

6 **Type** Question **and press Enter.**

You now customize each check box field.

7 **In the page, double-click the first check box field.**

The Check Box Properties dialog box appears (see Figure 9-7).

8 **In the Name text box, type** Feedback.

9 **In the Value text box, type** Comment.

The value is Comment because, by checking this field, a visitor indicates this particular bit of feedback is a comment.

10 **Click the Checked radio button.**

By doing so, you tell the Editor that you want the Comment check box to appear initially checked.

11 **Click OK.**

The Check Box Properties dialog box closes. Now you customize the second check box field.

12 **In the page, double-click the second check box field.**

The Check Box Properties dialog box appears.

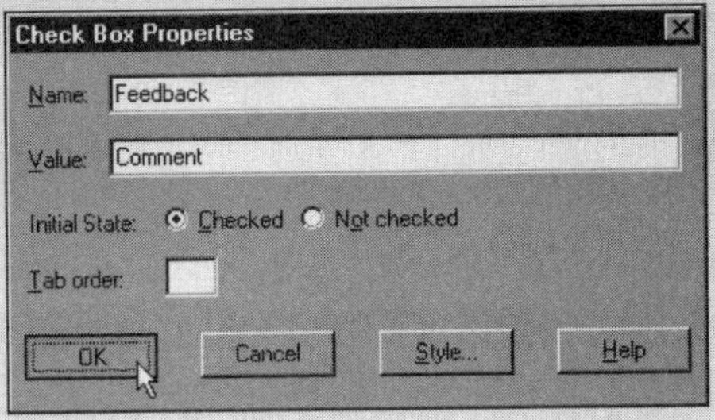

Figure 9-7: The Check Box Properties dialog box.

Figure 9-7

Notes:

13 In the **Name text box, type** Feedback.

14 In the **Value text box, type** Question.

15 Click OK.

The dialog box closes, and the fields are now complete.

When you use check box fields, keep in mind that you enable visitors to check more than one option — or no options at all. If you want visitors to choose a single option, or if you want to take away the option of *not* choosing, use a group of radio button fields instead (Lesson 9-5 shows you how).

extra credit

Push button fields

The Submit and Reset buttons sitting on your form are members of a group of fields called *push button fields.* Push button fields create a rectangular button in a page, which, when clicked, does something. In a working form, clicking the Submit button submits the information entered into the form, and clicking the Reset button clears the form's contents.

If the labels *Submit* and *Reset* rub you the wrong way, you can change them. To do so, follow these steps:

1. **Double-click the button you want to change.**

The Push Button Properties dialog box appears.

2. **In the Value/Label text box, enter a new button label.**

3. **Click OK.**

The dialog box closes, and the new label appears on the button.

For more information about push button fields, refer to the FrontPage Help system by choosing Help➪Microsoft FrontPage Help, or by pressing F1.

☑ **Progress Check**

If you can do the following, you've mastered this lesson:

❑ Insert a check box field.

❑ Give the field a name and a value.

Recess

Form building isn't difficult, but it does involve a lot of steps. Click Save, take a break for awhile, and think about how much you've progressed since you started using this book. You really have come a long way. Reward yourself by turning on the liveliest music you can find and dancing with abandon. Who cares whether people stare? You get your blood flowing, and you're energized, renewed, and, I'll bet, in a good mood by the time you sit down to finish your form.

Don't laugh — I do this all the time.

Lesson 9-5

Adding a Group of Radio Buttons

radio button group =
choose one option
from a list of
choices

Radio Button
button

Unlike check boxes, *radio buttons* must appear in a group. Each group of radio buttons contains one option that appears initially marked. When a visitor clicks another radio button in the group, the first one becomes unmarked.

In this lesson, you use radio buttons to present visitors with a Yes/No answer choice to a question.

1 **In the page, place the cursor in the blank space between the group of check box fields and the Submit and Reset buttons.**

2 **Type** Would you like a response? **and press Enter.**

3 **Click Radio Button.**

A single radio button appears in your page.

4 **Type** Yes **and then press Shift+Enter.**

5 **Click the Radio Button button to insert a second radio button.**

6 **Type** No **and then press Enter.**

Now you customize the pair of radio button fields.

7 **In the page, double-click the first radio button field to customize it.**

The Radio Button Properties dialog box appears (see Figure 9-8).

8 **In the Group Name text box, type** Response.

9 **In the Value text box, type** Yes.

10 **Click OK to close the Radio Button Properties dialog box.**

11 **In the page, double-click the second radio button field to customize it.**

The Radio Button Properties dialog box appears.

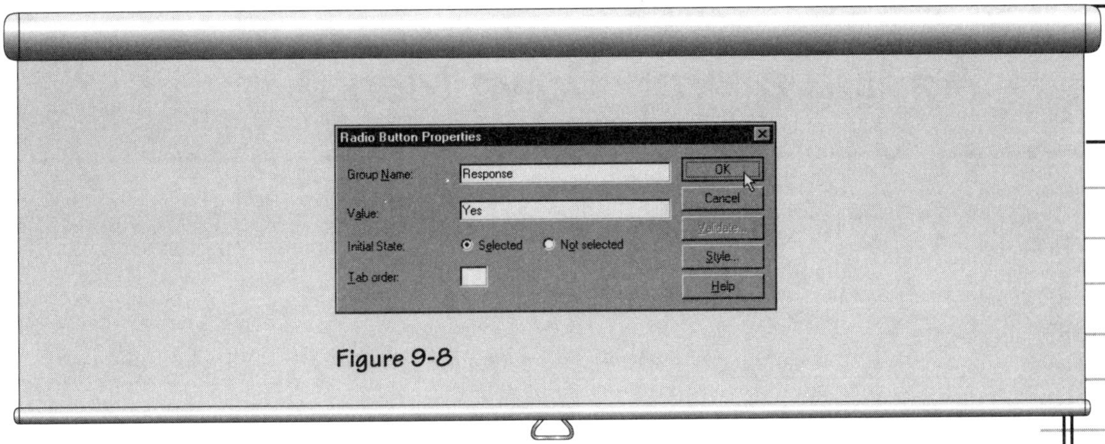

Figure 9-8

Figure 9-8: The Radio Button Properties dialog box.

Notes:

12 **In the Group Name text box, type** Response.

Unless all the radio button fields in the group have the same name, the fields won't function correctly.

13 **In the Value text box, type** No.

14 **Click OK.**

Bravo — you just created a fine radio button group. Your visitors can now tell you whether they expect you to respond to their question or comment. But wait a minute. . . . How can you respond if you don't know your visitor's e-mail address? Aha . . . time to add another text box field to your form.

1 **In the page, place the cursor in the empty space beneath the radio button group.**

2 **Type** If Yes, what is your e-mail address? **and then press Enter.**

3 **Click One-Line Text Box.**

A text box field appears in the page.

4 **In the page, double-click the text box field.**

The Text Box Properties dialog box appears.

5 **In the Name text box, type** Email.

6 **In the Initial Value text box, type** username@domain.com.

Here is a good example of using a field's initial value to model the type of response you want visitors to provide.

Keep in mind that if a visitor doesn't change the contents of the field before submitting the form information, the value of this field will be listed as `username@domain.com`.

7 **Click OK to close the Text Box Properties dialog box.**

Now you will be able to reply to your visitor's queries.

One-Line Text Box button

☑ Progress Check

If you can do the following, you've mastered this lesson:

❏ Insert a group of radio buttons.

❏ Give each field a name and a value.

❏ Add initial text to a text box field.

Lesson 9-6   Adding a Drop-Down Menu

drop-down menu =
choose one or more
items from a list of
choices

[icon]
Drop-Down Menu
button

Drop-down menus offer another way for visitors to choose an option from a list of choices that you define. The major difference between drop-down menus and radio button groups is cosmetic. Unlike radio buttons, however, you can set up a drop-down menu to accept more than one choice.

In this lesson, you add a drop-down menu to your feedback form to find out how your visitor found out about you.

1 **In the page, place the cursor to the right of the text box field you just inserted, and then press Enter.**

2 **Type** How did you find my site? **and press Enter.**

3 **Click Drop-Down Menu.**

A drop-down menu field appears in your page.

4 **Double-click the drop-down menu field in your page to customize it.**

The Drop-Down Menu Properties dialog box appears (as shown in Figure 9-9).

5 **In the <u>N</u>ame text box, type** Referred.

6 **To add choices to the drop-down menu, click <u>A</u>dd.**

The Add Choice dialog box appears (see Figure 9-10). In this dialog box, you enter the items you want to appear in the drop-down menu.

7 **In the Ch<u>o</u>ice text box, type** Web surfing.

Notice how the words Web surfing also appear in the Specify Value text box. If you wanted the field's value to be something different from the text displayed in the drop-down menu, you would check the Specify Value check box and then type a new value in the corresponding text box. In this example, you don't need to specify a different value.

8 **Click OK to close the Add Choice dialog box.**

The Drop-Down Menu Properties dialog box becomes visible again.

9 **Repeat Steps 6 through 8 to add two more menu choices.**

Name the choices **Search engine** and **Word of mouth**.

10 **Click OK to close the Drop-Down Menu Properties dialog box.**

The drop-down menu appears in your page, with the first menu item visible.

rearrange, modify,
or remove menu
items in the Drop-
Down Menu
Properties dialog
box by clicking the
item and then
clicking Move Up,
Move Down, Modify,
or Remove

Because you didn't use the following three items in the Drop-Down Menu Properties dialog box in the previous steps, they deserve some explanation:

▸ **Height text box:** By default, only the first menu item is visible when a drop-down menu appears in a page. To make more than one item initially visible, type a number in the Height text box. (You can also adjust the height and width of a drop-down menu — after you're finished defining its properties — by clicking the drop-down menu in your page and dragging the field's size handles.)

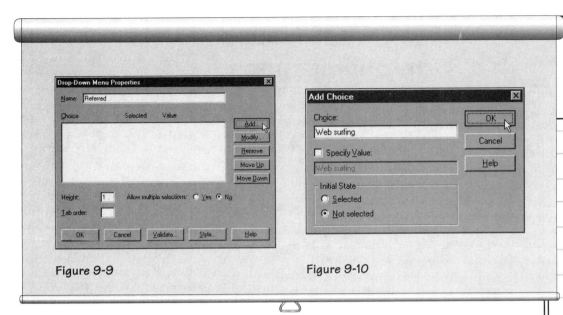

Figure 9-9

Figure 9-10

Figure 9-9: The Drop-Down Menu Properties dialog box.

Figure 9-10: The Add Choice dialog box.

Notes:

♦ **Allow multiple selections:** To enable visitors to choose more than one item from the drop-down menu, click the Yes radio button in the Allow Multiple Selections area. When visitors fill out the form, they can choose more than one option by holding down Ctrl or Ô as they click their selections.

♦ **Validation options:** Drop-down menu validation options enable you to require visitors to choose an item from the drop-down menu, and also let you to disallow the first menu item as an option (for example, the first menu item reads Choose one, and you don't want visitors to be able to choose that item as an option). To validate drop-down menu entries, click the Validate button to display the Drop-Down Menu Validation dialog box. To require that visitors choose an item from the list, click the Data Required check box. (In the case of multiple selection menus, you can specify a minimum and maximum number of choices.) To disallow the first menu choice as a valid selection, select the Disallow First Item check box. Click OK to close the Drop-Down Menu Validation dialog box.

extra credit

Using hidden fields

Hidden fields . . . sound mysterious? A hidden field isn't sinister; it is simply an invisible field that contains static information. Hidden fields enable you to send information along with form submissions that a) doesn't change, and b) visitors don't see. Most often, hidden fields are used in conjunction with custom form-handling scripts to pass information to the script to determine how the script functions (you find out more about the form-submission process in Lesson 9-7). To find out more about hidden fields, including how to add them to your form, refer to the FrontPage Help system by choosing Help⇨Microsoft FrontPage Help, or by pressing F1.

☑ **Progress Check**

If you can do the following, you've mastered this lesson:

❑ Insert a drop-down menu field.

❑ Give the field a name, and add items to the field's menu list.

Lesson 9-7

Choosing What Happens to Form Submissions

Congratulations — your form is almost complete. (Figure 9-11 shows how the form looks so far.) The final step is to set up what happens to the information visitors enter into the form after they click Submit — where the information goes and how it is processed.

To do so, you must set up a *form handler*. A form handler is a server-based program that receives the information submitted from forms, and then transforms the information into a readable format such as a text file, a Web page, or an e-mail message. In this lesson, you adjust the FrontPage form handler so it saves form results in a Web page in a private location in your Web site.

heads up

The examples in this book assume that you will eventually publish your finished Web site on a web server that supports FrontPage Server Extensions. If your web server doesn't support FrontPage Server Extensions, FrontPage's built-in form handler won't work. No problem — you can set up your Web site to work with a custom form-handling script. See the Extra Credit sidebar "Working with a custom script" later in this lesson for more information.

By default, FrontPage saves form submissions in a text file stored in your Web site's _private folder (this protected folder doesn't allow browsing access from the outside world, but you can open the file any time you want). The field names and their values are listed in this results file, which can be formatted as a text file or a Web page — or both. Each time a new visitor submits a form, the new form results are added to the file.

In addition to saving form results in a file, you can tell FrontPage to send individual form submissions to you (or another site administrator) in the form of an e-mail message. This message has the advantage of signaling you each time a visitor submits a form.

The built-in FrontPage form handler also generates a *confirmation page* (a page that tells visitors that the form is successfully submitted) or a *validation failure page* (a page that appears if data entered into the form is invalid).

In the following steps, you configure the FrontPage form handler to save form results in a Web page named results.htm.

1 **Right-click inside the form and then, from the shortcut menu that appears, choose Form Properties.**

The Form Properties dialog box appears (see Figure 9-12). In this dialog box, you specify how and where you want form results saved. The Editor's default setting saves form results in a text file named form_results.txt. You now change this setting to instead save form results in a Web page.

2 **In the dialog box, click Options.**

The Options for Saving Results of Form dialog box appears, with the File Results tab visible (see Figure 9-13).

how forms are submitted depends on setup of the web server on which site is published

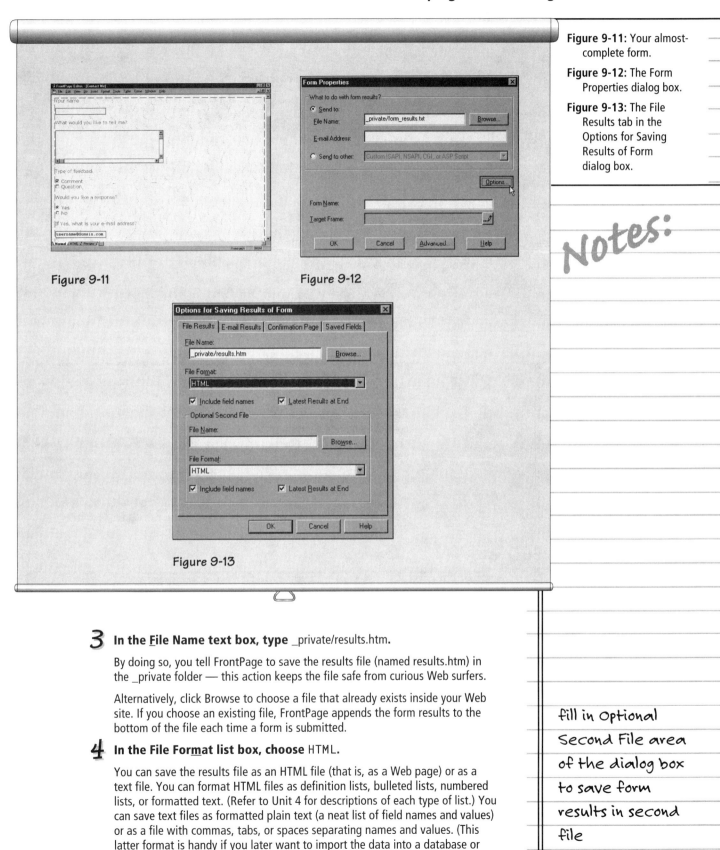

Figure 9-11

Figure 9-12

Figure 9-13

Figure 9-11: Your almost-complete form.

Figure 9-12: The Form Properties dialog box.

Figure 9-13: The File Results tab in the Options for Saving Results of Form dialog box.

Notes:

3 In the File Name text box, type _private/results.htm**.**

By doing so, you tell FrontPage to save the results file (named results.htm) in the _private folder — this action keeps the file safe from curious Web surfers.

Alternatively, click Browse to choose a file that already exists inside your Web site. If you choose an existing file, FrontPage appends the form results to the bottom of the file each time a form is submitted.

4 In the File Format list box, choose HTML**.**

You can save the results file as an HTML file (that is, as a Web page) or as a text file. You can format HTML files as definition lists, bulleted lists, numbered lists, or formatted text. (Refer to Unit 4 for descriptions of each type of list.) You can save text files as formatted plain text (a neat list of field names and values) or as a file with commas, tabs, or spaces separating names and values. (This latter format is handy if you later want to import the data into a database or spreadsheet.)

fill in Optional Second File area of the dialog box to save form results in second file

Figure 9-14: The Saved
Fields tab in the
Options for Saving
Results of Form dialog
box.

Notes:

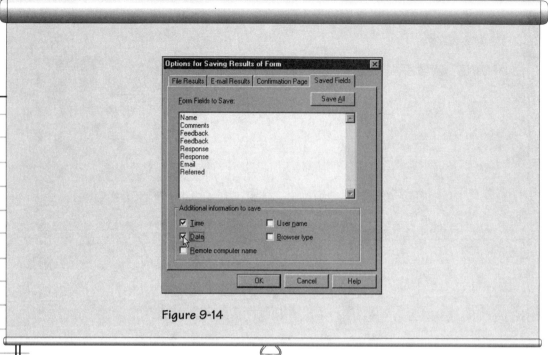

Figure 9-14

heads up

Be sure that the results filename visible in the File Name text box uses the
correct filename extension corresponding to the file type you choose in this
step. HTML files should be named with the filename extension .htm or .html,
and text files should be named with the extension .txt.

5 **At the top of the dialog box, click the Saved Fields tab.**

The Saved Fields tab appears (see Figure 9-14). This tab enables you to choose
which field results are saved in the results file. You can also tell FrontPage to
save additional information in the results file.

extra credit

Working with a custom script

If the web server on which you publish
your site doesn't support FrontPage Server
Extensions, or if you need special data-
processing capabilities that the FrontPage
form handler can't accommodate, you can
hook up your form to a custom *form-
handling script.* Like the FrontPage form
handler, the script receives and processes
form information and then outputs the

results. The script's internal programming
determines how form results are formatted and where they are stored.

To use a custom script, you need to work
with your ISP or system administrator. He
or she knows whether the web server
contains such a script, and if so, how it
works.

6 In the **F**orm Fields to Save box, highlight B1 **and then press the Delete key**.

B1 is the field name of the Submit button. You don't need to see the results of this field, because the button exists in your form only to activate the form handler.

7 In the Additional Information to Save area, mark the **D**ate and **T**ime check boxes.

8 Click OK to close the Options for Saving Results of Form dialog box.

9 Click OK to close the Form Properties dialog box.

Your form is now complete and is ready to be previewed and tested.

Previewing and Testing Your Form

Lesson 9-8

The proof is in the pudding — or should I say the preview? Previewing and testing your form in a web browser to be sure that it works properly is always wise. You do so in the steps that follow.

1 Save the Contact Me page.

2 Click Preview in Browser to preview the form page in your selected web browser.

Your web browser launches and displays the form page.

3 Fill out the form, entering any information you want into the form fields.

4 In the form, click Submit.

The FrontPage form handler springs into action, and in a moment, a confirmation page appears on-screen verifying your form submission (see Figure 9-15).

You now return to FrontPage to take a look at your form results file.

5 Switch back to the FrontPage Explorer, and choose **V**iew➪**R**efresh.

The Explorer updates the Web site display.

6 Open the file named results.htm (it's stored inside the _private folder).

The form results file opens in the Editor. The file contains a list of the field names along with the values that you chose, plus the date and time the form was submitted.

Save button

Preview in Browser button

Figure 9-15: A
confirmation page lets
you know that your
form has been
submitted successfully.

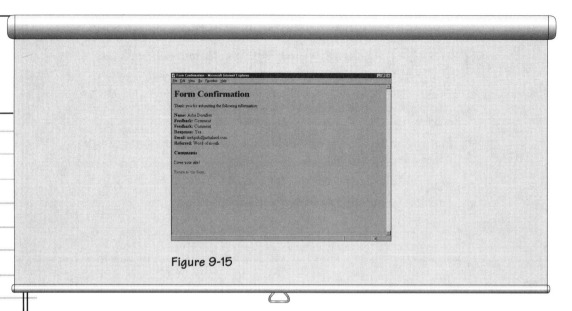

Figure 9-15

on the CD

Good job — you have just completed a fully functional interactive form. This example form works perfectly well, but could do with a cosmetic touch-up. Feel free to format the form field labels with text styles and formatting. Another excellent way to pretty up a page containing a form is to structure the form using an invisible table. Place the labels and fields inside individual table cells, and line up the cells however you like (for more information about tables, refer to Unit 8). For an example of how you can spruce up a form page with text formatting and tables, take a look at the file named form.htm sitting in the FP101 folder.

(After you're through, be sure to save your form page.)

☑ Progress Check

If you can do the following, you've mastered this lesson:

❑ Preview and test your form in a web browser.

❑ Open the form results file.

extra credit

Creating a custom confirmation page

The built-in FrontPage form handler generates a plain confirmation page each time a visitor submits a form. The confirmation page works, but it's not very attractive. Instead, why not design a custom confirmation page that fits in with the design of your site? It's easy. For details, refer to the FrontPage Help system by choosing Help➪Microsoft FrontPage Help or by pressing F1.

Unit 9 Quiz

Take this quiz to review the material you covered in this unit.

1. **Circle the letter next to the tasks you can accomplish by adding a form to your Web site.**

   A. Collect visitor opinions.

   B. Pay your taxes.

   C. Give visitors another way to correspond with you besides sending a regular e-mail message.

   D. Create a guest book.

   E. Impress your friends.

2. **How do you create a new form?**

   A. You choose Insert➪Form.

   B. You insert any type of form field into a Web page by choosing Insert➪Form Field➪*Field Type,* or by clicking a button on the Forms toolbar.

   C. You create a new page using the Feedback Form page template.

   D. On the Editor's Standard toolbar, you click the New Form button.

   E. You launch the Form Page Wizard.

3. **Which term refers to the places in a form where visitors enter information?**

   A. Boxes.

   B. Buttons.

   C. Meadows.

   D. Fields.

   E. Hotspots.

4. **In your form, you want visitors to choose an option from a list, but you want them to make only a single choice. Which field type should you use to collect the information?**

   A. A one-line text box.

   B. A drop-down menu.

   C. A group of radio buttons.

   D. A group of check boxes.

   E. A bulleted list.

Notes:

Notes:

5. **Which generic term describes the information that visitors enter in a field?**

   A. The field's name.

   B. The field's size.

   C. The field's value.

   D. The field's price.

   E. Stuff.

6. **What is the purpose of a form handler?**

   A. To format the form.

   B. To process the information sent from forms.

   C. To format form results.

   D. To confuse FrontPage users.

   E. To confuse everyone.

Unit 9 Exercise

1. In the Contact Me page open in the Editor, rename the Name field **FullName**.

2. Give the scrolling text box field a width of 40 characters and a height of 5 lines.

3. Add a new check box field to the existing group, and call it **Rant**.

4. In the radio button group, make the No radio button appear initially selected instead of the Yes radio button.

5. Change the initial value of the Email field from `username@domain.com` to `Enter your e-mail address here`. If the text is too long to be fully visible inside the text box field, increase the field's width.

6. Add a new item to the drop-down menu field that reads `A little voice inside my head told me`.

7. Change the form handler settings so the visitor's browser type appears in the form results file.

8. Save the page, and then preview and test the form using your Web browser.

9. Return to the Editor, and open the form results file. Say, "Oooooo. Ahhhh."

10. Save and close all open pages in the Editor, and exit FrontPage.

Framing Your Web Site

Objectives for This Unit

✓ Figuring out frames

✓ Creating a frames page

✓ Inserting content pages into frames

✓ Adjusting frames properties

✓ Creating a No Frames alternative

✓ Saving and previewing framed sites

Prerequisites

▶ Launching FrontPage (Lesson 1-2)

▶ Creating a new Web site from scratch (Lesson 1-3)

▶ Adding existing files to a FrontPage Web site (Lesson 1-5)

▶ Opening an existing Web site in the Explorer (Lesson 2-1)

▶ Launching the FrontPage Editor (Lesson 2-2)

▶ Previewing a page (Lesson 3-6)

▶ Saving a page that contains images (Lesson 6-5)

on the CD

▶ imagemap.htm

▶ imagemap.gif

Say the word *frames* to a novice Web publisher, and watch what happens. Chances are you'll see a bewildered expression followed by under-the-breath mumbling about how frames are too technical and complicated for a beginner to use.

No so with FrontPage. Want proof? In this lesson, you experience just how easily you can transform My Web Site into a framed Web site.

Frames Facts

A bit of explanation is in order before you begin, because frames require you to look at Web publishing in a whole new way.

Frames divide the browser window into individual sections, each of which displays a separate Web page. Figure 10-1 illustrates a simple, two-frame Web site.

Figure 10-1: A two-frame Web site.

Notes:

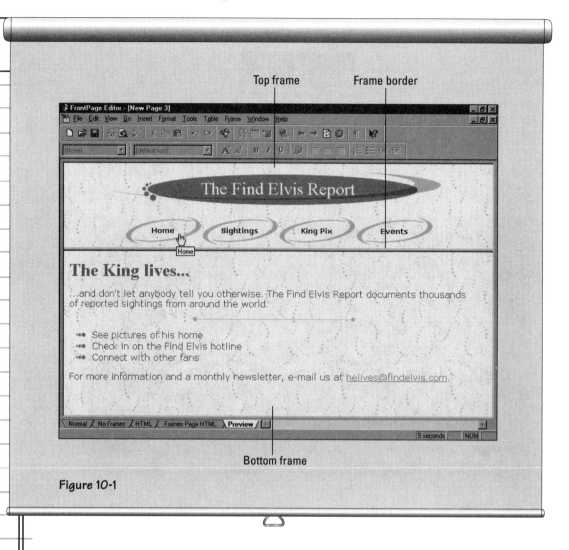

Figure 10-1

frames page defines frame layout and properties

frames display more than one page inside browser window

In Figure 10-1, each frame contains a distinct Web page. The top frame contains a page banner and a navigation bar, and the bottom frame holds the site's content. When you click a navigation bar button in the top frame, the link's destination page appears in the bottom frame.

A third Web page is at work here as well: the *frames page*. The frames page determines the placement and characteristics of the frames themselves, but it is otherwise transparent.

Frames require a cognitive leap because the browser window no longer displays a single page: It displays more than one page at the same time. Unlike shared borders, which exist inside the body of each page in the site, frames allow you to keep part of the browser window stable while other parts of the window change.

In this unit, you apply the two-frame layout shown in Figure 10-1 to My Web Site. In the top frame, you insert the image map page you created in Unit 7 (if you didn't follow the lessons in Unit 7, I have included a complete image map page named imagemap.htm in the FP101 folder).

First things first — you must set up your FrontPage workspace to get ready for the upcoming lessons.

1 Launch FrontPage, and open My Web Site.

If you're not sure how to open a Web site, refer to Lesson 2-1.

2 On the Explorer toolbar, click Show FrontPage Editor.

The Explorer launches, and a new, blank page becomes visible.

If you followed the lessons in Unit 7, choose File⇨Close to close the empty page, and then move on to Lesson 10-2. If you didn't follow the lessons in Unit 7, continue with Step 3.

3 Import the files named imagemap.htm and imagemap.gif from the FP101 folder into My Web Site.

If you don't remember how to import files, refer to Lesson 1-5.

You're now ready to build frames.

Show FrontPage
Editor button

☑ **Progress Check**

If you can do the following, you've mastered this lesson:

❑ Know what frames are and (basically) how frames work.

Creating a Frames Page

Lesson 10-2

on the test

The first step in creating a framed Web site is creating a *frames page*. The frames page is a special type of Web page that defines the size, placement, and properties of the site's frames. I say *special*, because although the frames page is indeed a Web page, its only purpose is to define the site's frames — the frames page contains no content of its own. The content you see when you look at a framed site belongs to the pages displayed inside each frame.

The Editor contains templates for the most common frames page layouts. You will now create a frames page using a simple, two-frame layout.

1 In the Editor, choose File⇨New (or press Ctrl+N).

The New dialog box appears.

2 In the dialog box, click the Frames tab.

The Frames tab becomes visible (see Figure 10-2).

3 In the dialog box, click the Header template.

A description of the template appears in the Description area, telling you how the frames page works. At the same time, a preview of the frames page layout appears in the Preview area.

4 Click OK.

The New dialog box closes, and a new frames page appears in the Editor (see Figure 10-3).

Figure 10-2: The Frames tab in the New dialog box.

Figure 10-3: A new, empty frames page.

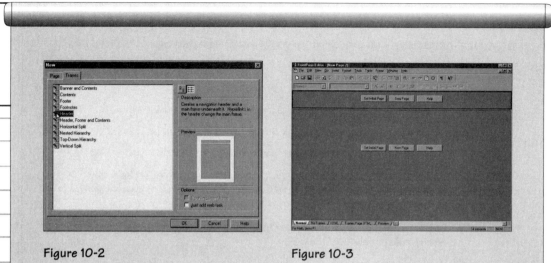

Figure 10-2   Figure 10-3

Notes:

☑ **Progress Check**

If you can do the following, you've mastered this lesson:

❑ Create a new frames page.

Notice the appearance of two new tabs at the bottom of the Editor window: No Frames and Frames Page HTML. The No Frames View contains a message that appears to those of your visitors who use browsers that can't display frames. (I talk more about No Frames messages in Lesson 10-5.) The Frames Page HTML View displays the HTML code of the frames page.

Lesson 10-3   Adding Content Pages

content pages appear inside each frame

After you create a frames page, you must fill each frame with an *initial content page.* Initial content pages appear inside the frames the first time a visitor views the frames page with a web browser (after that, the content pages change depending on how the visitor navigates through the site).

In the following steps, you fill each frame with a page from your Web site.

1 **In the top frame, click the Set Initial Page button (or, click inside the frame and then choose Frame⇨Set Initial Page).**

The Create Hyperlink dialog box appears.

2 **In the dialog box, double-click imagemap.htm.**

The dialog box closes, and the image map page appears inside the top frame.

3 **In the bottom frame, click the Set Initial Page button.**

The Create Hyperlink dialog box appears again.

4 **In the dialog box, double-click the home page icon.**

The dialog box closes, and the home page appears inside the bottom frame.

That's it. Each page is now visible and can be edited (just click the page you want to change and go to work). For extra editing room, click the page you want to edit and then choose Frame⇨Open Page in New Window to expand the page into a new Editor window.

In this lesson you used existing pages as the frames page's initial content pages. You can just as easily fill frames with new, blank pages. To do so, instead of clicking the Set Initial Page button as you did in Step 3, you would click the New Page button.

heads up

If you imported the complete image map page into My Web Site at the beginning of this unit, the page appears without the Arcs theme you applied to My Web Site in Unit 6. To apply the theme to the page, click inside the top frame, and then choose Format⇨Theme. In the Choose Theme dialog box that appears, mark the Use Theme From Current Web radio button, and then click OK. The dialog box closes, and FrontPage applies the Arcs theme to the page.

Recess

Working with frames can numb your mind, not because frames are difficult, but because they require a hefty shift in perspective. If you feel the brain fog rolling in, lean back, close your eyes, and stretch your arms high over your head. Keep stretching until you feel the synapses crackling again.

☑ **Progress Check**

If you can do the following, you've mastered this lesson:

❑ Insert initial content pages into frames.

Adjusting the Frames Page

Lesson 10-4

To keep things simple, I chose a two-frame layout as the example for this unit. When creating your own framed Web site, don't feel constrained by layouts presented by the Editor's frames page templates. You can arrange frames in any layout you want, and you can adjust the settings of each individual frame.

In this lesson, I show you the ways in which you can change the frames page. Because the frames page you created in Lesson 10-2 doesn't require much tweaking, I begin with general instructions in Table 10-1, and at the end of the lesson, I take you through specific steps for adjusting your frames page.

Table 10-1	How to Change the Frames Page
Tweak	*How to Do It*
Resizing frames	To resize a frame, click and drag the frame borders.
Splitting frames	To create a new frame, you split an existing frame in two. To do so, while pressing Ctrl, click a frame border and drag the border to a new position. When you release the mouse button, a new frame appears.

(continued)

drag frame borders to resize frames

Ctrl + drag frame borders to split frame

Notes:

Table 10-1 *(continued)*

Tweak	How to Do It
Deleting frames	To delete a frame, click the frame, and then choose Frame⇨Delete Frame. (When you delete a frame, you remove only the frame from the frames page. You don't affect the content page that's visible in the frame.)
Changing individual frame settings	You can change many of the properties of individual frames by using the Frame Properties dialog box (see Figure 10-4). To display the Frame Properties dialog box, click the frame you want to adjust, and then choose Frame⇨Frame Properties.

The Frame Properties dialog box contains all sorts of goodies you can use to reign in the selected frame. Specifically, you can adjust the following settings:

- **Name:** The frame name is a label that describes the frame's content or position.

- **Show Scrollbars:** This list box lets you control when (or if) the frame contains scrollbars. Your choices are Always (scrollbars are always visible), Never (scrollbars never appear), and If Necessary (scrollbars appear only if the visitor's browser window is too small to display the entire contents of the frame).

- **Resizable in Browser:** The state of this check box determines whether visitors can drag frame borders while viewing the site in a web browser.

- **Frame Size:** You can specify precise width and height dimensions using absolute (pixel), proportional (percentage of browser window), or relative (based on the other frames in the page) measurements.

- **Margins:** You can adjust the amount of space separating frame content from frame borders.

- **Show Borders:** By clicking the Frames Page button, you display the Frames Page Properties dialog box, in which you can specify that frame borders are invisible.

- **Frame Spacing:** The Frames Page Properties dialog box also lets you adjust the amount of space between frame borders.

Now that you know what's possible, you are ready to adjust the frames in your frames page.

heads up

In the following steps, you don't change every frame setting — only those that improve the look or function of your frames page.

1 **In the page, click the top frame.**

By doing so, you specify that the adjustments you are about to make apply only to the top frame.

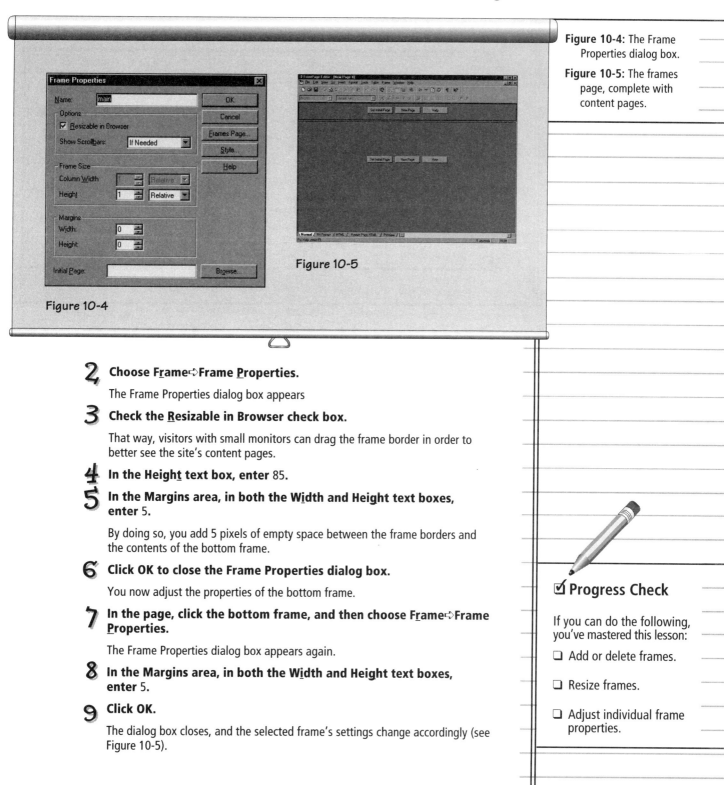

Figure 10-4: The Frame Properties dialog box.

Figure 10-5: The frames page, complete with content pages.

Figure 10-5

Figure 10-4

2 **Choose Frame➪Frame Properties.**

The Frame Properties dialog box appears

3 **Check the Resizable in Browser check box.**

That way, visitors with small monitors can drag the frame border in order to better see the site's content pages.

4 **In the Height text box, enter** 85.

5 **In the Margins area, in both the Width and Height text boxes, enter** 5.

By doing so, you add 5 pixels of empty space between the frame borders and the contents of the bottom frame.

6 **Click OK to close the Frame Properties dialog box.**

You now adjust the properties of the bottom frame.

7 **In the page, click the bottom frame, and then choose Frame➪Frame Properties.**

The Frame Properties dialog box appears again.

8 **In the Margins area, in both the Width and Height text boxes, enter** 5.

9 **Click OK.**

The dialog box closes, and the selected frame's settings change accordingly (see Figure 10-5).

☑ **Progress Check**

If you can do the following, you've mastered this lesson:

❑ Add or delete frames.

❑ Resize frames.

❑ Adjust individual frame properties.

Notes:

extra credit

Changing the target frame

In this frames page, clicking a link in the top frame causes the contents of the bottom frame to change. In Web publishing lingo, the bottom frame is referred to as the top frame's *target frame*. Each frames page template contains default target frame settings that work with that particular frame layout, so 99 percent of the time, you don't need to change the target frame setting. If you want the frames to function differently, however, you can change the target frame setting for the entire page or for selected hyperlinks inside the page. You can even specify the target frame for form results or for image map hotspots.

To find out how to change target frame settings, refer to the FrontPage Help system by choosing Help➪Microsoft FrontPage Help or by pressing F1.

Lesson 10-5   Creating a No Frames Message

No Frames message appears in browsers that can't display frames

Using frames involves an unfortunate flip side: Not all your visitors can see frames. Older browsers can't display frames; instead, these browsers (gasp!) show an empty page.

This problem is shrinking as more Web surfers switch to frames-capable browsers such as Microsoft Internet Explorer (version 3.01 or later) and Netscape Navigator (version 2.0 or later), but you still must provide an alternative for those of your visitors who choose not to use one of these browsers. The alternative comes in the form of the *No Frames message*.

The No Frames message appears to visitors whose browsers don't display frames. The No Frames message can be as simple as a single line of text (To view this site, you must use a frames-capable browser), or it can contain text, hyperlinks, images — anything that can appear inside a regular Web page.

FrontPage adds a basic No Frames message to each frames page. In the steps that follow, you adjust the No Frames message for My Web Site.

1 **In the Editor, click the No Frames tab.**

The No Frames View appears.

2 **Place the cursor at the end of the current message, and then press Enter to create a new line.**

3 **Type** I recommend downloading and installing one of the following web browsers: **and then press Enter.**

4 **Click Bulleted List.**

A list bullet appears.

Bulleted List
button

5 **Type** Microsoft Internet Explorer (version 3.01 or later), at http://
www.microsoft.com/ie/default.asp, **and then press Enter.**

The URL turns into a link to the Microsoft site.

6 **Type** Netscape Navigator (version 2.0 or later), at http://www.netscape.com,
**and then press the spacebar to turn the URL into a hyperlink to the
Netscape Web site.**

Now visitors need only click a single link to go to the download sites for the
two most popular frames-capable browsers.

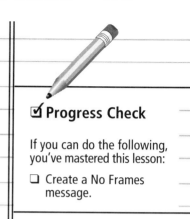

☑ Progress Check

If you can do the following,
you've mastered this lesson:

❏ Create a No Frames
message.

Saving and Previewing the Framed Site

Lesson 10-6

When you save a framed Web site, you save any changes to the content pages
(or if the content pages are new, you save the pages for the first time), and you
also save the frames page.

In the following steps, you save your framed site:

1 **Click Save.**

The Save As dialog box appears (see Figure 10-6). The right side of the dialog
box contains a diagram of the frames page. The entire diagram appears
highlighted, because you are currently saving the frames page. (If any of the
content pages are new, one of the frames inside the frames diagram appears
highlighted.)

2 **In the dialog box's U̲RL text box, enter** frames.htm.

3 **In the T̲itle text box, enter** My Web Site.

heads up

In a framed site, choosing a meaningful title is especially important, because
the title of the frames page is the only title visible as a visitor views the site
with a web browser. The titles of the individual content pages don't appear.

4 **Click OK.**

The dialog box closes, and the Editor saves the frames page.

To save changes in a single content page without saving the entire site, click
the page's frame and then choose Fra̲me➪S̲ave Page.

Don't forget to preview your site to test the links and make sure that the whole
site works properly. You can preview a framed Web site using the Preview
View or a separate web browser (for more information about previewing your
site, see Lesson 3-6).

Save button

Preview in
Browser button

Figure 10-6: The Save As dialog box.

Notes:

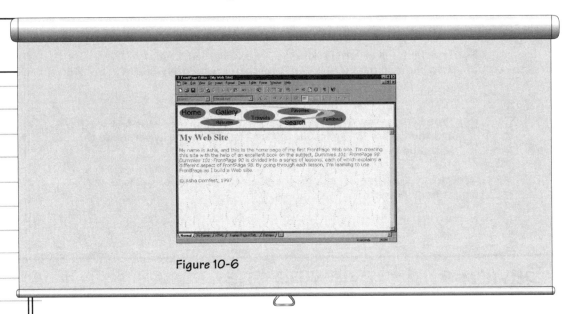

Figure 10-6

☑ Progress Check

If you can do the following, you've mastered this lesson:

❏ Save a framed Web site.

❏ Preview a framed Web site.

This unit introduced you to frames. Framing your site involves more than just setting up the frames page. Depending on your site's design, you may need to tweak the content and layout of each page so the page looks nice inside the frame. For example, you may need to adjust the placement of hyperlinks or navigation bars inside your pages.

You also need to decide how you want visitors to browse your framed site. One option is to transform the frames page into the site's home page, so that visitors see the framed version of the site when they first arrive. Another option is to leave the home page as it is and add a link from the home page to the frames page. This way, visitors can choose whether they want to see the framed version of the site.

Bottom line: If you use frames in your Web site, be sure to thoroughly preview and test the site to be sure it works the way you want.

heads up

In the following units, you set aside the frames page and return to working with the nonframed version of My Web Site, just to keep the steps in each unit simple and straightforward.

Unit 10 Quiz

Take this quiz to review the material you covered in this unit.

1. **What is a frames page?**

   A. A page that defines the placement and layout of the frames in a Web site.

   B. A subsection of a page inside which a content page appears.

   C. A Web page.

   D. A content page.

   E. The first page visible inside a frame when a visitor views the site with a web browser.

2. **How do you create a frames page?**

   A. Choose Frames⇨New Frames Page.

   B. Click the Frames Page button on the toolbar.

   C. Choose File⇨New, and then click the Frames tab.

   D. Create a new, blank page, and then use table drawing tools to draw frame borders.

   E. Invite your computer genius friend over for coffee, and then discreetly lead her to the keyboard.

3. **Which settings can be changed using the Frame Properties dialog box?**

   A. Scrollbars.

   B. Frame background color.

   C. Frame size.

   D. Hyperlink destinations.

   E. Brightness and contrast.

4. **How do you change the size of a frame?**

   A. Press Ctrl, and then drag a frame border.

   B. Drag a frame border.

   C. In the Frame Properties dialog box, enter dimensions in the Width and Height text boxes.

   D. Feed it ice cream.

   E. You can't change frame sizes.

5. **What is the purpose of a No Frames message?**

   A. To alert all your visitors about the presence of frames in your site.

   B. To save visitors using frames-impaired browsers from staring at a blank screen.

   C. To provide an alternate method for getting around the site.

   D. To berate visitors who use limited browsers.

   E. To tell other Web publishers not to use frames in their Web sites.

Unit 10 Exercise

1. In the frames page open in the Editor, split the bottom frame in two.

2. In the new frame, insert a new page.

3. In the new page, type any text you want. Include at least one hyperlink to a page in your Web site or to a URL on the Web.

4. Resize the top frame by dragging the frame border.

5. Make the frame borders invisible.

6. Save your changes, and then preview the site using your web browser.

7. Return to the Editor, save and close all open pages, and then exit FrontPage.

Getting Dynamic with FrontPage Components and Active Elements

Objectives for This Unit

✓ Getting familiar with the capabilities of FrontPage Components and Active Elements

✓ Creating a hover button

✓ Using the Scheduled Include Page FrontPage Component

✓ Enabling visitors to search your site for keywords

✓ Inserting a hit counter

Prerequisites

◗ Launching FrontPage (Lesson 1-2)

◗ Creating a new Web site from scratch (Lesson 1-3)

◗ Opening an existing Web site in the Explorer (Lesson 2-1)

◗ Launching the FrontPage Editor (Lesson 2-2)

◗ Saving a page (Lesson 2-6)

◗ Working with the *Dummies 101: FrontPage 98* example files (Lesson 3-1)

◗ Previewing a page (Lesson 3-6)

on the CD

◗ home.htm

◗ unit11a.htm

◗ unit11b.htm

FrontPage 98 goes beyond the basics of Web page creation. In addition to simplifying all the core tasks that go into building a Web site, the Editor lets you take advantage of dynamic design effects and interactive features that were previously available only to designers and programmers.

These extras, called *FrontPage Components* and *Active Elements*, add a new level of energy to your site. This unit introduces you to FrontPage Components and Active Elements.

Lesson 11-1

Understanding FrontPage Components and Active Elements

Active Elements and FrontPage Components add dynamic or interactive effects to Web pages

Insert FrontPage Component button

Active Elements is what FrontPage calls a group of dynamic design goodies you can add to your page. These items live in the Insert⇨Active Elements section of the Editor menu bar. Each Active Element creates a different effect, as follows:

▶ **Hover Button:** A hover button is an animated button that, when clicked, activates a hyperlink.

▶ **Banner Ad Manager:** The Banner Ad Manager helps you maintain a rotating display of graphic advertisements (often referred to as *banner ads,* because they typically create a rectangular banner at the top of a page).

▶ **Marquee:** A marquee is a rectangular box that contains a scrolling text message.

▶ **Search Form:** A search form enables visitors to search your site for keywords.

▶ **Hit Counter:** A hit counter keeps track of the number of visits your page receives.

▶ **Video:** This Active Element helps you insert AVI video files into your page.

FrontPage Components save you time and brain power by simplifying or automating common Web publishing tasks. FrontPage Components are stored in the Insert FrontPage Component dialog box (shown in Figure 11-1), which you display by clicking Insert FrontPage Component or by choosing Insert⇨ FrontPage Component.

FrontPage Components do the following amazing things:

▶ **Comment:** Comments are reminders that are visible to you in the Editor but invisible when the page is viewed with a web browser. In Unit 4, I showed you how to insert comments.

▶ **Confirmation Field:** This component works with an interactive form to confirm information that visitors enter into form fields. I showed you how to build forms in Unit 9.

▶ **Include Page:** This component, added to a Web page, replaces itself with the contents of a second page.

▶ **Insert HTML:** This component helps you insert HTML tags into your page without using the Editor's HTML View.

▶ **Page Banner:** This component, when used in conjunction with a FrontPage theme, creates a graphical page banner. You used this component in Unit 6.

▶ **Scheduled Include Page:** This component works just like the Include Page FrontPage Component, except that the inclusion appears only during a specified time period.

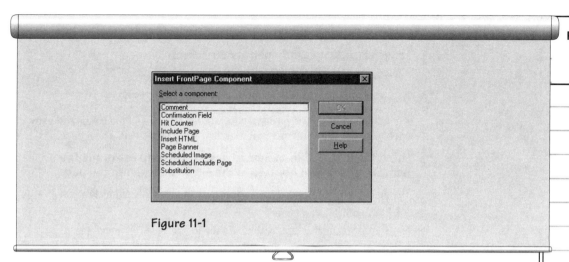

Figure 11-1: The Insert FrontPage Component dialog box.

Figure 11-1

Notes:

- ◗ **Scheduled Image:** This component works just like the Scheduled Include Page FrontPage Component, except that it includes an image rather than the contents of a Web page.

- ◗ **Substitution:** This component enables you to display certain types of standard information in your Web pages.

To use an Active Element or FrontPage Component, you simply drop the item into your page, and then customize the item according to how you want it to look or function. Afterwards, you sit back and let your visitors think that you spent hours programming to achieve the same effect.

heads up

Some of the effects produced by Active Elements and FrontPage Components are visible only in advanced web browsers such as Internet Explorer and Netscape Navigator. Be sure to preview your pages using a few different browser flavors to see how the effects look to different visitors.

Furthermore, certain features require that you publish your Web site on a web server that supports FrontPage Server Extensions. I alert you to these features here, and I provide a complete list in Unit 13.

Active Elements and FrontPage Components are subject to browser and server limitations

heads up

The rest of the lessons in this unit show you how to use a selection of Active Elements and FrontPage Components that I find most helpful. Even though each Active Element and FrontPage Component works differently, the skills you gain in this unit prepare you to use the other features (should you want to) in your own Web site.

For a complete list of instructions, refer to the FrontPage Help system by choosing <u>H</u>elp⇨Microsoft FrontPage <u>H</u>elp, or by pressing F1. If you prefer the *...For Dummies* approach, turn to my other book, *FrontPage 98 For Dummies* (IDG Books Worldwide, 1997). In it, I explain how to use each Active Element and FrontPage Component.

on the CD

In this unit, you work with two example files: one named unit11a.htm, and another named unit11b.htm, both of which are currently sitting in the FP101 folder. In the following steps, you set up your FrontPage workspace so you're ready to follow the rest of the lessons in this unit.

Show FrontPage
Editor button

☑ **Progress Check**

If you can do the following,
you've mastered this lesson:

❑ Understand the basic
capabilities of Active
Elements and FrontPage
Components.

1 **Launch FrontPage, and open My Web Site.**

If you're not sure how to open a Web site, refer to Lesson 2-1.

2 **On the Explorer toolbar, click Show Front PageEditor.**

The Editor launches, and presents you with a new page. (If the Editor is already open, click the New button on the standard toolbar to create a new page.)

3 **Using the Insert⇨File command, insert the contents of the file named unit11a.htm (located in the FP101 folder) into the page.**

The dialog box closes, and FrontPage inserts the contents of unit11a.htm into the page.

For detailed instructions on how to use the Insert⇨File command, see Lesson 3-1.

4 **Save the new page as part of your Web site, title the page Moving Sale Announcement, and name the page moving.htm.**

Okay — you're ready to go.

Lesson 11-2 | Creating a Hover Button

hover button is a
type of Java applet

Notes:

A *hover button* is an animated button that, when clicked, activates a hyperlink. Here's the fun part: When the visitor passes the pointer over the button (an activity known as *hovering*), the button changes color.

FrontPage achieves this effect by inserting a *Java applet* into the page. A Java applet is a separate program (written in the Java programming language) that the Web page references. When a Web browser that understands Java encounters the applet, it displays the applet's effect on the page.

heads up

Unfortunately, only Internet Explorer (Version 3.0 or later) and Netscape Navigator (Version 2.0 or later) know how to deal with Java applets. Other browsers ignore the applet and therefore don't display the hover button.

In the steps that follow, you insert a hover button into the Moving Sale Announcement page:

1 **In the page, place the cursor at the end of the sentence and press Enter.**

2 **Choose Insert⇨Active Elements⇨Hover Button.**

A hover button appears in the page, and at the same time, the Hover Button dialog box appears (see Figure 11-2).

3 **In the Button Text text box, enter E-mail me for details!.**

4 **Click Font.**

The Font dialog box appears.

5 **In the Color list box, select Yellow, and then click OK.**

The dialog box closes, and the Hover Button dialog box becomes visible again.

6 **In the Link To text box, type** mailto: **followed by your e-mail address.**

My mailto link looks like this: `mailto:webpub@ashaland.com`.

7 **In the Button Color list box, select Maroon.**

8 **Leave the Background Color list box alone.**

9 **In the Effect list box, select Color Fill.**

10 **In the Effect Color list box, select Teal.**

11 **In the Width text box, enter** 170.

12 **Leave the value in the Height text box alone.**

13 **Click OK.**

The Hover Button dialog box closes, and the hover button changes accordingly (see Figure 11-3).

14 **Click Save.**

The Editor saves the page.

To see how the hover button works, preview the page using the Editor's Preview View or a Java-enabled web browser. When you pass the pointer over the button, it turns from maroon to teal. When you click the button, your e-mail program launches, and a new message addressed to your e-mail address appears (assuming your browser knows how to work with e-mail).

extra credit

More fun with hover buttons

The Hover Button Active Element enables you to use graphics to create a hover button — perfect if you like the hover effect but don't want your button to look like a box. You can even specify a sound that plays when a visitor clicks or hovers over the button.

For details, in the Hover Button dialog box, click Custom to display the Custom dialog box. In the Custom dialog box, click Help.

mailto hyperlinks tell visitor's browser to launch the associated e-mail program in order to send a message

Save button

Preview in Browser button

☑ **Progress Check**

If you can do the following, you've mastered this lesson:

❑ Insert a hover button into a page.

❑ Preview and test the hover button.

Figure 11-2: The Hover Button dialog box.

Figure 11-3: A hover button.

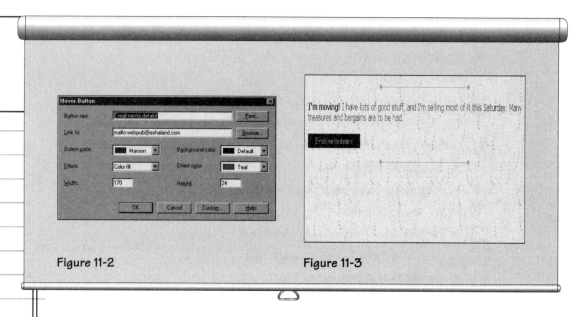

Figure 11-2

Figure 11-3

Lesson 11-3

Simplifying Site Updates with the Scheduled Include Page Component

Of all the FrontPage Components, the three I find most handy belong to the Include family. Each of these components — Include Page, Scheduled Include Page, and Scheduled Include Image — simplifies inserting the same information in more than one page in your Web site.

on the test

After you insert an Include component into your page, the component is replaced by the contents of a second page (or in the case of the Scheduled Include Image component, a graphic of your choice). Unlike shared borders, which are confined to the edges of each page, you can stick an Include component anywhere you want. (I described shared borders in Unit 5.)

All the Include components work basically the same way: You place the cursor where you want the included content to appear, and then you specify the page or image you want to include. Unlike with the Insert⇨File command, in which the inserted content is pasted into the body of the host page, content inserted using an Include component remains distinct. You can edit the included page or image at any time — even *after* the material has been included in a host page. After you save the included page or image and then refresh the display of the host page, the edits appear in the host page.

The Scheduled Include components add an interesting twist: The included material is only visible in the host page for a limited time (the duration of which you specify), after which it disappears from view. In this way, you can include time-sensitive announcements in your Web site, and you don't have to remember to remove the announcements after they expire.

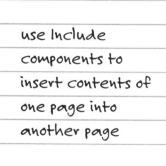
use Include components to insert contents of one page into another page

In this lesson, you use the Scheduled Include Page component to insert the contents of the Moving Sale Announcement into the home page of My Web Site. Because the announcement has a limited shelf life, you specify the time period you want the announcement to be visible.

on the CD

1 **In the Editor, open the home page of My Web Site.**

If you didn't follow the lessons in Units 3 and 4, a complete version of the home page text is available in the FP101 folder. In the Editor, open your existing home page, and then insert the contents of the file named home.htm into the page using the Insert⇨File command (refer to Lesson 3-1 for directions). Then proceed with Step 2.

2 **Place the cursor at the end of the main body paragraph.**

3 **On the Standard toolbar, click Insert FrontPage Component.**

The Insert FrontPage Component dialog box appears.

4 **In the Select a Component area, click Scheduled Include Page, and then click OK.**

The Insert FrontPage Component dialog box is replaced by the Scheduled Include Page Component Properties dialog box (see Figure 11-4).

5 **In the Page URL to Include text box, type** moving.htm.

Or click Browse to choose the page from the Current Web dialog box.

6 **The Starting Date and Time area displays the current date and time. Leave this area alone, because in this example, you want the inclusion to begin as soon as you close the dialog box.**

7 **If not already visible, in the Ending Date and Time area, from the Year, Month, and Day list boxes, choose the current year, month, and day.**

In the real world, you would choose an ending date and time that occurs right after the announcement is no longer valid. But because I want you to see the effects of the component, you choose today as the ending date, and a time five minutes from now as the ending time.

8 **In the Time text box, click the notation, and specify the time five minutes from now.**

In other words, if it's 10:00 p.m. right now, you specify 10:05 p.m.

9 **Click OK.**

The dialog box closes, and the contents of the Moving Sale Announcement page appear inside the home page (see Figure 11-5).

10 **Click Save to save the page.**

Go ahead — preview the page. You'd never know that the content is part of a separate page, would you?

After you finish the next lesson, during Recess time, you will return to the home page to see what happens when the scheduled inclusion expires.

Notes:

Insert FrontPage
Component button

Save button

return to home
page after Recess

Figure 11-4: The Scheduled Include Page Component Properties dialog box.

Figure 11-5: The contents of the included page (moving.htm) appear inside the home page.

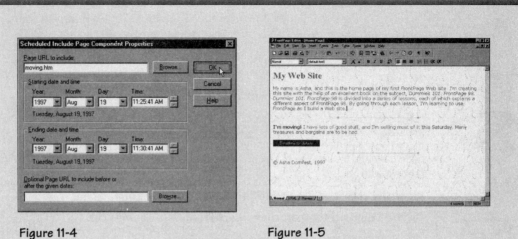

Figure 11-4   Figure 11-5

important warning about Scheduled Include components

☑ Progress Check

If you can do the following, you've mastered this lesson:

❑ Use the Scheduled Include Page FrontPage component.

If you use the Scheduled Include Page and the Scheduled Include Image FrontPage Components in your site, you need to be aware of one unfortunate but unavoidable complication. For the components to work correctly, the site must be updated *during the scheduled inclusion time* to begin the inclusion and again *after the scheduled include time* to cause the inclusion to disappear. If you update your site every day, this requirement is no problem, but if you don't, you need to refresh the Web site by hand — a fact that defeats the purpose of the scheduled include because you need to remember the scheduled date and time.

To refresh the Web site by hand, in the Explorer, choose Tools⇨Recalculate Hyperlinks. The Recalculate Hyperlinks dialog box appears, warning you that recalculating hyperlinks may take several minutes. Click Yes to close the dialog box and proceed with recalculation. After the recalculation is complete, republish your Web site to make the changes visible on the Web. (I show you how to publish your Web site in Unit 13.)

Lesson 11-4

Adding a Keyword Search to Your Web Site

As your site expands (more quickly than you may think!), visitors may need help finding the information they want. To help them cut through the clutter, include a *keyword search* in your Web site.

The Search Form Active Element creates a simple form visitors use to enter words or phrases they want to find. They then click a button to activate the search. In a moment, a new Web page appears containing links to all the Web site pages containing the requested words.

heads up

For the Search Form Active Element to work properly, you must publish your Web site on a server that supports FrontPage Server Extensions. For details about how to publish your Web site, skip ahead to Unit 13.

on the CD

In the following steps, you add a Search page to My Web Site. Steps 1-2 take you through inserting the file unit11b.htm (stored in the FP101 folder) into a new Web page. This task saves you from having to type introductory text in the page. After that, you construct your search form.

1 In the Editor, click New.

A new page appears.

2 Using the Insert⇨File command, insert the contents of unit11b.htm (located in the FP101 folder) into the page.

The dialog box closes, and FrontPage inserts the contents of unit11b.htm into the page.

For detailed instructions on how to use the Insert⇨File command, see Lesson 3-1.

3 Press Enter to create a new line.

4 Choose Insert⇨Active Elements⇨Search Form.

The Search Form Properties dialog box appears, with the Search Form Properties tab visible (see Figure 11-6).

5 Leave the Label for Input text box alone.

6 In the Width in Characters text box, type 30.

7 Leave the Label for "Start Search" Button text box alone.

8 In the Label for "Clear" Button text box, type Clear Form.

9 In the dialog box, click the Search Results tab.

The Search Results tab becomes visible (see Figure 11-7).

10 Leave the Word List to Search text box alone.

11 Mark the Score (Closeness of Match), File Date, and File Size (in K bytes) check boxes.

By doing so, you specify the search results page, in addition to listing the linked titles of pages that match the search, lists of the files' scores, the dates the pages were last updated, and the file sizes.

12 Click OK to close the Search Form Properties dialog box.

A search form appears in your page (see Figure 11-8).

13 Click Save.

The Save As dialog box appears, prompting you to save the new page.

14 Name the page search.htm, title the page Search, and then click OK.

The dialog box closes, and the Editor saves the page.

Notes:

New button

the default settings in Search Form Properties dialog box work well in most forms

Save button

Figure 11-6: The Search
Form Properties dialog
box.

Figure 11-7: The Search
Results tab of the
Search Form Properties
dialog box.

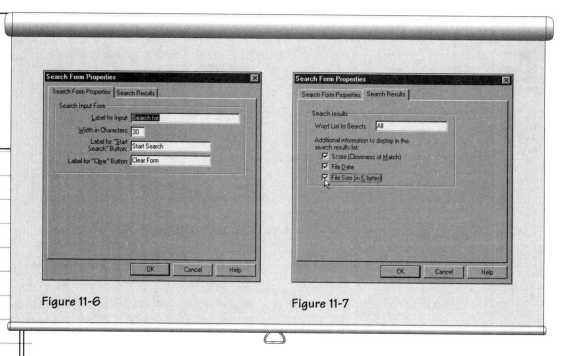

Figure 11-6   Figure 11-7

Preview in Browser
button add
keyword search
using Search Page
template

☑ Progress Check

If you can do the following,
you've mastered this lesson:

❑ Add a keyword search
function to your Web
site.

❑ Preview and test the
search function.

15 **Click Preview in Browser.**

Your web browser launches, and the Search page is visible.

16 **In the form's Search For text box, type** dummies, **and then click the form's Start Search button.**

A brief pause occurs as the Personal Web Server processes the search, and then the search results page appears, listing all the matching pages (see Figure 11-9).

 If you don't want certain pages in your site to appear in search results, store those pages in your Web site's _private folder. (In Unit 12, I show you how to move pages into folders.)

on the test

In this lesson, you added the Search Form Active Element to an empty page. Another option is to create a new page using the Editor's Search Page template (available by choosing File➪New). The template already contains the Search Form Active Element, plus directions for operating the search and sample queries.

Recess

If you need it, feel free to take a break right now. In fact, take a break even if you don't think you need it. Your eyes will thank you, plus you can be sure that five minutes have passed to see what happened with the Scheduled Include Page Component you used in Lesson 11-3.

[Insert five-minute break here.]

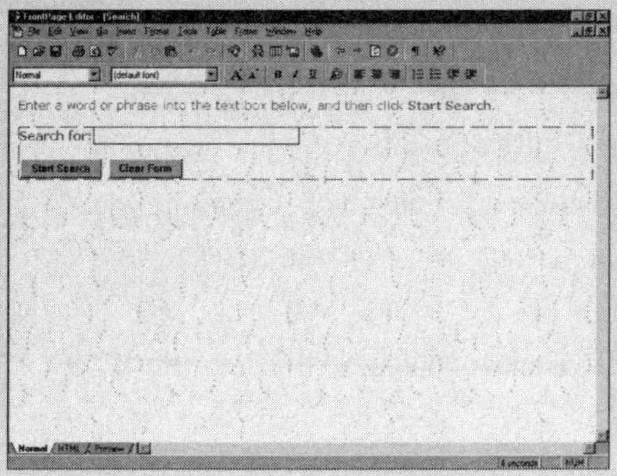

Figure 11-8

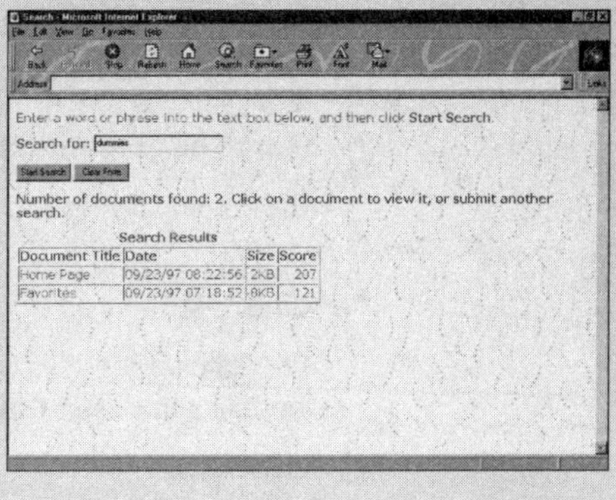

Figure 11-9

Figure 11-8: The Search Form Active Element adds a search form to your Web site.

Figure 11-9: The search results page contains a list of all the pages that contain the words you specified.

Okay, now that five minutes are up, return to the Editor, and make the home page visible. On the Standard toolbar, click Refresh. The FrontPage Editor dialog box appears asking if you want to save changes to the page; click Yes. The Editor refreshes the page display, and the message [Expired Scheduled Include Page] replaces the moving sale announcement. For the full effect, preview your page in a web browser. The included content is gone.

Refresh button

Inserting a Hit Counter

Lesson 11-5

The easiest way to let the world know how popular you are is to include a *hit counter* in your site's home page. A hit counter keeps track of the numbers of visits, or *hits*, your page receives, and then displays that number in the page.

heads up

For the hit counter to work properly, you must publish your Web site on a server that supports FrontPage Server Extensions. For details about how to publish your Web site, skip ahead to Unit 13.

In this lesson, you insert a hit counter into the home page of My Web Site.

1 **If it's not already open or visible, in the Editor, open the home page.**

Because the message has expired, if you like, go ahead and delete the Scheduled Include Page component by clicking [Expired Scheduled Include Page] and then pressing Delete.

2 **Place the cursor at the end of the last body paragraph in the page, and then press Enter to create a new, blank line.**

3 Type **Number of visitors so far: and then press Shift+Enter.**

Notes:

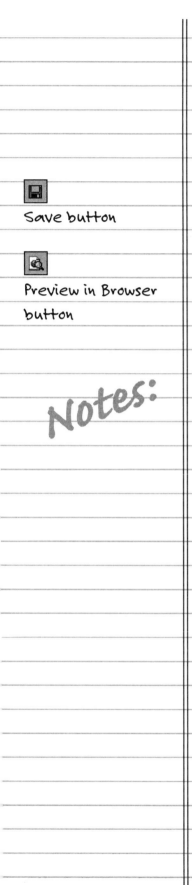

Save button

Preview in Browser button

Notes:

heads up

4   **Choose Insert⇨Active Elements⇨Hit Counter.**

The Hit Counter Properties dialog box appears (see Figure 11-10).

5   **In the Counter Style area, click the second radio button.**

6   **Mark the Fixed Number of Digits check box.**

The accompanying text box (containing the number 5) comes into view. That's good.

7   **Click OK.**

The dialog box closes, and a placeholder appears in the page (the placeholder looks like this: **[Hit Counter]**).

8   **Click Save.**

9   **Click Preview in Browser.**

Your web browser launches, and in a moment, the home page becomes visible. The hit counter reads 1 (see Figure 11-11).

If you don't see the hit counter, click your browser's Reload or Refresh button to update the browser display.

10   **In your browser, click the Refresh or Reload button to refresh the page display.**

The page reloads, and the hit counter now reads 2.

After you publish your Web site, the hit counter increases by one every time a new visitor drops by.

To reset the hit counter, in the page open in the Editor, double-click the [Hit Counter] placeholder in the page to display the Hit Counter Properties dialog box. In the dialog box, mark the Reset Counter To check box, and then, in the accompanying text box, enter the number you want the counter to display. Click OK to close the dialog box.

You can use your own image in place of the Editor's preset counter graphics. To do so, in the Hit Counter Properties dialog box, click the Custom Image radio button, and then, in the accompanying text box, enter the image's file name and location. The image you choose must be a single graphic that contains the numbers 0–9, and the numbers must be evenly spaced inside the image.

You now have a good sense for the exciting effects Active Elements and FrontPage Components can add to your Web site. Before you move on to Unit 12, choose File⇨Save All to save all your pages.

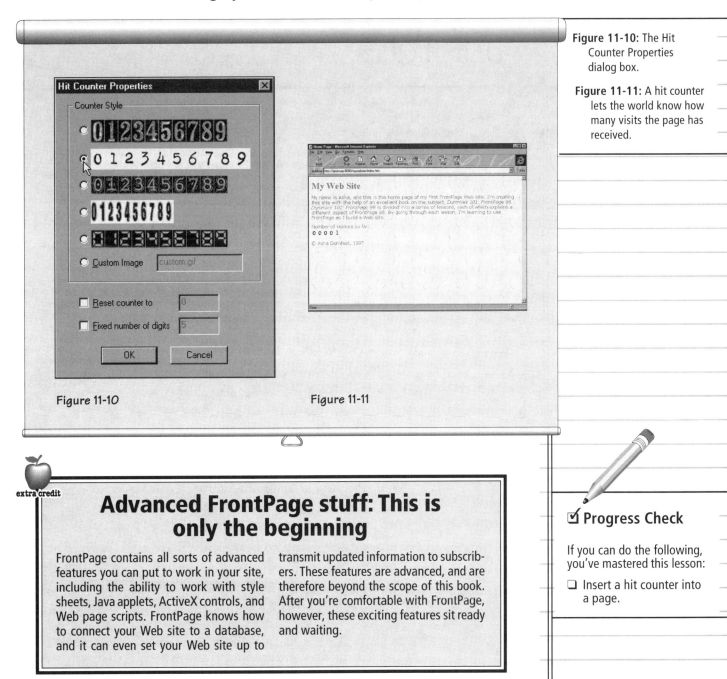

Figure 11-10

Figure 11-11

Figure 11-10: The Hit Counter Properties dialog box.

Figure 11-11: A hit counter lets the world know how many visits the page has received.

Advanced FrontPage stuff: This is only the beginning

FrontPage contains all sorts of advanced features you can put to work in your site, including the ability to work with style sheets, Java applets, ActiveX controls, and Web page scripts. FrontPage knows how to connect your Web site to a database, and it can even set your Web site up to transmit updated information to subscribers. These features are advanced, and are therefore beyond the scope of this book. After you're comfortable with FrontPage, however, these exciting features sit ready and waiting.

☑ **Progress Check**

If you can do the following, you've mastered this lesson:

❑ Insert a hit counter into a page.

Unit 11 Quiz

Take this quiz to review the material you covered in this unit. (Each question may have more than one right answer.)

1. **What are Active Elements and FrontPage Components?**

   A. Complicated technical gizmos that require programming expertise to use.

   B. Items represented in the Periodic Table of Elements.

   C. Items you can drop into a Web page to produce a dynamic design effect.

   D. Unique FrontPage features.

   E. Features that are subject to the specifics of the visitor's web browser as well as the server on which the Web site is published.

2. **In the context of this unit, what does *hover* mean?**

   A. To linger annoyingly over the shoulder of a coworker or child.

   B. To levitate slightly above one's chair.

   C. To pass the pointer over an object without clicking the object.

   D. To click an object, and then drag the object to a new location.

   E. To cause an object to fly around inside the page.

3. **What do the Include family of FrontPage Components do?**

   A. Copy and paste an image or the contents of a page into a second page, merging the two files into a single file.

   B. Help new FrontPage users feel welcome and comfortable.

   C. Insert an image or the contents of a page into a second page while keeping the included content distinctly separate.

   D. Simplify adding standard text and images to many pages in a Web site.

   E. Make possible updating the content of a single page, and have that update automatically appear in many pages in the Web site.

4. **How do you hide a page from a keyword search?**

   A. Store the page in the Images folder of your Web site.

   B. Store the page in the _private folder of your Web site.

   C. Store the page in a closet.

   D. Insert the word *Hidden* in the page title.

   E. Choose File⇨Save as Hidden.

5. **What is the purpose of a hit counter?**

   A. To increase site traffic.

   B. To record the number of visits that page has received.

   C. To privately keep track of site traffic.

   D. To record the number of visits the entire site has received.

   E. To let your visitors know how popular you are.

Unit 11 Exercise

1. In the Editor, open the Moving Sale Announcement page.

2. In the page, double-click the hover button to display the Hover Button dialog box.

3. Change the button color and the event color.

4. Change the effect.

5. Preview the resulting button using a web browser.

6. Return to the Editor, and then use the Include Page FrontPage Component to include the contents of the Moving Sale Announcement page in another page of your choice. (You should have no problem using this component because it is a simplified version of the Scheduled Include Page FrontPage Component.)

7. Open the Search page.

8. Change the search result settings so that only the page title and file size appear in the search results page.

9. Save the page, and test the updated search function using a web browser.

10. Return to the Editor, and open the home page.

11. Choose a new counter digit style, and set the number of visible digits to 4.

12. Save the page, and test the updated counter using a web browser.

13. Return to the Editor, save and close all pages, and exit FrontPage.

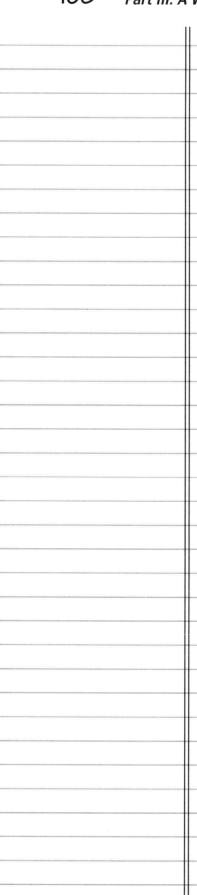

Part III Review

Unit 9 Summary

▶ **What is a form?** A form enables visitors to fill information into spaces in a Web page and then send the information back to you. The spaces into which visitors enter information are called *fields*.

▶ **Form handler:** A *form handler* is a program that sits on the web server hosting the Web site. When form information is submitted, the form handler receives the form data and then does something with it, such as formatting the information and sending it to you in an e-mail message or adding the information to a Web page.

▶ **Creating a new form:** You can create a new form by using the Form Page Wizard, a form page template, or by adding individual form fields to a Web page. To use the Form Page Wizard or a form page template, in the Editor, choose File➪New to display the New dialog box. In the dialog box, double-click Form Page Wizard or the name of a template.

▶ **Inserting individual form fields:** You can add the following types of fields to a form: a one-line text box, a scrolling text box, check boxes, radio buttons, drop-down menus, push buttons, and hidden fields. To insert most types of fields into a Web page, choose Insert➪Form Field, and then choose the name of the field you want to insert. Or click a button on the Forms toolbar.

▶ **Customizing form fields:** After you insert a form field in a page, you must customize the field. To do so, double-click the field to display the field's Properties dialog box. In the dialog box, specify the field's properties, and then click OK to close the dialog box.

▶ **Setting up a form handler:** To choose and set up a form handler, right-click inside the form, and then, from the shortcut menu that appears, choose Form Properties. In the Form Properties dialog box, choose the form handler you want to use, and then click Options to customize the form handler.

Unit 10 Summary

▶ **What are frames?** Frames divide the browser window into individual sections, each of which displays a separate Web page. Frames can interact, so that clicking hyperlinks in one frame causes the contents of a second frame to change.

▶ **Frames page:** The frames page is a special type of Web page that defines the size, placement, and properties of the site's frames. To create a frames page, choose File➪New to display the New dialog box. At the top of the dialog box, click the Frames tab. In the Frames tab, double-click a frames page template. After you create a frames page, you can adjust the page's layout, properties, and the way it works by choosing Frame➪Frame Properties.

▶ **Content pages:** Content pages are what appear inside each frame in a framed Web site. You can fill frames with new or existing content pages. Each frame has an *initial content page*, the page that's visible the first time a visitor views a framed Web site.

▶ **No Frames message:** The No Frames message appears to visitors whose browsers don't display frames. To create a No Frames message, add text, hyperlinks, and other elements to the Editor's No Frames view (to access the No Frames view, click the No Frames tab in the lower-left corner of the Editor window). The No Frames message can contain all the elements of a regular Web page.

Part III Review

Unit 11 Summary

▶ **What are Active Elements and FrontPage Components?** Active Elements and FrontPage Components are ready-made dynamic and interactive features you can drop into your Web site. For example, you can use the Search Form Active Element to add a keyword search to your Web site, and you can use the Include Page FrontPage Component to include the contents of a page inside another page.

▶ **Inserting an Active Element:** To insert an Active Element, choose Insert➪Active Elements, and then choose the name of the Active Element you want to use in your page.

▶ **Inserting a FrontPage Component:** To insert a FrontPage Component, click the Insert FrontPage Component button. The Insert FrontPage Component dialog box appears. In the dialog box, double-click the component you want to use.

Part III Test

Take this test as a review of the material covered in Part III, Units 9 through 11. If you'd like to check your answers, refer to Appendix B.

True   False

T   F   1. For all Active Elements to work, the Web site must be published on a web server that supports FrontPage Server Extensions.

T   F   2. A frames page is invisible except for the layout and placement of the frames.

T   F   3. When you include a page inside another page using the Scheduled Include Page FrontPage Component, the included page's content merges with the host page's content, and can't be removed later on.

T   F   4. A form handler is a web server-based program.

T   F   5. A form handler processes the information visitors submit using interactive forms.

T   F   6. A form handler is a piece of software you buy to help you do your taxes.

T   F   7. The layout of a frames page template is set; if you don't like the templates provided by FrontPage, you're out of luck.

Part III Test

T   F   8. A hover button is a type of Java applet.

T   F   9. A hit counter keeps track of the number of times you hit your computer.

T   F   10. Pages stored inside the _private folder are searched by the Search Form Active Element.

Multiple Choice

For each of the following questions, circle the correct answer or answers.

11. In what formats can information submitted from forms be saved?

A. A Web page.

B. A comma-delimited text file.

C. A FrontPage Component.

D. An e-mail message.

E. A bulleted list in a Web page.

12. Which of the following items are form fields?

A. A hover button.

B. A scrolling text box.

C. A check box.

D. A jack-in-the-box.

E. A drop-down menu.

13. Which of the following features or effects can be created using a FrontPage Component or an Active Element?

A. A keyword site search.

B. A graphical button that, when clicked, transports the visitor to a new location.

C. A decorative page banner.

D. An image map.

E. A row of numbers that records the number of visits the page receives.

14. Which aspects of a frames page can be changed?

A. The presence of scrollbars inside frames.

B. Frame dimensions.

C. Whether the frame uses content pages.

D. The presence of frame borders.

E. Frame margins.

Matching

15. Match each of the following buttons with its name:

A.   1. Drop-Down-Menu

B.   2. Radio Button

C.   3. Scrolling Text Box

D.   4. One-Line Text Box

E.   5. Insert FrontPage Component

16. Match each FrontPage Component or Active Element with what it does.

A. Search Form   1. Records the number of visits a page receives

B. Hit Counter   2. Creates a clickable button

C. Page Banner   3. Inserts an invisible annotation

D. Comment   4. Creates a keyword site search

E. Hover Button   5. Creates a decorative page banner

Part III Test

17. **Match each category of information with the form field type that would best collect that information in a form.**

    A. Colors the visitor likes   1. A one-line text box

    B. A visitor's gender   2. A group of check boxes

    C. A visitor's age   3. A group of radio buttons

    D. A visitor's life story   4. A drop-down menu

    E. The answer to a Yes or No question   5. A scrolling text box

Part III Lab Assignment

This lab assignment gives you a chance to apply your ever-deepening FrontPage skills to the real-world project you began at the end of Part I. At the end of Part II, you opened your pet Web site and added lots of new content. In this assignment, you embellish the site with forms, frames, and dynamic extras.

If one of the following steps stumps you, go ahead and page back through this part to refresh your memory.

Step 1: Launch FrontPage, and open the Web site you created in the Part I Lab Assignment

Step 2: Create a new form page

Use the Form Page Wizard or a template, or build your own form.

Step 3: Customize the form

Use the form in any way you like. Survey your visitors or collect their opinions. Or try out the Guest Book template if you want to share visitor feedback with everyone who stops by.

Part III Lab Assignment

Step 4: Save the form page, and preview and test the page using a web browser

Step 5: Return to the Editor, and, if you like, create a new frames page

(If you don't want to use frames in your Web site, skip to Step 8.)

I say *if you like* here because you may not want your site to use frames. Not everyone does, to be sure. If you *do* want to use frames in your site, however, this is a good time to do it.

Step 6: Fill the frames with content pages

Step 7: Adjust the layout and properties of each frame

Step 8: Insert at least one Active Element and one FrontPage Component in your site

Take your pick!

Step 9: Preview the site to see how your Web site is shaping up

Step 10: Switch back to the Editor and save all your pages

Step 11: Exit FrontPage

Publishing and Maintaining Your Web Site

Part IV

In this part . . .

Sure, tinkering with FrontPage on your computer is fun, but the moment of truth arrives when you actually publish your Web site on the World Wide Web. In this part, you sift through your Web site to make sure that it's primed and ready for publication, and finally, in Lucky Unit 13, you make the leap to cyberspace.

Unit 12

The Final Pass

Objectives for This Unit

✓ Tidying up your Web site's file system
✓ Checking spelling
✓ Making sure that your site contains no broken hyperlinks
✓ Readying your site for its worldwide debut

Prerequisites

▶ Launching FrontPage (Lesson 1-2)

▶ Creating a new Web site from scratch (Lesson 1-3)

▶ Adding existing files to a FrontPage Web site (Lesson 1-5)

▶ Opening an existing Web site in the Explorer (Lesson 2-1)

▶ Launching the FrontPage Editor (Lesson 2-2)

▶ Saving a page (Lesson 2-6)

▶ Previewing a page (Lesson 3-6)

▶ Enough FrontPage fluency to tweak any aspect of your Web site (Parts II and III)

on the CD

▶ All the files stored inside the Complete subfolder of the FP101 folder: art.htm, favorite.htm, feedback.htm, frames.htm, imagemap.htm, index.htm, moving.htm, resume.htm, search.htm, travel.htm, backgrnd.gif, fish.gif, fish2.gif, imagemap.gif, painter.gif.

Ahhhh. The page building is done, and the hard work is over. Right?

Well, almost. Just as you wouldn't spend three weeks agonizing over a report, and then turn in the report without proofreading it, you wouldn't want to bare your Web site to the world without first giving the site a thorough once-over.

In this unit, you let FrontPage help you do the last-minute checking that ensures that your site is typo- and glitch-free when it finally goes public.

Cleaning Up the File System

Lesson 12-1

In the previous units, I encouraged you to focus on the workings of FrontPage and the content of your pages, and in so doing, ignored the Web site's *file system* (the organization of the files and folders in your Web site).

The result: Your site looks like a jumbled heap of Web pages and graphic files all thrown together.

I confess: The omission was intentional because I wanted you to have a nice, messy Web site to sort out in this lesson. You'll now organize your pages and files into neat little piles so they aren't so cluttered.

on the test

In the past, changing the Web site's file system *after* the site was complete caused serious problems. If you changed the location or filename of a page that contained hyperlinks or graphics (or was itself the destination of a hyperlink in another page), you risked breaking the links because the links no longer pointed to a file's current location. The Explorer sidesteps this problem. If you move a page into a folder or rename a page, the Explorer automatically updates the page's incoming and outgoing hyperlinks and its graphic references. This powerful feature lets you organize your site's file system however you want to without having to worry about broken links.

Moving files into folders

The best way to tidy up your Web site's file system is to store related groups of files inside folders. If you have ever organized the files on your hard drive (or the paper files in your filing cabinet, for that matter), you know what I mean: Creating a logical system of folders makes finding the file you want much easier.

FrontPage understands this fact and gets you started by providing you with the images and the _private folders. The images folder is a good holding place for all your Web site graphics (with graphics and pages stored in separate folders, you can quickly survey the contents of your site). The _private folder hides the files it contains from Web surfers and from the Search Form Active Element. Use the _private folder to store pages that are in progress, included pages (that is, pages you include inside other pages using the Include Page FrontPage Component), or pages you don't want to appear in keyword search results.

In the following steps, you streamline the My Web Site file system by storing files inside folders.

on the CD

In the lessons in this unit, I assume you've gone though the previous units in order. If you haven't completed the previous units, your Web site's file system contains different files than the ones I describe in this unit. That's okay — your main objective is to get comfortable with the final pre-publishing cleanup process. If you prefer to work with a full set of files, however, in the FP101 folder, you find a folder named Complete. Inside the Complete folder is a complete copy of the Web site you built throughout the course of this book. Import all the files from the FP101/Complete folder into My Web Site, replacing any existing files contained there (if you're not sure how to import files into your Web site, refer to Lesson 1-4). After the import process is complete, apply the Arcs theme to the Web site (for a refresher, turn to Lesson 6-6). Then, proceed with the steps in this lesson.

heads up

If you replace the files you created with files from the FP101/Complete folder, any changes you made to those pages will be overwritten by the new files.

file system = the way files and folders in Web site are arranged

when you move or rename a page, the Explorer automatically updates page's associated links and graphic references

_private folder hides pages from web browsers and keyword site searches

Folders button

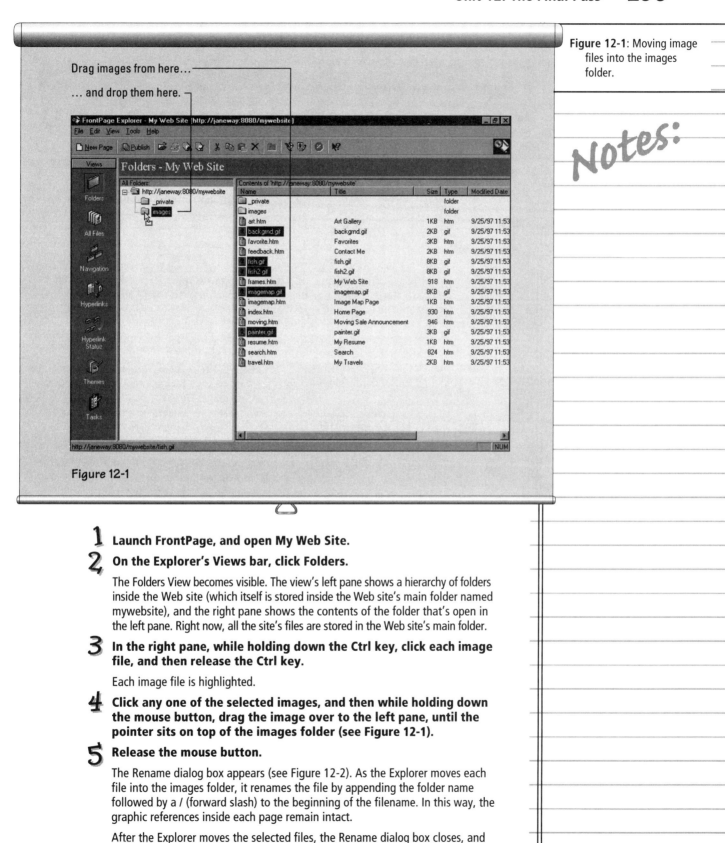

Drag images from here...

... and drop them here.

Figure 12-1

Figure 12-1: Moving image
files into the images
folder.

Notes:

1 **Launch FrontPage, and open My Web Site.**

2 **On the Explorer's Views bar, click Folders.**

The Folders View becomes visible. The view's left pane shows a hierarchy of folders
inside the Web site (which itself is stored inside the Web site's main folder named
mywebsite), and the right pane shows the contents of the folder that's open in
the left pane. Right now, all the site's files are stored in the Web site's main folder.

3 **In the right pane, while holding down the Ctrl key, click each image
file, and then release the Ctrl key.**

Each image file is highlighted.

4 **Click any one of the selected images, and then while holding down
the mouse button, drag the image over to the left pane, until the
pointer sits on top of the images folder (see Figure 12-1).**

5 **Release the mouse button.**

The Rename dialog box appears (see Figure 12-2). As the Explorer moves each
file into the images folder, it renames the file by appending the folder name
followed by a / (forward slash) to the beginning of the filename. In this way, the
graphic references inside each page remain intact.

After the Explorer moves the selected files, the Rename dialog box closes, and
the Folders view displays the new contents of the images folder.

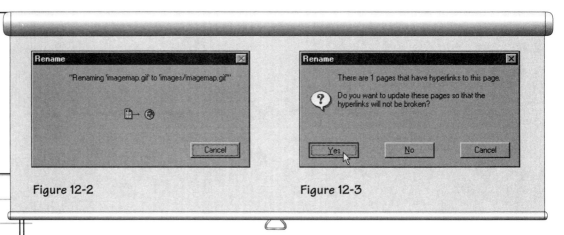

Figure 12-2: The Rename dialog box.

Figure 12-3: The Rename dialog box looks different if the page you're moving or renaming is linked to from other pages in the site.

If you want more practice moving files into folders, I recommend storing the Moving Sale Announcement page (moving.htm) in the _private folder. That way, the page (which was never meant to be viewed on its own) stays hidden from your keyword site search.

You're not limited to the Explorer's standard folders; you can create your own folders as well. To do so, while in the Folders View or in the bottom pane of the Navigation View, choose File➪New➪Folder. A new folder appears with its name (New_Folder) highlighted. Type a new folder name, and then press Enter.

Renaming a file

Naming your files logically also helps to simplify your Web site's file system. Filenames that reflect the file's contents help you remember which pages do what.

heads up

The one exception is the site's home page. The home page's filename should match the name the web server recognizes as the site's default page (the page that automatically appears if someone types the site's URL into a web browser). Most (but not all) web servers recognize the filename index.htm (or index.html) as the site's home or default page (check with your ISP or system administrator if you're not sure what your home page's name should be).

Your Web site filenames are already fairly straightforward, but just to show you how renaming files works, in the following steps, you rename the Favorites page (favorite.htm).

1 **In the left pane of the Folders View, click the top folder.**

The contents of the Web site's main folder become visible in the right pane.

2 **In the right pane, click favorite.htm to select the file.**

3 **Choose Edit➪Rename (or press F2).**

The filename becomes highlighted.

4 **Type** links.htm**, and then press Enter.**

to create new folder, choose File→New→Folder

extra credit

Changing the FrontPage default home page filename

The FrontPage Personal Web Server uses the filename `index.htm` to identify the Web site's home page (the Microsoft Personal Web Server uses the filename `Default.htm`). The web server on which you publish your Web site may use a different home page filename than FrontPage uses. To save yourself the hassle of changing the filename of the home page in every site you are about to publish, change the filename FrontPage uses to recognize the home page.

If you use the FrontPage Personal Web Server, to change the filename, you make a tiny adjustment to one of the web server's configuration files. Adjusting the file is easy; just follow these steps:

1. **Launch your favorite word processor or text editor, such as Windows 95 Notepad.**

2. **Open the file named srm.cnf.**

   The file is located at C:\FrontPage Webs\Server\conf. (If you don't see the file, choose All Files (*.*) from the Files of type list box in the Open dialog box of your text editor or word-processing program.)

   Microsoft thoughtfully explains everything in the configuration file in the lines preceded by a #. Anything without a # at the beginning is an actual configuration setting used by the Personal Web Server.

3. **Look for a line that reads** # `DirectoryIndex` *filename* **where** *filename* **is the current home page filename that FrontPage recognizes.**

4. **Change** *filename* **to the filename that you want FrontPage to recognize as your home page.**

   For example, change the filename to **default.htm** or **index.html**. You should choose the home page filename recognized by the web server on which you will eventually publish your Web site.

5. **Delete the # sign in that line of text.**

   By doing so, you transform the line into a configuration setting.

6. **Save the file and close the text editor or word processing program.**

If you use the Microsoft Personal Web Server, the steps required to change the home page filename are different. See `www.microsoft.com/kb/articles/q169/0/86.htm` for complete instructions.

The next time you create a new FrontPage Web site, the site appears with the new home page filename. Existing Web sites keep the original home page filename; you must rename the home page by hand (see Lesson 12-1 for instructions).

The Rename dialog box appears (see Figure 12-3). Because the Favorites page is linked to from other pages in the Web site, the Explorer wants your permission to update the hyperlinks in the other pages to reflect the current page's new name.

5 **Click Yes.**

The Explorer renames the current file and updates all the files that link to the current file. When the operation is complete, the dialog box closes.

☑ **Progress Check**

If you can do the following, you've mastered this lesson:

❑ Move a page or file into a folder.

❑ Rename a page or file.

Lesson 12-2

Checking Spelling

FrontPage can spell check files one by one, or site-wide

Cross File Spelling button

Even the most lovingly prepared Web site can be marred by a typo. Spelling errors project an I-don't-care-about-quality image that can spoil an otherwise solid site.

FrontPage wards off typos with a powerful spell checking feature. You can activate the spell checker from within the Editor (to check the active page) or from the Explorer (to check every page in the Web site). Site-wide spell checking saves a lot of time, especially if your site contains many pages.

heads up Before you begin, if any pages are open in the Editor, switch to the Editor and choose File⇨Save All. Then, switch back to the Explorer.

Now try checking My Web Site's spelling.

1 **On the Explorer toolbar, click Cross File Spelling (or choose Tools⇨Spelling, or press F7).**

The Spelling dialog box appears. This dialog box enables you to choose which pages you want to check — those that are currently selected in the Explorer, or all pages.

2 **Click the All Pages radio button, and then click Start.**

FrontPage proceeds to check the spelling of all the text in your Web site. The Spelling dialog box records the progress of the spell-checker (see Figure 12-4). After the spell check is complete, the message `Finished checking pages` appears inside the dialog box, and the number of misspellings found in each page is listed in the dialog box's list box.

3 **To correct the misspellings, in the dialog box, click the Edit Page button.**

The dialog box closes, and the first page containing misspellings opens in the Editor. FrontPage highlights the misspelled word, and in the Editor, the Spelling dialog box appears (see Figure 12-5). You're probably familiar with how this dialog box works, because it looks very similar to the spell checking function in other Microsoft programs.

4 **To correct the misspelling, in the Change To text box, enter the correct spelling, or click the correctly spelled word in the Suggestions area.**

If the word is spelled correctly (as `Minnie` is in Figure 12-5), click the Ignore button to skip the word, or click the Add button to add the word to the dictionary. When the spell checker reaches the end of the page, The Continue with Next Document? dialog box appears.

5 **In the dialog box, click the Next Document button.**

FrontPage proceeds to check the spelling of the next page.

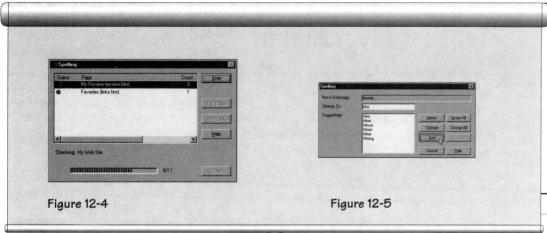

Figure 12-4

Figure 12-5

Figure 12-4: The Spelling dialog box records the number of misspellings found in your Web site.

Figure 12-5: The Editor's Spelling dialog box enables you to correct the misspelled word or to add a new word to the FrontPage spelling dictionary.

6 **Continue to check the spelling in each page until the check is complete.**

You know the check is complete when the Finished Checking Documents dialog box appears.

7 **Click OK to close the dialog box.**

When you return to the Explorer, the Spelling dialog box (which is still open) displays yellow Edited symbols next to each page. Click Close to close the dialog box.

extra credit

Finding and replacing text

In addition to spell checking, FrontPage knows how to find and replace text. To find or replace text in a single page, in the Editor, choose Edit⇨Find (or press Ctrl+F) or Edit⇨Replace (or press Ctrl+H). To find or replace text Web-wide, in the Explorer, choose Tools⇨Find (or click the Cross File Find button on the toolbar, or press Ctrl+F) or choose Tools⇨Replace (or press Ctrl+H).

Recess

If you want to take a break from Web site-cleaning for a while, be my guest. If you feel like having a diversion, check out the *...For Dummies* Web site at www.dummies.com, or drop by my virtual home at www.ashaland.com.

☑ Progress Check

If you can do the following, you've mastered this lesson:

❑ Check your Web site's spelling.

Notes:

Lesson 12-3 | # Testing Hyperlinks

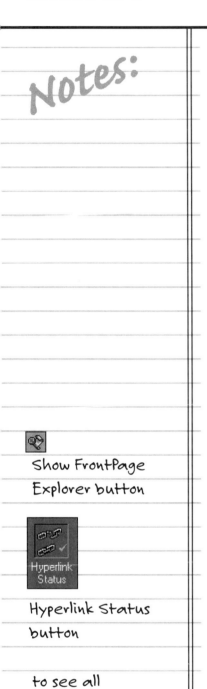

Notes:

Show FrontPage
Explorer button

Hyperlink Status
button

to see all
hyperlinks, choose
View→Show All
Hyperlinks

Even though the Explorer protects your site from broken hyperlinks due to changes in your site's file system, other situations that cause links to break are beyond the Explorer's control. For example, you can delete a page that is linked to from elsewhere in your site. Or a site on the Web to which you link can go down. In either case, if your visitors try to follow a broken link, they are slapped with an error message (an unpleasant experience, to be sure).

What's more, the battle against broken hyperlinks never ends, because you don't know when a site to which your page links changes location or disappears from the Web altogether. To assist you in the struggle, the FrontPage Explorer provides a powerful weapon: the Hyperlink Status View.

The Hyperlink Status View helps you find and repair broken hyperlinks, both to locations inside your Web site and out. Without this tool, you'd need to individually follow every link in your site to be sure that the link works (a time-consuming, tedious process). Not only that, but you would also need to repeat the process regularly. The Hyperlink Status View saves hours of your time by doing most of the work for you.

You now put the Explorer's link-checking tool to work on My Web Site.

Checking hyperlinks

The first thing to do is find the broken links in your Web site (if any exist). To do so, follow these steps:

1 **Activate your Internet connection.**

2 **If you haven't already, in the Editor, save all open pages by choosing File⇨Save All.**

3 **On the FrontPage Standard toolbar, click Show Explorer.**

4 **On the Explorer's Views bar, click Hyperlink Status.**

   The Hyperlink Status View becomes visible. The view displays a list of external hyperlinks in the Web site. (The Hyperlink Status View also displays broken internal hyperlinks, but My Web Site has none.)

5 **To verify external hyperlinks, click Verify Hyperlinks (or, choose Tools⇨Verify Hyperlinks).**

   The Verify Hyperlinks dialog box appears (see Figure 12-6). This dialog box gives the option of verifying all the site's external links or the currently selected URLs.

6 **In the dialog box, click the Verify Hyperlinks radio button and then click Start.**

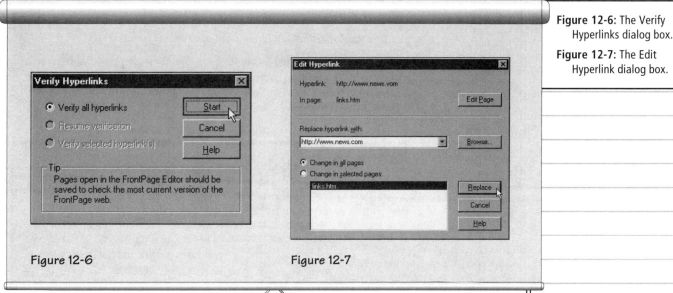

Figure 12-6

Figure 12-7

Figure 12-6: The Verify Hyperlinks dialog box.

Figure 12-7: The Edit Hyperlink dialog box.

The dialog box closes, and the Explorer checks each external link by contacting the destination web server (the Status bar displays a progress message letting you know what's going on). If the Explorer encounters server problems it can't understand, it lets you know by popping open a FrontPage Explorer dialog box containing an explanatory message. Click OK to close the dialog box and continue. As the Explorer checks each link, the link's Status label changes from a yellow circle to a green circle (the link is valid) or a red circle (the link is kaput).

To stop the verification process, click the Stop button on the toolbar. To resume verifying hyperlinks, click the Verify Hyperlinks button. When the verification process is complete, the Explorer lists a summary of its findings in the Status bar.

Fixing broken hyperlinks

I know for a fact the Explorer found at least *one* broken link in your Web site, because I planted an invalid URL in the Favorites page (clever, aren't I?). Now that you know that the broken link exists, you can repair it.

In the steps that follow, you fix one of your site's broken links.

1 **In the link list in the Hyperlink Status View, double-click the broken hyperlink with the URL** `http://www.news.vom`.

The Edit Hyperlink dialog box appears (see Figure 12-7). This dialog box enables you to correct the link's destination URL or to open the page containing the broken link so you can proceed with repairs in the Editor. In the following steps, you correct the link's destination URL.

2 **In the Replace Hyperlink <u>W</u>ith list box, enter** `http://www.news.com`.

Alternatively, click Browse to launch your web browser. Browse to the destination, and then switch back to the Explorer, and the destination URL automatically appears inside the Replace Hyperlink With list box.

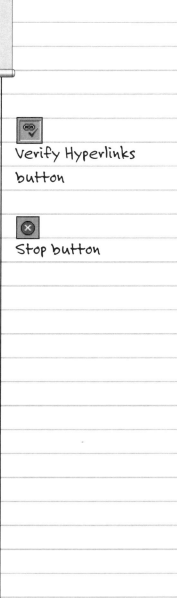

Verify Hyperlinks button

Stop button

☑ Progress Check

If you can do the following, you've mastered this lesson:

❑ Use the Explorer's Hyperlink Status View to verify the hyperlinks in your Web site.

❑ Fix any broken hyperlinks that appear in your site.

3 Click Replace.

The Explorer changes the link destination, and the dialog box closes. In the Hyperlink Status View, a yellow circle appears next to the new URL. The next time you verify hyperlinks, the Explorer will double-check to be sure that the new URL checks out.

extra credit

The Editor knows how to verify hyperlinks, too!

In the Editor, you can check individual hyperlinks inside your pages by holding down the Ctrl key and clicking the link you want to follow. In a moment, the destination page appears. To return to the original page, on the toolbar, click the Back button, or choose Go⇨Back. To go forward again, click the Forward button, or choose Go⇨Forward.

Lesson 12-4

Readying Your Site for Publication

This lesson is your last rest stop before launching into cyberspace. It's time to give each page in your Web site a final go-around to be sure that it's spotless. Your goal is to check each element in each page to make sure that the page is ready for prime time. Think of this task as the final tie-straightening or skirt-smoothing you do before entering a fancy dinner party.

The following steps are general guidelines. Feel free to do more. You can never be too careful.

1 In the Explorer's Navigation View, make sure that all the pages you want represented in navigation bars are part of the navigational structure.

I would add every page to the navigational structure except for the frames page.

2 In the Editor, open each page in your Web site, and check to see that the page's layouts are consistent.

You may need to insert a page banner here or there, add a navigational bar, reformat some text, or whatever.

3 Do any last-minute rewording now.

4 Double-check that your feedback form, your keyword search, and your image map work properly.

5 Preview the site in a web browser. Try to see your site as a new visitor would. Better yet, grab a friend or coworker and let that person critique your site.

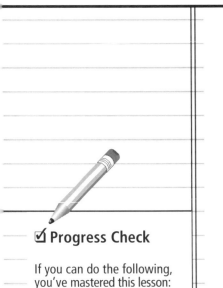

☑ Progress Check

If you can do the following, you've mastered this lesson:

❑ Fix any last-minute problems that creep into your site.

❑ Feel gratified by a job well done.

6 If you see anything you don't like, fix the problem in the Editor.

7 After you're satisfied, save everything, and, if you can reach, give yourself a hearty pat on the back (or ask your friend to do it for you).

Congratulations! You're finished with My Web Site. You have accomplished so much and have every reason to feel proud of yourself. The final job is to publish your Web site so the rest of the world can admire your savvy. You'll find out how to publish your Web site in Unit 13.

Unit 12 Quiz

Take this quiz to review the material you covered in this unit. (Each question may have more than one right answer.)

Notes:

1. **Which situation causes a hyperlink in your site to break?**

   A. In the Explorer, you change a page's filename.

   B. Your site links to another Web site, and the web server that houses that other site bites the dust.

   C. You delete a page in your Web site that is linked to from another page in your Web site.

   D. As you create a hyperlink, you mistype the link's URL in the URL text box in the Create Link dialog box.

   E. You drop the link on the floor.

2. **What is the purpose of the _private folder?**

   A. To keep your love letters out of your brother's grimy little fingers.

   B. To hide unfinished pages from visitors.

   C. To password-protect part of your Web site.

   D. To keep the contents of pages from appearing in keyword searches.

   E. To make pages transparent.

3. **What filename must you give your Web site's home page?**

   A. index.htm.

   B. home.htm.

   C. index.html.

   D. default.htm.

   E. It depends on settings specific to the web server on which you publish your Web site.

4. **How do you make sure that the hyperlinks in your Web site work properly?**

   A. Preview your Web site, and click each hyperlink to check it.

   B. In the Explorer's Hyperlinks View, click the Verify Hyperlinks button.

   C. In the Explorer's Hyperlink Status View, click the Verify Hyperlinks button.

   D. In the Editor, hold down the Ctrl key while clicking a hyperlink in a page.

   E. Choose File⇨Verify Hyperlinks.

5. **How do you know when your site is ready to publish?**

   A. You've checked each page, fixed any errors, and you feel good about your Web site.

   B. You're too sick of messing with your Web site to care about a few glitches.

   C. `You've fussed enough, so publish already` appears in the Explorer Status bar.

   D. You've asked friends and colleagues to offer feedback, and most of them liked what they saw.

   E. You just know.

Unit 12 Exercise

1. Rename art.htm to gallery.htm.

2. Add two more hyperlinks to the Favorites page.

3. Add text to any pages that seem skimpy.

4. Make any other design adjustments you want: apply a new theme to the Web site, change the site's navigation bars, or add some clip art.

5. After you're through, spell check your Web site.

6. Make sure that the Web site contains no broken hyperlinks.

7. Preview the Web site to make sure that it flows well.

8. Save and close all open pages, and exit FrontPage.

Going Public

Objectives for This Unit

✓ Understanding what "publishing your Web site" means

✓ Making your Web site visible on the World Wide Web

✓ Updating your Web site after it's "live"

Prerequisites

▶ Launching FrontPage (Lesson 1-2)

▶ Creating a new Web Site from scratch (Lesson 1-3)

▶ Opening a Web site in the Explorer (Lesson 2-1)

T his unit is the culmination of all the page building, tweaking, adjusting, and rearranging you've done in previous lessons: It's time to publish your Web site. In this unit, I take you through the steps required to make your new Web site visible on the World Wide Web.

What *Publishing Your Web Site* Means   Lesson 13-1

Publishing your Web site means moving your Web site from the privacy and comfort of your hard drive to the center stage of the World Wide Web — open for all to see.

publishing your Web
site = transferring
the site's files to
an ISP or company
Web server

find out whether
the web server
supports FrontPage
Server Extensions

on the test

To publish your Web site, you must copy all the site's files and folders to another computer called a *web server*. A web server is a computer that runs special server software and is plugged into the Internet 24 hours per day via a high-speed connection. If you're publishing a personal Web site, most likely you will transfer your files to a computer maintained by your ISP. If you're working on a corporate or intranet Web site, you may use your company's web server (an intranet is a company's internal network accessible only to employees).

After you have access to a dedicated web server, you need to ask your ISP's staff or your system administrator whether the server has *FrontPage Server Extensions* installed. FrontPage Server Extensions are special programs that add FrontPage-specific capabilities to the web server program. Many Internet service providers support FrontPage Server Extensions (Microsoft makes FrontPage Server Extensions available for free). (On the CD, I included trial software for one such ISP called MindSpring, a FrontPage-friendly ISP that serves the United States.)

heads up

If the web server *doesn't* support FrontPage Server Extensions, you can still publish your Web site, but a few FrontPage features are off limits in your Web site, as follows:

> **The _private folder:** Pages stored inside the _private folder are fully accessible on web servers without FrontPage Server Extensions installed.

> **FrontPage image maps:** Instead, use the image map style specific to your dedicated web server.

> **The built-in FrontPage form handler:** Instead, use a custom form-handling script.

> **The Confirmation Field FrontPage Component**

> **The Search Form Active Element**

> **The Hit Counter Active Element**

> **FrontPage discussion groups**

> **FrontPage user registration systems**

> **Permissions:** If you want to adjust your Web site's permissions, you need to discuss your options with your ISP or your system administrator.

> **Opening or creating Web sites stored on a computer other than your own**

> **The Tasks View:** You can use the Tasks View to organize your own tasks, but you can't share the Tasks View with a Web-building team.

(You may not be familiar with a few items in the previous list because I didn't cover every single FrontPage feature in this book's lessons. For a down-to-earth reference guide to FrontPage 98, check out my other book, *FrontPage 98 For Dummies,* published by IDG Books Worldwide.)

You don't need to memorize the preceding list — if you attempt to publish a Web site containing a FrontPage-specific feature on a web server that doesn't support FrontPage Server Extensions, a warning dialog box appears during the publishing process, alerting you to the situation and prompting you to change the features or publish the site with the understanding that those features won't work.

☑ **Progress Check**

If you can do the following, you've mastered this lesson:

❑ Understand what happens when you publish your Web site.

❑ Know what FrontPage Server Extensions are.

❑ Know which FrontPage features are off limits if your web server doesn't support FrontPage Server Extensions.

Publishing Your Web Site (Finally!)   Lesson 13-2

The promised hour has arrived. In this lesson, I show you how to publish your Web site. The steps you follow in this lesson depend on whether your web server supports FrontPage Server Extensions. Either way, FrontPage reduces publishing your Web site to working with a few easy dialog boxes.

Because publishing procedures vary widely among ISPs and company web servers, I provide only general instructions in this lesson. Double-check the specifics with your ISP or system administrator.

If your web server supports FrontPage Server Extensions

Ideally, your web server supports FrontPage Server Extensions, giving you access to all of the FrontPage bells and whistles. If so, follow the steps in this section to publish your Web site.

If your ISP or company web server uses an older version of the FrontPage Server Extensions (those built for FrontPage 1.1 or FrontPage 97), some of the features in your FrontPage 98 Web site may not work properly. Check the FrontPage 98 Web site at www.microsoft.com/frontpage for the latest information about compatibility issues.

To publish your Web site for the first time, follow these steps:

1 **Activate your Internet connection.**

2 **Launch FrontPage and, in the Explorer, open My Web Site.**

3 **On the toolbar, click Publish FrontPage Web (or, choose File⇨Publish FrontPage Web, or press Ctrl+B).**

The Publish FrontPage Web dialog box appears (see Figure 13-1).

If, instead of the Publish FrontPage web dialog box, the Publish dialog box appears, it means you have already attempted to publish this Web site using FrontPage. For instructions on how to use the Publish dialog box, skip ahead to Lesson 13-3.

4 **In the Please Specify the Location to Which You Want to Publish Your FrontPage Web list box, type the destination URL.**

The destination URL is the URL of the location on the web server to which you're publishing. If you don't know your destination URL, check with your ISP or system administrator.

5 **Click OK.**

The Publish FrontPage Web dialog box closes. A pause occurs as FrontPage contacts the dedicated web server. In a moment, the Name and Password Required dialog box appears.

Publish FrontPage Web button

in Publish FrontPage Web dialog box, click big square button to view listing of FrontPage-enabled ISPs on Microsoft's Web site

Notes:

Publish FrontPage Web button

in Publish dialog box, click big square button to view listing of FrontPage-enabled ISPs on Microsoft's Web site

6 **In the Name and Password text boxes, enter the user name and password you chose at the time you established your Internet account and then click OK.**

Depending on the Web site's settings, the Name and Password Required text box may appear again, this time requesting your FrontPage administrator name and password. If this occurs, in the Name and Password text boxes, enter your FrontPage administrator name and password and then click OK.

The dialog box closes, and FrontPage copies all your Web site files to the web server. After the work is done, the Status bar displays the message `Published to` followed by the destination URL.

Congratulations — you've arrived!

If your web server doesn't have FrontPage Server Extensions installed

If the world were a simple place, every web server would support FrontPage Server Extensions. Alas, this isn't so. But don't fret — it's almost as easy to publish your Web site if your ISP or company web server doesn't support FrontPage Server Extensions.

To publish your Web site on a non-FrontPage server for the first time, do the following:

1 **Activate your Internet connection.**

2 **Launch FrontPage and, in the Explorer, open My Web Site.**

3 **On the toolbar, click Publish FrontPage Web (or, choose File⇨Publish FrontPage Web, or press Ctrl+B).**

The Publish FrontPage Web dialog box appears (see Figure 13-1).

If, instead of the Publish FrontPage Web dialog box, the Publish dialog box appears, it means you have already attempted to publish a Web site using FrontPage. For instructions on how to use the Publish dialog box, skip ahead to Lesson 13-3.

4 **In the Please Specify the Location to Which You Want to Publish Your FrontPage Web list box, type the Web site's destination URL.**

The destination URL is the URL of the location on the web server to which you're publishing. If you don't know your destination URL, check with your ISP or system administrator.

5 **Click OK.**

The Publish FrontPage Web dialog box closes. A pause occurs as FrontPage contacts the dedicated web server. After FrontPage figures out that the server does not support FrontPage Server Extensions, the Microsoft Web Publishing Wizard dialog box appears (see Figure 13-2).

6 **In the FTP Server Name text box, enter the name of the destination web server.**

If you're not sure which URL to enter here, double-check with your ISP.

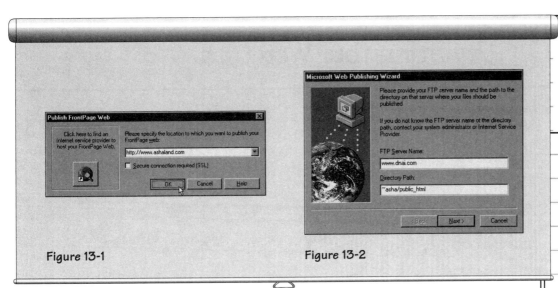

Figure 13-1

Figure 13-2

Figure 13-1: The Publish FrontPage Web dialog box.

Figure 13-2: The Microsoft Web Publishing Wizard dialog box.

7 **In the <u>D</u>irectory Path text box, enter the location of the web server folder that holds your Web site files.**

All web servers contain a special folder that holds Web site files. An ISP's web server, which hosts many users' Web sites, contains individual folders for each user. (Most web servers name this folder `public_html`, but some servers use other names.)

My ISP maintains both FrontPage and non-FrontPage web servers. As an example, if I were to publish a Web site on my ISP's non-FrontPage server, I would enter `~asha/public_html` in the Directory Path text box. The resulting Web site URL would be `www.dnai.com/~asha` (visitors don't need to type `public_html` in the Web site URL because the web server distributes only pages that are stored inside that folder).

Again, if you're not sure what to enter here, check with your ISP.

8 **Click Next.**

The second Microsoft Web Publishing Wizard dialog box appears.

9 **In the User Name and Password text boxes, enter the user name and password you chose at the time you established your Internet account, and then click Finish.**

The dialog box closes, and FrontPage verifies your user name and password with the server. If everything checks out, FrontPage proceeds to publish your Web site. After the work is done, the Status bar displays the message `Published to` followed by the destination URL.

Congratulations — your site is now open for visitors!

Recess

If you have an old mortarboard and graduation gown in your attic, dust them off and put them on, and then lift your head high and stride around the house or office (ask your friend or coworker to hum the tune to "Pomp and Circumstance"). You've graduated to the real world. Congratulations on your achievement.

☑ Progress Check

If you can do the following, you've mastered this lesson:

❑ Ascertain your Web site's destination URL.

❑ Publish your Web site.

Lesson 13-3   Updating Your Web Site

to update site,
change and then
publish site again

Just because your Web site is public doesn't mean you won't want to update the site in the future. New content and occasional design changes keep visitors interested in your site. FrontPage makes it easy to update your now-published Web site.

Updating your site involves making changes to your Web site and then publishing the site again. If you simply want to update the site's changed pages, a single button-click does the trick. To publish the entire site again (including pages that haven't changed), or to publish the site to a different location, the steps are slightly more involved (but not much.)

Updating pages that have changed

To update your site's changed pages, follow these steps:

Publish

Publish FrontPage
Web button

1 **Activate your Internet connection.**

2 **Launch FrontPage and open the Web site you want to update.**

3 **Make whatever changes you want to the site.**

Be sure to save all the pages you change by choosing File⇨Save All.

4 **In the Explorer, click Publish FrontPage Web.**

Depending upon whether the destination server supports FrontPage Server Extensions, one of the following things happens:

- If the web server supports FrontPage Server Extensions, the Name and Password Required dialog box appears. In the Name and Password text boxes, enter the user name and password you chose at the time you established your Internet account, and then click OK.

  Depending on the Web site's settings, the Name and Password Required text box may appear again, this time requesting your FrontPage administrator name and password. If this occurs, in the Name and Password text boxes, enter your FrontPage administrator name and password, and then click OK.

- If the web server does not support FrontPage Server Extensions, the Microsoft Web Publishing Wizard dialog box appears. In the User Name and Password text boxes, enter the user name and password you chose at the time you established your Internet account, and then click Finish.

  The dialog box closes, and FrontPage copies the changed pages to the web server.

Publishing the entire Web site again

To publish the entire Web site again, or to publish the Web site to a new location, follow these steps:

1 **Activate your Internet connection.**

2 **Launch FrontPage and open the Web site you want to update.**

3 **Make whatever changes you want to the site.**

Be sure to save all the pages you change by choosing File➪Save All.

4 **In the Explorer, choose File➪Publish FrontPage Web (or press Ctrl+B).**

Do *not* click the Publish FrontPage Web button in this step. Otherwise, FrontPage will publish the site using its current settings (as described in the previous set of steps).

The Publish dialog box appears (see Figure 13-3). The Publish Web To box contains all the locations to which you have previously published FrontPage 98 Web sites (the current Web site's URL is highlighted). By clicking each item in the box, you display the site's destination URL in the space beneath the Publish Web To box.

To publish the Web site to a new location, continue with Step 4. To publish the Web site to the same location, but with different settings, skip ahead to Step 6.

5 **To publish the Web site to a new location, click the More Webs button.**

The Publish FrontPage Web dialog box appears.

6 **In the Please Specify the Location to Which You Want to Publish Your FrontPage Web list box, type the Web site's destination URL, and then click OK.**

The dialog box closes, and the Publish dialog box becomes visible again.

7 **To publish the entire Web site (not just the pages that have changed), uncheck the Publish Changed Pages Only check box.**

8 **Click OK.**

Depending on your Web site's permission settings and the type of web server to which you're publishing, a dialog box (the Name and Password Required dialog box or the Microsoft Web Publishing Wizard dialog box) may appear requesting your user name and password. Enter the user name and password you chose when you set up your account, and then click OK to complete the publishing process.

Your site is now refreshed.

Notes:

congrats!

☑ Progress Check

If you can do the following, you've mastered this lesson:

❑ Update the contents of your Web site.

❑ Publish the updated site to the same or a different location.

Figure 13-3: The Publish dialog box.

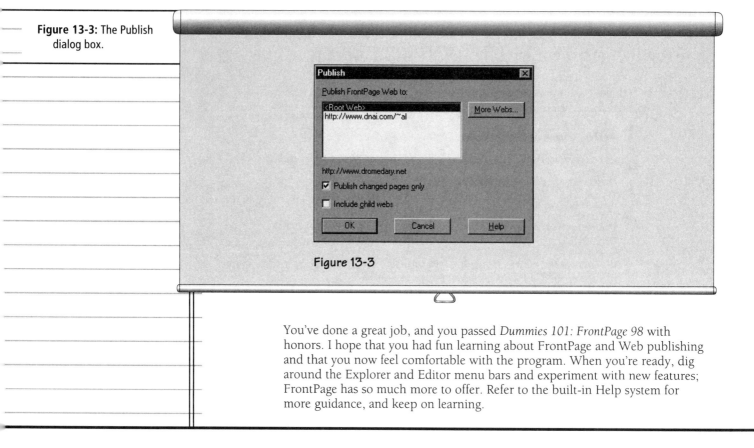

Figure 13-3

You've done a great job, and you passed *Dummies 101: FrontPage 98* with honors. I hope that you had fun learning about FrontPage and Web publishing and that you now feel comfortable with the program. When you're ready, dig around the Explorer and Editor menu bars and experiment with new features; FrontPage has so much more to offer. Refer to the built-in Help system for more guidance, and keep on learning.

Unit 13 Quiz

Take this quiz to review the material you covered in this unit. (Each question may have more than one right answer.)

1. **What happens when you publish a Web site?**

   A. You become eligible for the Nobel Prize.

   B. Your Web site is visible to people surfing the Web.

   C. FrontPage copies your Web site files onto a different computer.

   D. You can no longer edit the contents of your Web site.

   E. You can forget about the site — it's out of your hands.

2. **What are FrontPage Server Extensions?**

   A. A set of programs installed on the destination web server that enable certain FrontPage features to work.

   B. Optional Web site additions, such as hit counters and search forms.

   C. A set of programs that must be installed on the destination web server if you are to publish your FrontPage Web site on that server.

D. Applications, such as Microsoft Internet Explorer, that work well with FrontPage.

E. Small metal rods you attach to the web server to make the server bigger.

3. How do you publish a Web site using FrontPage?

A. In the Explorer, click the Publish FrontPage Web button.

B. In the Editor, choose File↪Publish Page.

C. In the Explorer, choose File↪Publish FrontPage Web.

D. In the Explorer, press Ctrl+B.

E. You need to use a separate program to publish your Web site.

4. What happens after your site is visible on the Web?

A. Visitors send you appreciative e-mail.

B. Visitors send you critical e-mail.

C. Visitors send you inquisitive e-mail.

D. Visitors send you challenging e-mail.

E. Visitors send you flowers.

Unit 13 Exercise

1. Launch your web browser and visit your Web site at its new World Wide Web URL.

2. Explore the Web site. If you see anything you want to change, return to FrontPage and change the Web site.

3. If you changed the Web site, update the site to make the changes visible on the Web.

4. Think of two items or features you will add to your Web site within the next two weeks.

5. Save and close all pages that are currently open in the Editor, and exit FrontPage.

6. Breathe a sigh of satisfaction.

Notes:

Part IV Review

Unit 12 Summary

- **Readying the site for publication:** Before you publish your Web site, go through the site page by page to be sure that it looks and works perfectly.

- **Explorer Folders View:** Use this view to clean up your Web site's system of files and folders. For example, use this view to move Web graphics into a separate images folder or rename pages. When you rename or move pages, the Explorer automatically updates the file's associated graphic references and hyperlinks.

- **Moving files into folders:** The left pane of the Folders View displays the Web site's folders, and the right pane displays the files stored inside the folder open in the left pane. To move a file, drag the file from the right pane and drop it into a folder visible in the left pane.

- **Renaming a page:** In the Folders, All Files, or Navigation views, choose Edit⇨Rename.

- **Checking spelling:** To check the spelling of your entire Web site, in the Explorer, click the Cross File Spelling button. To spell check a single page, in the Editor, click the Check Spelling button.

- **Verifying repairing hyperlinks:** The Explorer's Hyperlink Status View helps you find and repair broken hyperlinks in your Web site. To verify hyperlinks, in this view, click the Verify Hyperlinks button. After the verification process is finished, repair broken hyperlinks by double-clicking the hyperlink's listing in the Hyperlink Status View.

Unit 13 Summary

- **What happens when you publish your Web site?** When you publish your Web site, you copy your Web site files to another computer called a web server. Generally, your ISP or your company maintains the web server and keeps the server connected to the Internet or company intranet 24 hours per day.

- **FrontPage Server Extensions:** FrontPage Server Extensions are special programs that add FrontPage-specific capabilities to the web server. For certain FrontPage 98 features to work, your ISP staff or system administrator must install FrontPage Server Extensions on the web server. Most FrontPage features will work on servers with or without FrontPage Server Extensions installed.

- **To publish a Web site:** With the Web site open in the Explorer, click the Publish FrontPage Web button, or choose File⇨Publish FrontPage Web, or press Ctrl+B.

- **To update a Web site that has already been published:** Make any changes you want to the Web site, and save the changes. Then republish the Web site by clicking the Publish FrontPage Web button, or choosing File⇨Publish FrontPage Web, or pressing Ctrl+B.

Part IV Test

Take this test as a review of the material covered in Part IV, Units 12 and 13. If you'd like to check your answers, refer to Appendix B.

True   False

T   F   1. The web server on which you publish a FrontPage 98-authored Web site must have FrontPage Server Extensions installed.

T   F   2. FrontPage is able to check the spelling of every page in the Web site.

T   F   3. To rename a page, in the Explorer's Hyperlink Status View, click a page icon, and then choose Edit⇨Rename.

T   F   4. Every FrontPage-created Web site contains a folder named images.

T   F   5. When you move a page into a folder, you must update by hand any hyperlinks associated with that page.

T   F   6. You must use a separate program to publish your FrontPage Web site.

T   F   7. To publish a Web site, you must have access to a web server. For most people, this means getting an account with an ISP or working with a web server maintained by their company.

T   F   8. After you verify that your site's hyperlinks work properly, you never need to do so again.

Multiple Choice

For each of the following questions, circle the correct answer or answers.

9. **Which tasks should you do before publishing your Web site?**

   A. Check the spelling of your Web pages.

   B. Preview each page.

   C. Clean up the Web site's file system.

   D. Verify the site's hyperlinks.

   E. Dust off your tuxedo or evening gown.

10. **How do you publish a Web site?**

    A. In the Explorer, press Ctrl+B.

    B. Get an agent.

    C. In the Editor, choose File⇨Publish FrontPage Web.

    D. In the Explorer, choose File⇨Publish FrontPage Web.

    E. On the Explorer toolbar, click Publish FrontPage Web.

11. **Which features do not work properly unless the web server has FrontPage Server Extensions installed?**

    A. The Search Form Active Element.

    B. The Hit Counter Active Element.

    C. Shared Borders.

    D. The _private folder.

    E. The built-in FrontPage form handler.

Part IV Test

12. **What does the Explorer's Verify Hyperlinks View do?**

    A. It performs background checks on suspicious-looking hyperlinks.

    B. It checks links leading to places outside the Web site to make sure that those links are valid.

    C. It lists broken internal hyperlinks.

    D. It enables you to fix broken hyperlinks.

    E. Nothing.

Matching

13. **Match each of the following buttons with its name:**

A. 	1. Check Spelling (Editor)
B. 	2. Verify Hyperlinks
C. 	3. Refresh
D. 	4. Cross File Spelling (Explorer)
E. 	5. Publish FrontPage Web

14. **Match each Web site problem with its solution:**

A. You misspelled your boss's name in one of your site's 700 pages, and you can't remember which page.	1. Preview the page in a web browser, and click the image map's hotspots.
B. Your Web site contains a link to another Web site that is no longer in service.	2. Open the page and add last-minute information.
C. You're not sure whether your image map works.	3. Sort your pages and files into folders.
D. You are having trouble sorting through your Web site's file system.	4. On the Explorer toolbar, click the Cross File Spelling button.
E. You forgot to add your e-mail address to your site's home page.	5. In the Explorer, choose Tools➪Verify Hyperlinks.

Part IV Lab Assignment

This is your final lab assignment — it's time to finish up the Web project you began at the end of Part I. In this assignment, you add any finishing touches your site needs, double-check its perfection, and publish the Web site.

Step 1: Launch FrontPage, and open the Web site you created in the Part I Lab Assignment

Step 2: Check the Web site's spelling

Step 3: Organize the Web site's file system

Start by moving any images into the images folder. If you need to create more folders, go ahead.

Step 4: Verify the Web site's hyperlinks

If any broken hyperlinks appear, fix them.

Step 5: Open each page and double-check the page's layout and contents

If you want to add or change anything, do so now.

Step 6: Save all your pages

Step 7: Publish your Web site

Step 8: Visit the Web site at its new URL, just to be absolutely sure that it published okay

If anything is amiss, make changes to the copy of the Web site on your computer, and then publish the site again.

Step 9: Exit FrontPage

Appendixes

Part V

In this part . . .

This final part contains three appendixes. Appendix A tells you a little bit about the other programs hitching a ride on the FrontPage program CD. Appendix B contains all the answers to the quizzes and tests. Appendix C explains how to use the CD included with this book.

The FrontPage 98 Supporting Cast

You got a bonus when you bought FrontPage — four programs that work together with FrontPage to extend FrontPage's capabilities as a Web publishing dynamo.

Because everyone loves bonuses, in this appendix I tell you a bit about each program. I don't go into detail; if I did, I'd end up writing four entire books. Instead, I give you a little teaser about each program and graciously pass you on to the programs' Web sites for more information. For installation instructions, refer to the documentation that comes with FrontPage.

Microsoft Internet Explorer 3.0 with Internet Mail and Internet News

Microsoft Internet Explorer is a powerful web browser you can use to surf the Web or preview the Web sites you build by using FrontPage. Internet Explorer supports many Web design effects, including text formatting and color, tables, forms, frames, ActiveX, Java, Web page scripts, and much more. Internet Explorer also comes with a built-in e-mail program and a news reader so that you can easily send and receive e-mail messages and read and post articles to Usenet newsgroups, all from within the same tightly integrated program.

Everything you ever wanted to know about Internet Explorer and its associates is available at www.microsoft.com/ie.

By the time you read this, Internet Explorer 4.0 will be available for free download from the Microsoft Web site. FrontPage 98 supports several Web design effects that work hand-in-hand with Internet Explorer 4.0.

Microsoft Image Composer 1.5 with GIF Animator

If you want to create good-looking images for your Web site, look no further than Microsoft Image Composer. This potent image-editing program carries a steep learning curve but is well worth the time. By using Image Composer, you can create your own images or you can assemble images out of clip art and other components. You embellish images with text and art effects, such as charcoal sketch, embossing, or neon glow. Best of all, Image Composer ties in nicely with FrontPage so that you can easily switch between the two programs while you create your Web site's pages and graphics.

Visit the Image Composer Web site at `www.microsoft.com/ imagecomposer` for more information, more free art, and general inspiration.

Microsoft Personal Web Server

FrontPage comes with its own built-in web server — the FrontPage Personal Web Server — so that you can both build and test FrontPage Web sites on your own computer. Although the FrontPage Personal Web Server is a fully functional web server program, it can't handle the amount of traffic buzzing around the Internet or a corporate intranet. Folks who want a more powerful web server to use with FrontPage can instead try the Microsoft Personal Web Server. Use this web server as the basis for a small-scale intranet or to share files with other Web site authors.

Visit `www.microsoft.com/ie/pws` for more information about the Microsoft Personal Web Server.

Microsoft Web Publishing Wizard

The Web Publishing Wizard works inside FrontPage to automate transferring Web site files from your computer to web servers that don't support FrontPage Server Extensions. I show you how to publish your Web site in Unit 13.

The Web Publishing Wizard home page at `www.microsoft.com/windows/ software/webpost` contains lots more information.

Quiz and Test Answers

Unit 1 Quiz Answers

Question	Answer	If You Missed It, Try This
1.	A, B	Review Lesson 1-1.
2.	B, D, E	Review Lesson 1-2.
3.	A, B	Review Lesson 1-3.
4.	B, C	Review Lesson 1-3.
5.	B	Review Lesson 1-4.
6.	B, D	Review Lesson 1-6.
7.	B, D	Review Lesson 1-6.
8.	E	Review Lesson 1-6.

Unit 2 Quiz Answers

Question	Answer	If You Missed It, Try This
1.	B, D	Review Lesson 2-1.
2.	A, B, D	Review Lesson 2-2.
3.	A	Review Lessons 2-2, 2-3, and 2-5.
4.	C	Review Lesson 2-5.
5.	B, C, D	Review Lesson 2-6.

Part I Test Answers

Question	Answer	If You Missed It, Try This
1.	False	Review Lesson 1-2.
2.	True	Review Lesson 1-2.
3.	True	Review Lesson 1-1.
4.	False	Review Lesson 1-4.
5.	False	Review Lesson 1-2.
6.	True	Review Lesson 1-6.
7.	True	Review Lesson 1-3.
8.	True	Review Lesson 2-5.
9.	False	Review Lesson 2-3.
10.	False	Review Lesson 2-6.
11.	C, D, E	Review Lesson 2-2.
12.	B	Review Lesson 1-2.
13.	A, B, C, D, E	Review Lesson 2-3.
14.	A-4, B-3, C-1, D-5, E-2	Review Lesson 1-6.
15.	A-3, B-4, C-2, D-5, E-1	Review Lessons 1-6, 2-1, 2-2, 2-4, and 2-6.

Unit 3 Quiz Answers

Question	Answer	If You Missed It, Try This
1.	A, C	Review Lesson 3-2.
2.	A, B, C, E	Review Lesson 3-2.
3.	A, D	Review Lesson 3-2.
4.	B, C	Review Lesson 3-3.
5.	A, B, D, E	Review Lesson 3-6.

Unit 4 Quiz Answers

Question	Answer	If You Missed It, Try This
1.	B	Review Lesson 4-1.
2.	C, D	Review Lesson 4-1.
3.	A, C, E	Review Lesson 4-2.
4.	A, C	Review Lesson 4-3.
5.	A, B, C	Review Lesson 4-4. (By the way, a *straight* line — which is not necessarily horizontal — is the shortest distance between two points.)

Unit 5 Quiz Answers

Question	Answer	If You Missed It, Try This
1.	A, B, D, E	Review Lesson 5-1.
2.	C, D	Review Lesson 5-1.
3.	A, B, C, D, E	Review Lesson 5-2.
4.	C	Review Lesson 5-4.
5.	A, B	Review Lesson 5-4.
6.	E	Review Lesson 5-4.

Unit 6 Quiz Answers

Question	Answer	If You Missed It, Try This
1.	A, D, E	Review Lesson 6-1.
2.	D	Review Lesson 6-1.
3.	C, E	Review Lesson 6-2.
4.	A, B, C, E	Review Lesson 6-3.
5.	B	Review Lesson 6-4.
6.	C, D	Review Lesson 6-5.

Unit 7 Quiz Answers

Question	Answer	If You Missed It, Try This
1.	B, D	Review Lesson 7-1.
2.	C, D	Review Lesson 7-1.
3.	B	Review Lesson 7-2.
4.	C	Review Lesson 7-3.

Unit 8 Quiz Answers

Question	Answer	If You Missed It, Try This
1.	C, D, E	Review Lesson 8-1.
2.	A, B, C, D, E	Review Lesson 8-1.
3.	C	Review Lesson 8-2.
4.	C	Review Lesson 8-2.
5.	A, B, C, E	Review Lesson 8-2.

Part II Test Answers

Question	Answer	If You Missed It, Try This
1.	True	Review Lesson 3-2.
2.	True and False	A trick question! If you have Microsoft Internet Explorer installed on your computer, the answer is False, because you have access to the Editor's Preview View. If you *don't* have Internet Explorer installed, the answer is True; the only way you can preview a page is to launch a separate browser. Review Lesson 3-6 for details.
3.	False	How you answer every question on a quiz or test matters, even though no one is grading you!
4.	False	Review Unit 5.

Question	Answer	If You Missed It, Try This
5.	True	Review Lesson 5-2.
6.	False	Review Unit 6.
7.	True	Review Lesson 6-1.
8.	False	Review Unit 7.
9.	True	Review Lesson 8-2.
10.	True	Review Lesson 2-4.
11.	A, D, E	Review Lessons 4-2 and 4-3.
12.	C	Review Lesson 5-4.
13.	A, B, C, D, E	Review Lesson 6-5.
14.	B	Review Lesson 8-2.
15.	A-3, B-4, C-5, D-1, E-2	Review the toolbar buttons listed in Units 3, 5, 6, and 8.
16.	A-4, B-3, C-1, D-5, E-2	Review the toolbar buttons listed in Units 2, 3, 6, and 8.
17.	A-4, B-2, C-5, D-3, E-1	Review Units 3, 6, and 8.

Unit 9 Quiz Answers

Question	Answer	If You Missed It, Try This
1.	A, C, D, E	Review Lesson 9-1.
2.	B, C, E	Review Lesson 9-1.
3.	D	Review Lesson 9-1.
4.	C	Review Lesson 9-2.
5.	C	Review Lesson 9-5.
6.	B, C	Review Lesson 9-7.

Unit 10 Quiz Answers

Question	Answer	If You Missed It, Try This
1.	A, C	Review Lesson 10-1.
2.	A, C -	Review Lesson 10-2.
3.	A, C	Review Lesson 10-4.

Question	Answer	If You Missed It, Try This
4.	B, C	Review Lesson 10-4.
5.	B, C	Review Lesson 10-5.

Unit 11 Quiz Answers

Question	Answer	If You Missed It, Try This
1.	C, D, E	Review Lesson 11-1.
2.	C	Review Lesson 11-2.
3.	C, D, E	Review Lesson 11-3.
4.	B	Review Lesson 11-4.
5.	B, E	Review Lesson 11-5.

Part III Test Answers

Question	Answer	If You Missed It, Try This
1.	False	Review Lesson 11-1.
2.	True	Review Lesson 10-1.
3.	False	Review Lesson 11-3.
4.	True	Review Lesson 9-7.
5.	True	Review Lesson 9-7.
6.	False	Review Lesson 9-7.
7.	False	Review Lesson 10-2.
8.	True	Review Lesson 11-2.
9.	False	Review Lesson 11-5.
10.	False	Review Lesson 11-4.
11.	A, B, D, E	Review Lesson 9-7.
12.	B, C, E	Review Unit 9.
13.	A, B, C, E	Review Unit 11.
14.	A, B, D, E	Review Lesson 10-4.
15.	A-3, B-2, C-5, D-1, E-4	Review the toolbar buttons listed in Units 9 and 11.
16.	A-4, B-1, C-5, D-3, E-2	Review Unit 11.
17.	A-2, B-3, C-1, D-5, E-4	Review Unit 9.

Unit 12 Quiz Answers

Question	Answer	If You Missed It, Try This
1.	B, C, D	Review Lesson 12-3.
2.	B, D	Review Lesson 12-1.
3.	E	Review Lesson 12-1.
4.	A, C, D	A works, but why go through all that effort? Review Lesson 12-3 for details.
5.	A, D	Review Lesson 12-4.

Unit 13 Quiz Answers

Question	Answer	If You Missed It, Try This
1.	B, C	Review Lesson 13-1.
2.	A	Review Lesson 13-1.
3.	A, C, D	Review Lesson 12-2.
4.	A, B, C, D, E	Review Lesson 13-3.

Part IV Test Answers

Question	Answer	If You Missed It, Try This
1.	False	Review Lesson 13-1.
2.	True	Review Lesson 12-2.
3.	False	Review Lesson 12-1.
4.	True	Review Lesson 12-1.
5.	False	Review Lesson 12-1.
6.	False	Review Lesson 13-2.
7.	True	Review Lesson 13-1.
8.	False	Review Lesson 12-3.
9.	A, B, C, D	Review Unit 12.

Question	Answer	If You Missed It, Try This
10.	A, D, E	Review Lesson 13-2.
11.	A, B, D, E	Review Lesson 13-1.
12.	B, C, D	Review Lesson 12-3.
13.	A-2, B-5, C-4, D-1, E-3	Review the toolbar buttons listed in Units 12 and 13.
14.	A-4, B-5, C-1, D-3, E-2	Review Unit 12.

Appendix C

About the CD

The *Dummies 101: FrontPage 98* companion CD contains all the exercise files you use while you're following along with the lessons in the book, plus a bonus: sign-up software for MindSpring Enterprises (MindSpring provides FrontPage-friendly Internet service to the United States).

Before you can use any of the CD files, you need to install them on your computer. The installation process is easy and quick.

System Requirements

Before using the CD, make sure that your computer matches up to the minimum requirements listed here.

- ◆ A PC with a 486 or faster processor
- ◆ *At least* 8MB of total RAM (16MB recommended)
- ◆ Microsoft Windows 95, or Windows NT (version 4.0 or later)
- ◆ FrontPage 98
- ◆ At least 5MB of free hard drive space available if you want to install all the items from this CD (you need less space if you don't install every item)
- ◆ CD-ROM drive — double-speed (2x) or faster
- ◆ Monitor capable of displaying at least 256 colors or grayscale

Installing the CD Files onto Your Computer

The exercise files are practice Web pages and files you use while following along with the lessons in the book. You need to put these files on your hard drive before you begin using the book.

Notes:

Installing the exercise files

1 Insert the *Dummies 101: FrontPage 98* **CD (label side up) into your computer's CD drive.**

2 **In the taskbar, click the Start button to display the Start menu, and then choose** <u>R</u>**un.**

3 **In the dialog box that appears, type** d:\setup.exe **and then click OK. (If your CD drive is not listed as drive D, substitute the appropriate letter for** d**.)**

If this is the first time you are installing files from this CD, a license agreement appears.

4 **Read the license agreement and then click the Accept button.**

If you don't agree to the terms of the license agreement, you can't continue with the installation. After you click Accept, the CD Launcher dialog box appears.

5 **Click OK to launch the CD installer.**

The dialog box closes, and then, in few moments, the colorful *Dummies 101: FrontPage 98* installation window appears.

6 **Click Install Exercise Files.**

Another message appears, asking whether you want to go ahead and copy the exercise files to your hard drive.

7 **Click OK.**

The dialog box closes, and the files are saved to the FP101 folder on your hard drive.

After the exercise file installer is done, the Install completed dialog box appears to let you know the installation finished successfully.

8 **Click the Exit button in the lower-right corner of the window.**

The program asks whether you really, really want to exit.

9 **Click Yes to close the installation window.**

The window closes.

heads up

The exercise files are meant to accompany the book's lessons. If you open a file prematurely, you may accidentally make changes to the file, preventing you from following along with the steps in the lessons. So please don't try to open or view a file until you've reached the point in the lessons where I explain how to use the file.

If at some point you accidentally modify an exercise file and want to reinstall the original version, just follow the steps for installing exercise files for your computer. If you want to save your modified version of an exercise file, move the file to another folder before reinstalling the original.

Installing MindSpring sign-up software

MindSpring Enterprises is a popular and fast-growing national ISP. Even more exciting, MindSpring supports FrontPage Web hosting. MindSpring's FrontPage services are geared toward business users and therefore come with a *virtual domain name* of your choice (www.yourdomain.com), plus many other services.

Note: Although MindSpring provides great service, there are hundreds of FrontPage-friendly ISPs, all of whom offer different account options at different prices. If you just want a plain vanilla Internet account, many ISPs offer less expensive plans. Microsoft maintains an index of ISPs around the country who support FrontPage. See www.microsoft.com/frontpage for more information.

For details about MindSpring Internet service, visit www.mindspring.com.

heads up

If you already have an Internet service provider, please note that MindSpring software makes changes to your computer's current Internet configuration and may replace your current provider's settings.

To install the MindSpring software included on the CD, start up the CD as described in "Installing the CD Files onto Your Computer," earlier in this appendix. In the main CD installation window, click the Choose Software button and then click the category that you want to install. Next, click the appropriate button for more information about the program. To install the software, click the Continue button and follow the on-screen instructions.

heads up

The MindSpring setup program requires you to restart your computer. Be sure to close all open programs before you begin the installation process.

Removing the *Dummies 101: FrontPage 98* CD Files from Your Computer

After you're finished with the book, you can easily remove the CD files.

Removing the exercise files

After you're finished with the lessons in the book, you may want to delete the exercise files. To do so, follow these steps:

Notes:

1 On your Windows 95 desktop, double-click My Computer.

2 In the My Computer window, double-click the Drive C icon.

3 In the Drive C window, click once on the FP101 folder.

4 Choose File⇨Delete.

Depending on your Windows settings, a message may appear asking whether you really want to delete these items. Click Yes.

Removing the MindSpring software

To remove the MindSpring software, click the Start button, and then choose Settings⇨Control Panel. The Control Panel window appears. In the window, double-click the Add/Remove Programs icon. Listed on the Install/Uninstall tab of the window are any programs that Windows 95 can remove for you, including MindSpring. Click MindSpring, and then click the Add/Remove button. Follow the on-screen instructions to uninstall the program.

If You Have Problems (Of the CD Kind)

I tried my best to include files and programs that work on most computers with the minimum system requirements. Alas, your computer may differ, and something may go wrong.

The two likeliest problems are that you don't have enough memory (RAM) for the programs you want to use, or you have other programs running that are affecting the CD's installation program. If you get error messages such as Not enough memory or Setup cannot continue, try one or more of these methods, and then try running the installer again:

▶ Turn off any antivirus software that you have on your computer. Installers sometimes mimic virus activity and may make your computer incorrectly believe that it is being infected by a virus.

▶ Close all running programs. The more programs you're running, the less memory is available to other programs. Installers also typically update files and programs. So if you keep other programs running, installation may not work properly.

▶ Consider having your local computer store add more RAM to your computer. Adding more memory can really help the speed of your computer and allow more programs to run at the same time.

If you still have trouble with installing the items from the CD, please call the IDG Books Worldwide Customer Service phone number: 800-762-2974 (outside the U.S.: 317-596-5430).

Index

•D•

•E•

⟨S⟩

◆ T ◆

IDG Books Worldwide, Inc., End-User License Agreement

READ THIS. You should carefully read these terms and conditions before opening the software packet(s) included with this book ("Book"). This is a license agreement ("Agreement") between you and IDG Books Worldwide, Inc. ("IDGB"). By opening the accompanying software packet(s), you acknowledge that you have read and accept the following terms and conditions. If you do not agree and do not want to be bound by such terms and conditions, promptly return the Book and the unopened software packet(s) to the place you obtained them for a full refund.

1. **License Grant.** IDGB grants to you (either an individual or entity) a nonexclusive license to use one copy of the enclosed software program(s) (collectively, the "Software") solely for your own personal or business purposes on a single computer (whether a standard computer or a workstation component of a multiuser network). The Software is in use on a computer when it is loaded into temporary memory (RAM) or installed into permanent memory (hard disk, CD-ROM, or other storage device). IDGB reserves all rights not expressly granted herein.

2. **Ownership.** IDGB is the owner of all right, title, and interest, including copyright, in and to the compilation of the Software recorded on the disk(s) or CD-ROM ("Software Media"). Copyright to the individual programs recorded on the Software Media is owned by the author or other authorized copyright owner of each program. Ownership of the Software and all proprietary rights relating thereto remain with IDGB and its licensers.

3. **Restrictions on Use and Transfer.**

    (a) You may only (i) make one copy of the Software for backup or archival purposes, or (ii) transfer the Software to a single hard disk, provided that you keep the original for backup or archival purposes. You may not (i) rent or lease the Software, (ii) copy or reproduce the Software through a LAN or other network system or through any computer subscriber system or bulletin-board system, or (iii) modify, adapt, or create derivative works based on the Software.

    (b) You may not reverse engineer, decompile, or disassemble the Software. You may transfer the Software and user documentation on a permanent basis, provided that the transferee agrees to accept the terms and conditions of this Agreement and you retain no copies. If the Software is an update or has been updated, any transfer must include the most recent update and all prior versions.

4. **Restrictions on Use of Individual Programs.** You must follow the individual requirements and restrictions detailed for each individual program in the "About the CD" section of this Book. These limitations are also contained in the individual license agreements recorded on the Software Media. These limitations may include a requirement that after using the program for a specified period of time, the user must pay a registration fee or discontinue use. By opening the Software packet(s), you will be agreeing to abide by the licenses and restrictions for these individual programs that are detailed in the "About the CD" section and on the Software Media. None of the material on this Software Media or listed in this Book may ever be redistributed, in original or modified form, for commercial purposes.

5. **Limited Warranty.**

    (a) IDGB warrants that the Software and Software Media are free from defects in materials and workmanship under normal use for a period of sixty (60) days from the date of purchase of this Book. If IDGB receives notification within the warranty period of defects in materials or workmanship, IDGB will replace the defective Software Media.

(b) IDGB AND THE AUTHOR OF THE BOOK DISCLAIM ALL OTHER WARRANTIES, EXPRESS OR IMPLIED, INCLUDING WITHOUT LIMITATION IMPLIED WARRANTIES OF MERCHANTABILITY AND FITNESS FOR A PARTICULAR PURPOSE, WITH RESPECT TO THE SOFTWARE, THE PROGRAMS, THE SOURCE CODE CONTAINED THEREIN, AND/OR THE TECHNIQUES DESCRIBED IN THIS BOOK. IDGB DOES NOT WARRANT THAT THE FUNCTIONS CONTAINED IN THE SOFTWARE WILL MEET YOUR REQUIREMENTS OR THAT THE OPERATION OF THE SOFTWARE WILL BE ERROR FREE.

(c) This limited warranty gives you specific legal rights, and you may have other rights that vary from jurisdiction to jurisdiction.

6. Remedies.

(a) IDGB's entire liability and your exclusive remedy for defects in materials and workmanship shall be limited to replacement of the Software Media, which may be returned to IDGB with a copy of your receipt at the following address: Software Media Fulfillment Department, Attn.: *Dummies 101: FrontPage 98*, IDG Books Worldwide, Inc., 7260 Shadeland Station, Ste. 100, Indianapolis, IN 46256, or call 800-762-2974. Please allow three to four weeks for delivery. This Limited Warranty is void if failure of the Software Media has resulted from accident, abuse, or misapplication. Any replacement Software Media will be warranted for the remainder of the original warranty period or thirty (30) days, whichever is longer.

(b) In no event shall IDGB or the author be liable for any damages whatsoever (including without limitation damages for loss of business profits, business interruption, loss of business information, or any other pecuniary loss) arising from the use of or inability to use the Book or the Software, even if IDGB has been advised of the possibility of such damages.

(c) Because some jurisdictions do not allow the exclusion or limitation of liability for consequential or incidental damages, the above limitation or exclusion may not apply to you.

7. U.S. Government Restricted Rights. Use, duplication, or disclosure of the Software by the U.S. Government is subject to restrictions stated in paragraph (c)(1)(ii) of the Rights in Technical Data and Computer Software clause of DFARS 252.227-7013, and in subparagraphs (a) through (d) of the Commercial Computer–Restricted Rights clause at FAR 52.227-19, and in similar clauses in the NASA FAR supplement, when applicable.

8. General. This Agreement constitutes the entire understanding of the parties and revokes and supersedes all prior agreements, oral or written, between them and may not be modified or amended except in a writing signed by both parties hereto that specifically refers to this Agreement. This Agreement shall take precedence over any other documents that may be in conflict herewith. If any one or more provisions contained in this Agreement are held by any court or tribunal to be invalid, illegal, or otherwise unenforceable, each and every other provision shall remain in full force and effect.

Accessing the CD-ROM Files

See Appendix C for all the CD-ROM details. Follow the instructions in each unit of the book to use the CD-ROM files with FrontPage 98.

Dummies 101 CD Installation Instructions

The CD-ROM at the back of this book contains the exercise files that you use while you work through the lessons in this book. It also contains a handy installation program that copies the files to your hard drive in a very simple process. See Appendix C for complete details about the CD (especially system requirements for using the CD).

heads up

This CD does *not* contain FrontPage 98. You must already have FrontPage 98 installed on your computer.

With Windows 95 running, follow these steps to install the exercise files:

1 **Insert the *Dummies 101: FrontPage 98* CD (label side up) into your computer's CD drive.**

2 **Click the Start button to display the Start Menu, and then choose <u>R</u>un.**

3 **In the dialog box that appears, type** d:\setup.exe **(if your CD drive is not drive D, substitute the appropriate letter for** d**) and then click OK.**

The End-User License Agreement dialog box appears.

4 **Read the agreement and then click Accept to continue with the installation process.**

The CD Launcher dialog box appears.

5 **In the dialog box, click OK.**

The dialog box closes, and after a moment, The *Dummies 101: FrontPage 98* Welcome screen appears. From this screen, you can choose to install the exercise files or choose software (in this case, *software* refers to the MindSpring trial software also included on the CD).

6 **Click Install Exercise Files.**

7 **In the next dialog box that appears, click Yes to continue with the installation or click Cancel to stop the installation.**

If you click Cancel, you can install the files later by following these steps again (see Step 3 for instructions on how to get back to the installation window).

The installation program copies the files onto your computer in the folder location C:\FP101. When installation is complete, the Installer Complete dialog box appears, to let you know the installation finished successfully.

8 **Click the Exit button in the lower-right corner of the window.**

9 **In the window asking whether you want to quit, click Yes.**

You don't have to do anything with the exercise files yet — I tell you when you need to open the first file (in Unit 1).

If you have problems with the installation process, you can call the IDG Books Worldwide, Inc. Customer Support number: 800-762-2974 (outside the U.S.: 317-596-5430).

Note: The files are meant to accompany the book's lessons. If you open a file prematurely, you may accidentally make changes to the file, which may prevent you from following along with the steps in the lessons.

Discover Dummies Online!

The Dummies Web Site is your fun and friendly online resource for the latest information about ...*For Dummies*® books and your favorite topics. The Web site is the place to communicate with us, exchange ideas with other ...*For Dummies* readers, chat with authors, and have fun!

Ten Fun and Useful Things You Can Do at www.dummies.com

1. Win free ...*For Dummies* books and more!
2. Register your book and be entered in a prize drawing.
3. Meet your favorite authors through the IDG Books Author Chat Series.
4. Exchange helpful information with other ...*For Dummies* readers.
5. Discover other great ...*For Dummies* books you must have!
6. Purchase Dummieswear™ exclusively from our Web site.
7. Buy ...*For Dummies* books online.
8. Talk to us. Make comments, ask questions, get answers!
9. Download free software.
10. Find additional useful resources from authors.

Link directly to these ten fun and useful things at
http://www.dummies.com/10useful

For other technology titles from IDG Books Worldwide, go to
www.idgbooks.com

Not on the Web yet? It's easy to get started with *Dummies 101*®: *The Internet For Windows*®*95* or *The Internet For Dummies*®, 4th Edition, at local retailers everywhere.

Find other ...*For Dummies* books on these topics:
Business • Career • Databases • Food & Beverage • Games • Gardening • Graphics
Hardware • Health & Fitness • Internet and the World Wide Web • Networking
Office Suites • Operating Systems • Personal Finance • Pets • Programming • Recreation
Sports • Spreadsheets • Teacher Resources • Test Prep • Word Processing

IDG BOOKS WORLDWIDE BOOK REGISTRATION

Register This Book and Win!

We want to hear from you!

Visit **http://my2cents.dummies.com** to register this book and tell us how you liked it!

- ✔ Get entered in our monthly prize giveaway.

- ✔ Give us feedback about this book — tell us what you like best, what you like least, or maybe what you'd like to ask the author and us to change!

- ✔ Let us know any other ...*For Dummies* topics that interest you.

Your feedback helps us determine what books to publish, tells us what coverage to add as we revise our books, and lets us know whether we're meeting your needs as a ...*For Dummies* reader. You're our most valuable resource, and what you have to say is important to us!

Not on the Web yet? It's easy to get started with *Dummies 101*®: *The Internet For Windows*® *95* or *The Internet For Dummies*®, 4th Edition, at local retailers everywhere.

Or let us know what you think by sending us a letter at the following address:

...*For Dummies* Book Registration
Dummies Press
7260 Shadeland Station, Suite 100
Indianapolis, IN 46256
Fax 317-596-5498

BUSINESS AND
GENERAL
REFERENCE
BOOK SERIES
FROM IDG

COMPUTER
BOOK SERIES
FROM IDG